IMAGES
of America

MIDDLEFIELD
OTSEGO LAKE'S EASTERN SHORE

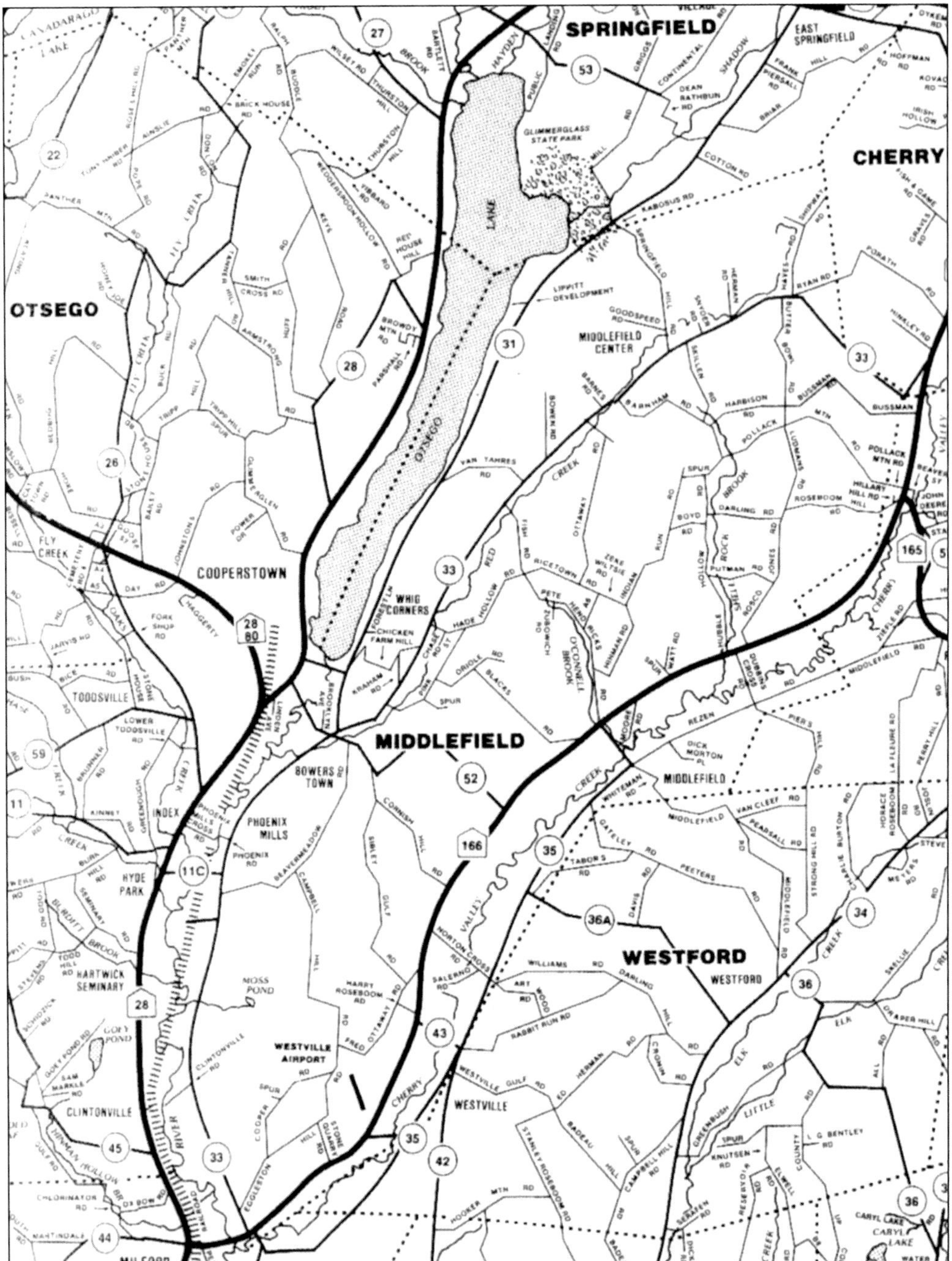

This map shows Middlefield, the town with the largest geographical area in Otsego County.

IMAGES
of America

MIDDLEFIELD OTSEGO LAKE'S EASTERN SHORE

Dominick J. Reisen

ARCADIA
PUBLISHING

ISBN 978-0-7385-1234-1

Published by Arcadia Publishing,
Charleston, South Carolina

Printed in the United States of America

Library of Congress Catalog Card Number: 2003105120

For all general information, contact Arcadia Publishing:
Telephone 843-853-2070
Fax 843-853-0044
E-mail sales@arcadiapublishing.com
For customer service and orders:
Toll-free 1-888-313-2665

Visit us on the Internet at www.arcadiapublishing.com.

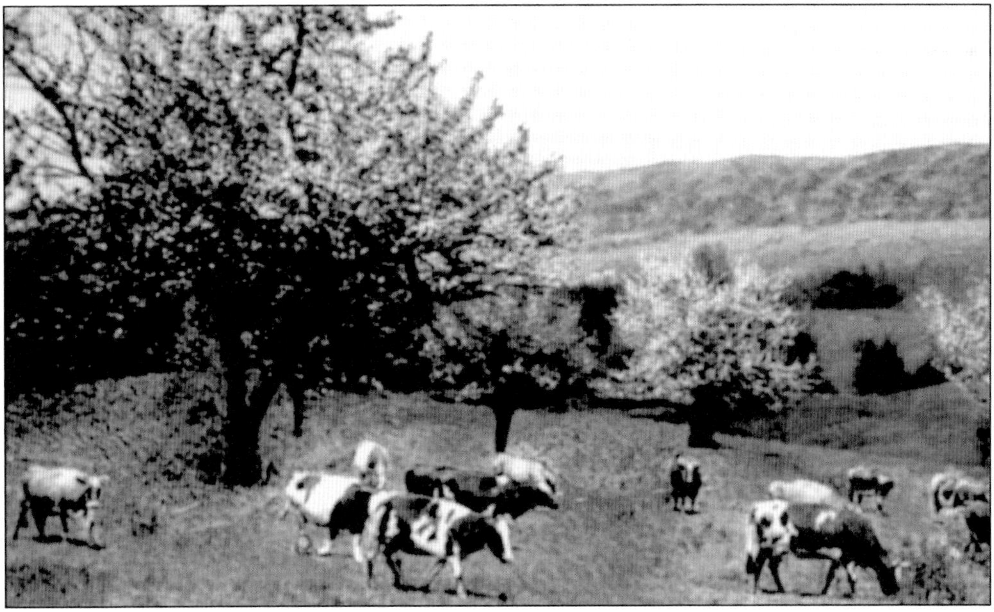

This early-20th-century postcard features the town of Middlefield.

Contents

Acknowledgments

In the writing of this book, I am greatly indebted first and foremost to the Town of Middlefield Historical Association for the generous use of its photograph archive. Thanks to the efforts of many over a long span of years, the association has assembled the single most comprehensive collection of photographs of the town of Middlefield. I would like to express my gratitude to Rodney and Jean Johnson for the use of their extensive collection of postcards and photographs of the hamlet of Middlefield, as well as to David Petri for the use of his many rare photographs. Finally, I would like to thank Albert and Sandra Bullard, Pearl Pollette, John and Becky Sears, the First Baptist Society in Middlefield, the *Freeman's Journal*, and the New York State Historical Association for their contributions of photographs and other images, and information to help make this book a success.

Caption acknowledgments are for institutional collections and are abbreviated as follows:

NYSHA Courtesy of the New York State Historical Association, Cooperstown.
TMHA Courtesy of the Town of Middlefield Historical Association, Middlefield.

INTRODUCTION

The town of Middlefield is located in the heart of the Leatherstocking Region of New York State. It runs along the east side of Otsego Lake, the beautiful "Glimmerglass" of James Fenimore Cooper's Leatherstocking Tales. It is made up of two picturesque valleys cut by the meandering Cherry Valley and Red Creeks as they wind their way to the Susquehanna River.

In the mid-18th century, Middlefield was carved into several large tracts of land, called land patents, which took their name from the individuals who purchased them through royal land grants. The Godfrey Miller Patent encompassed much of the northwest portion of Middlefield. The John Bowers Patent was on the southwest. The Volkert Outhout, or Long Patent, a narrow strip of land running the entire length of the eastern side of the town and straddling the Cherry Valley Creek, was acquired by George Clarke, lieutenant governor of New York in the 1740s.

A mere 20 years after John Lindsay settled with a small group of people in Cherry Valley, the first pioneers entered the area that later came to be known as Middlefield. During the Revolutionary War, the area was under constant threat of attack by Indians who were allied with the British. In 1779, the neighboring settlement at Cherry Valley was nearly wiped out by an attack known as the Cherry Valley Massacre. Although the region was virtually evacuated at this time, after the conclusion of hostilities, eager settlers flooded back to the area. Among these post-Revolutionary War settlers were some notable men who shaped the early history of Middlefield. Looming large in this group are Benjamin Gilbert, Col. Moses Rich, Joshua Pinney, Dr. Sumner Ely, and Dr. Obadiah Dunham. Middlefield was set off from the town of Cherry Valley in 1797, and Samuel Griffin was elected the first town supervisor.

Religious fervor took hold in Middlefield at an early date, when people banded together to form tiny congregations. In 1802, the Reverend William Colbert preached probably the first Methodist sermon in Middlefield Center at the home of Daniel McCollum. In 1832, a Methodist congregation built a church in the hamlet of Middlefield at a cost of $2,000 on land donated by George Clarke of Springfield, great-grandson of the lieutenant governor. The Baptists were building their congregation at the same time as the Methodists. Elder Benjamin Sawin preached in the hamlet of Clarksville *c.* 1806. By 1810, when the Baptists established the First Baptist Society in Middlefield, they were regularly meeting in the schoolhouse Joshua Pinney had helped to establish on the hill overlooking the hamlet (across from the present Baptist church). In 1826, they built their present church, also on lands donated by George Clarke. Their church design was based on the designs of Asher Benjamin, the noted Boston architect. It was also c. 1806 that the Presbyterians built their first church in Middlefield Center. They formally organized in 1821 and, by 1843, needed to erect a new church for their membership of some 89 people.

The early 19th century saw some significant business activity in the town. In 1815, the Phoenix cotton mill was established; it became a woolen mill c. 1866. Middlefield Center became home to one of the largest shoe last factories in New York State. In 1828, the Otsego County Farm, or Poor House, was set up along the Susquehanna River to help care for those who had fallen on hard times. Population and business growth induced the United States Postal Service to open offices throughout the town. These offices were established in Clarksville (renamed Middlefield), Middlefield Center, Westville, and Lentsville.

Agriculture remained the backbone of the economy, however. The early settlers grew a variety of grains, particularly wheat, for sale. As the 1820s dawned, farming began to steadily covert to dairying and its ancillary products such as cheese making. This diversity in agriculture almost completely vanished as hop-growing mania swept Otsego County. Farmers quickly gave up other crops to grow hops. Fantastic profits could be made with hops: fortunes were made and lost. After the century ran its course and soil exhaustion took its toll on the land, farmers returned to dairying.

As the population in the town stabilized from its Civil War–era decline, larger schoolhouses were needed. In 1875, George Hyde Clarke, son of the man who donated land for the Baptist and Methodist churches, donated land for a new school. The schoolhouse was built on a rise of land near the mill in the hamlet of Middlefield. It opened in 1875 and operated until 1954, when it was centralized with the Cherry Valley district. Small school districts were consolidated at Middlefield District No. 1 and Westville District No. 2, and a new building was erected in Westville to accommodate these students.

Three major fires marked the first half of the 20th century. In 1934, the American Hotel suffered the loss of its main section, and in 1942, the store of Charles Hearn was gutted by a fire that started in the Roberts house next door. Frances Roberts barely made it out alive after reentering the house to retrieve her purse. Finally, when the Morton house lost a wing to fire in 1955, a group of men banded together to form the Middlefield Volunteer Fire Department.

Although many people and businesses had left Middlefield by the mid-20th century, the town witnessed a resurgence in activity as the century came to a close: the Old District No. 1 Schoolhouse became headquarters for the Middlefield Historical Association; the Baptist and Methodist churches formed a cooperative parish and began alternating services at both buildings; the hamlet of Middlefield was listed on the National Register of Historic Places in the 1980s.

Throughout its history Middlefield has remained the quintessential rural town. Referred to as the "Land of Steady Habits," its residents have been industrious and content in the place they call home.

One

The Town and Its Hamlets

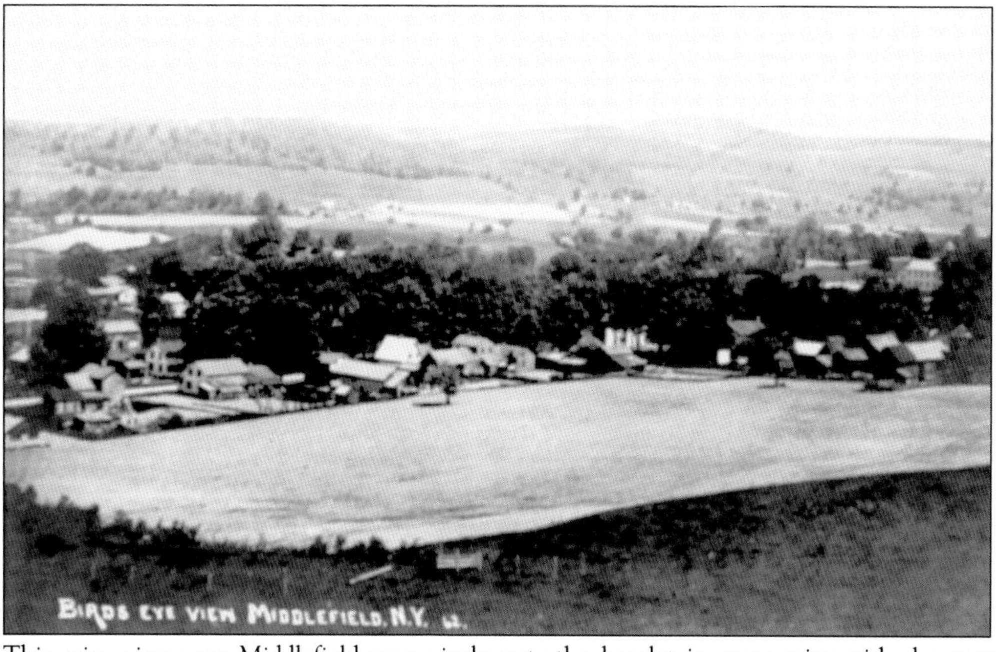

This crisp view over Middlefield very nicely puts the hamlet in perspective with the vast agricultural lands surrounding it.

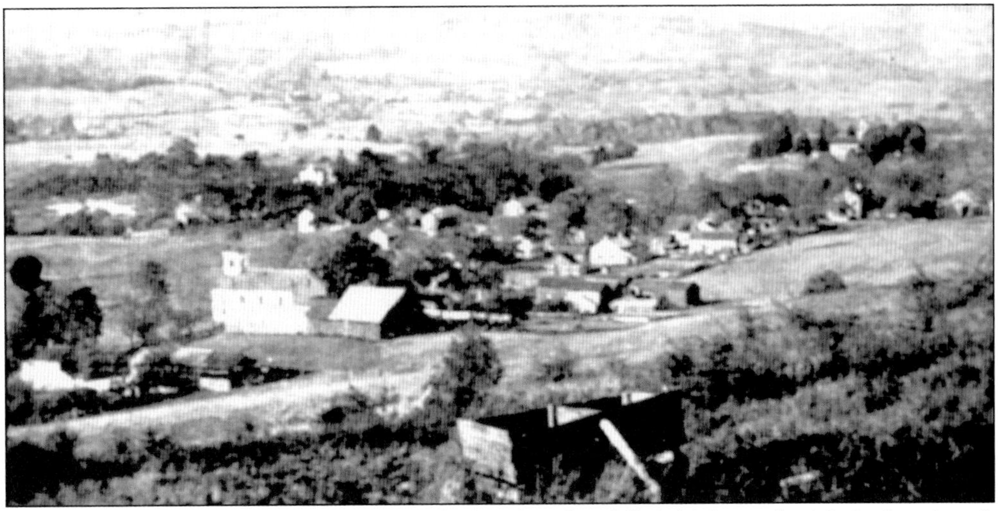

This c. 1911 view looking northeast over the hamlet of Middlefield shows the Methodist church in the center left. Straight back from the Methodist church can be made out the District No. 1 Schoolhouse. In the upper right corner is the Baptist church. In the foreground is a box for collecting hops, the golden cash crop of Otsego County, used in making beer.

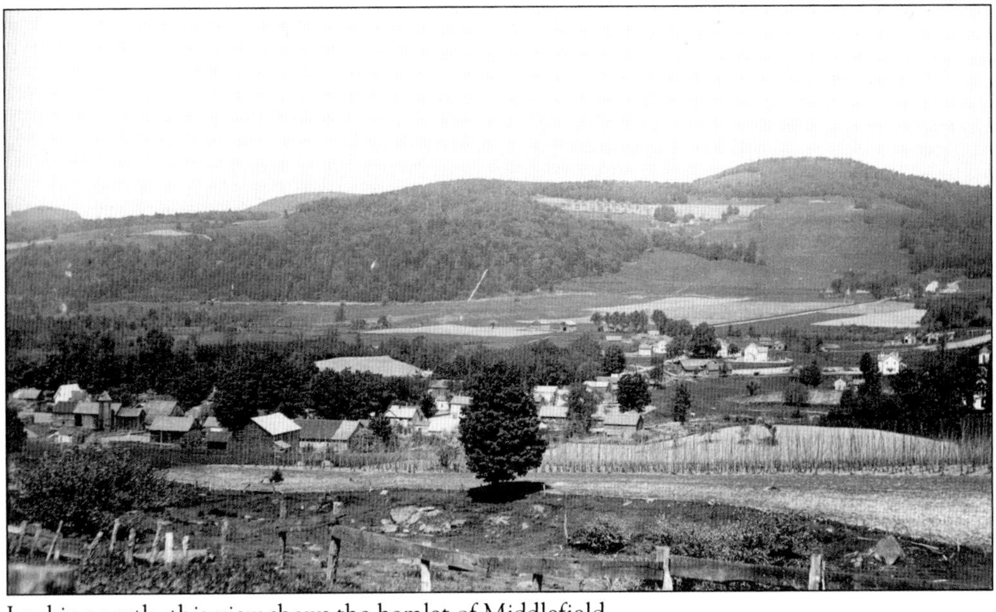

Looking north, this view shows the hamlet of Middlefield.

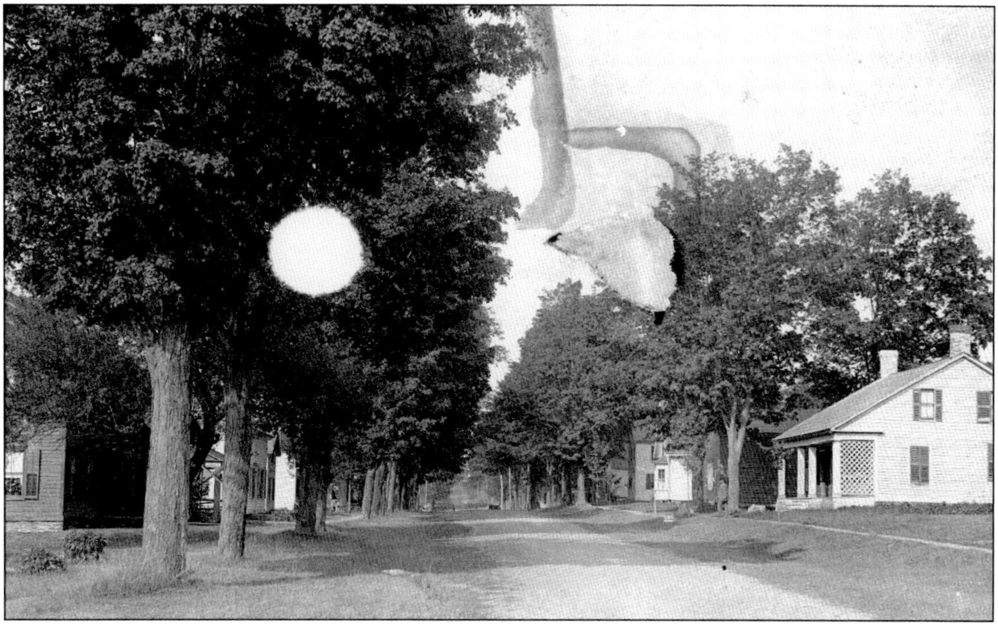

This photograph was taken heading into the hamlet of Middlefield from the southwest on what was once known as the Long Patent Road. On the left is the house built *c.* 1821 by Daniel Cummings, a prosperous wagon maker. On the right is the home built by Elijah Rich *c.* 1816, shown with its later Greek Revival portico.

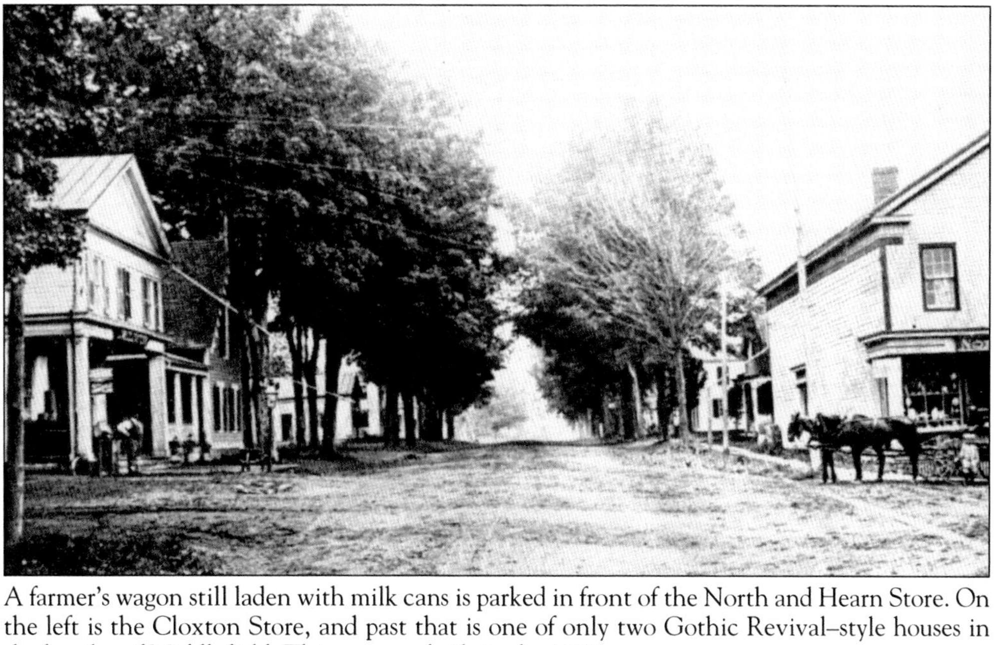

A farmer's wagon still laden with milk cans is parked in front of the North and Hearn Store. On the left is the Cloxton Store, and past that is one of only two Gothic Revival–style houses in the hamlet of Middlefield. This one was built in the 1850s.

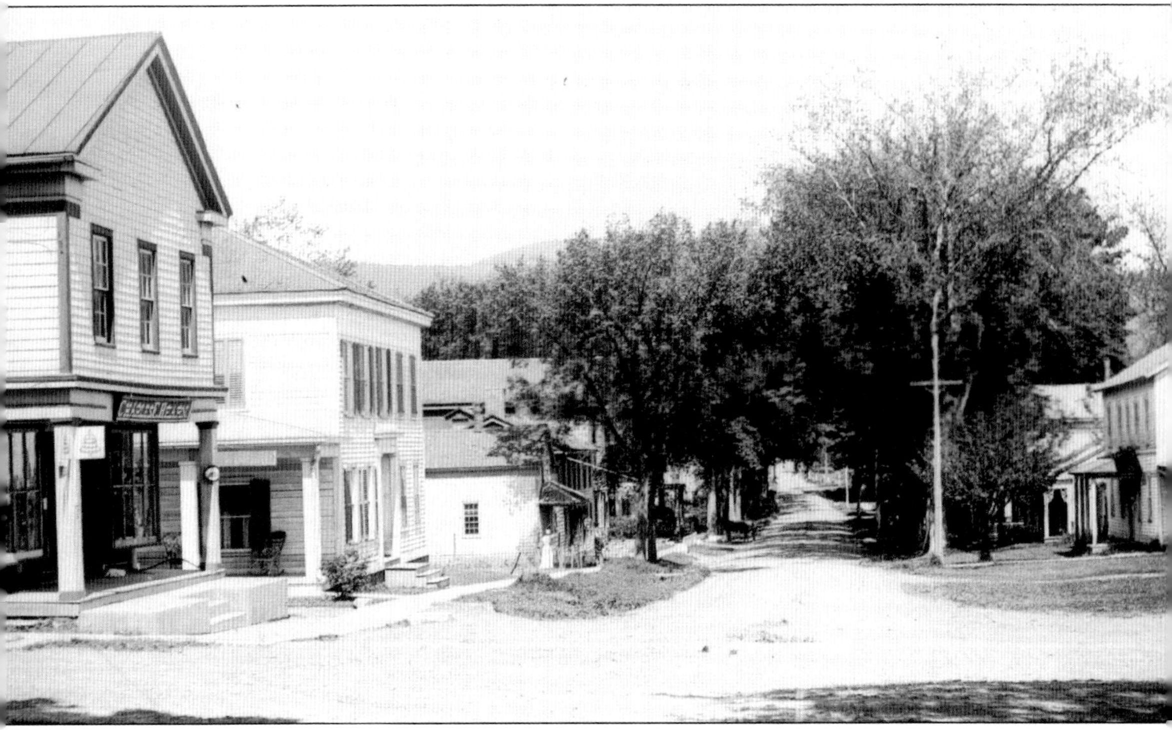

This view looks north past the North and Hearn Store, which was destroyed by fire in 1942. Visible beyond the store is the house built in the 1840s by Manning and Mortimer Gilbert, who first ran the store and then the American Hotel, before fire struck it in 1934. On the right is the Central Hotel.

The doorway to the Manning and Mortimer Gilbert house has an uncanny resemblance to plate 28 of Asher Benjamin's *The Architect, or Practical House Carpenter*, first published in 1830. Asher Benjamin was the architect whose plans were used for the Baptist church in 1826.

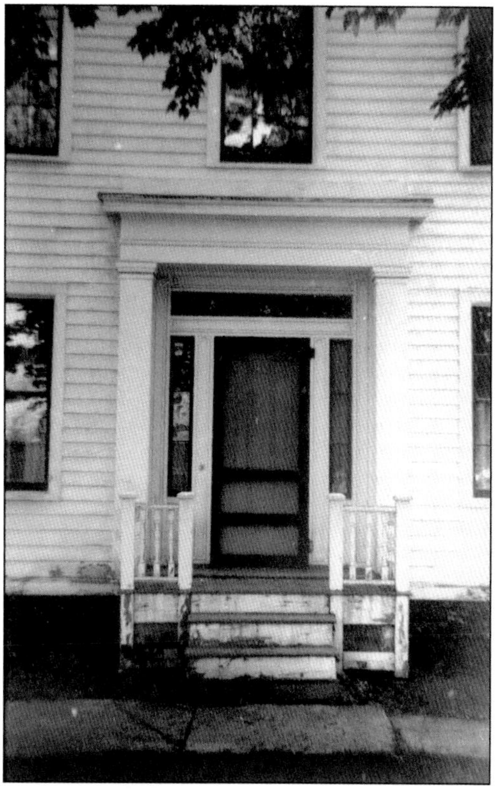

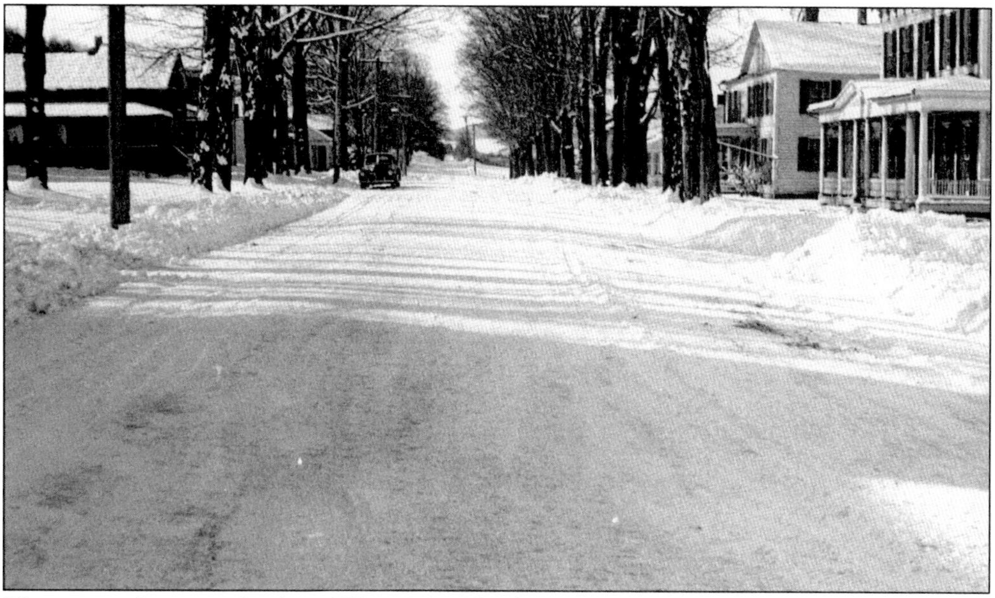

This postcard was sent by Aunt Ella to Mrs. Floyd Pitts, who during World War II was living in Cooperstown. It shows the Long Patent Road leading out of the hamlet of Middlefield in the winter of 1944. On the right, with the addition of a full front porch, is the house built in 1859 by Harrison North, a very prosperous merchant. (Courtesy TMHA.)

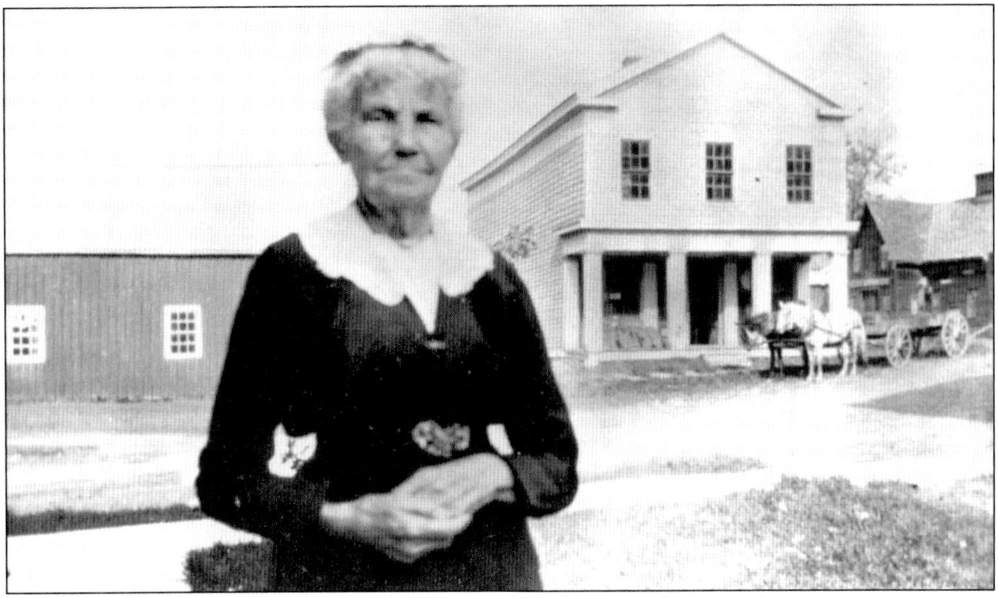

In 1923, the *Otsego Farmer* asked, "Who is the oldest resident of Otsego County?" Ann Shipman Pitts of Middlefield, at 95, won this honor, beating George Dewey of Cooperstown by two months. She was born on August 22, 1828, and is seen outside the American Hotel. This photograph provides an interesting vantage of the crossroads. Still relying on horse-drawn wagons, a customer has stopped at the store. The barn on the left has been razed to make way for the firehouse. In the right background is a wagon shop which no longer exists.

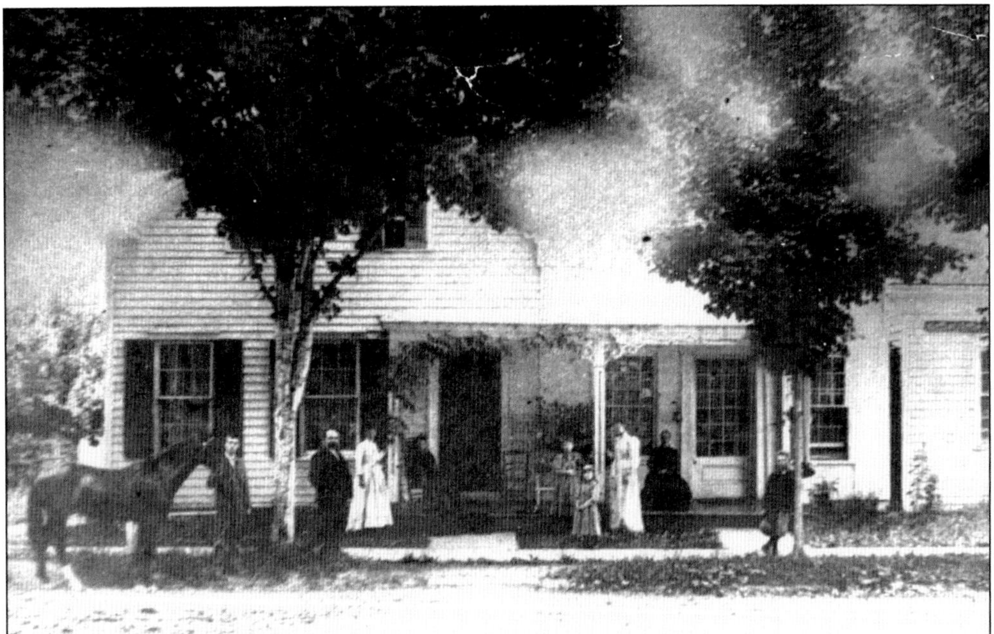

The 1942 fire started here. It leveled this house and destroyed the Hearn Store on the corner. This 1891 photograph shows, from left to right, Charles Hearn, Thomas Hearn, Lora VanHuzen, Maggie Denton (sitting), Grace Hearn Pollette, Helen North, Clara Hearn Fake, Ruth VanHuzen (sitting), and Charles Yager. (Courtesy TMHA.)

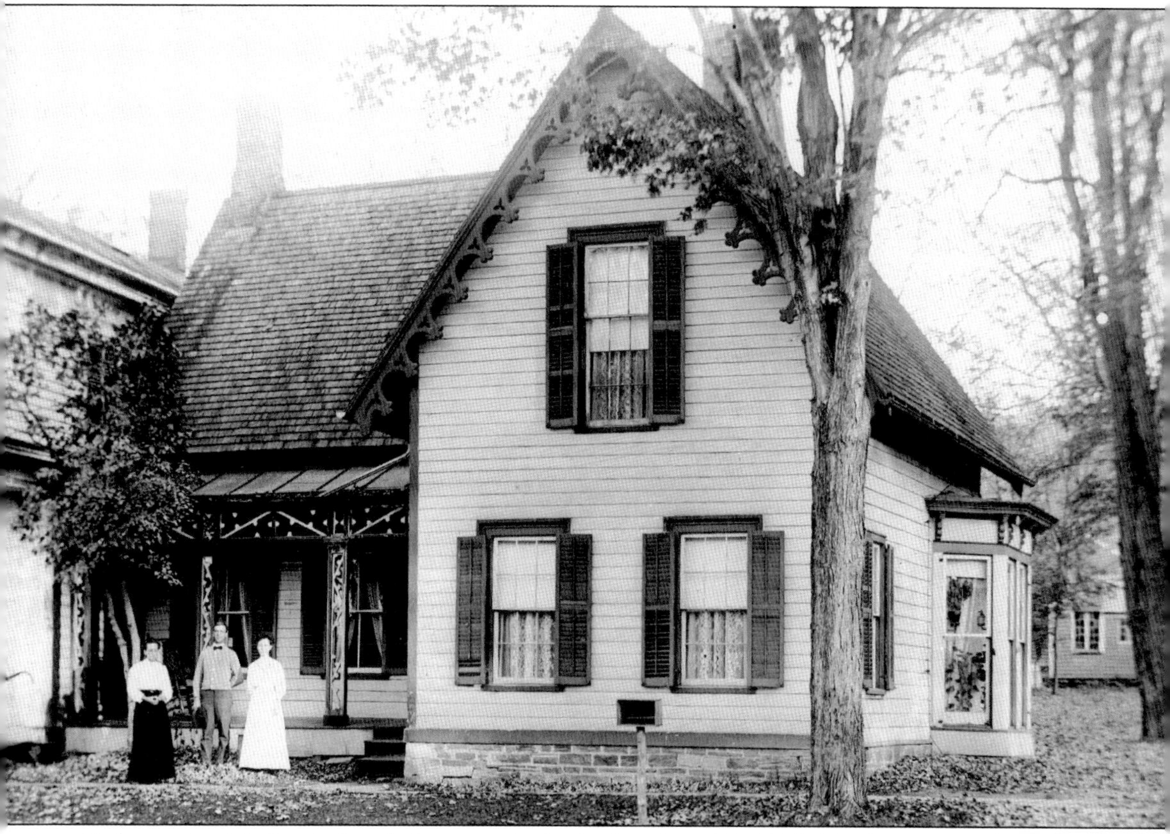

Only two Gothic Revival–style houses exist in the hamlet of Middlefield. This one was built by Alexander Murray in the 1850s. At that time Murray owned the still that tavern keeper Joshua Pinney had set up in the early 19th century. Murray is rumored to have let people drink for free at the tap. Laura Chapin added the bow window on the right before Charles Hearn bought the house. To the left can be seen the corner of the Cloxton Store, which was later moved. (Courtesy TMHA.)

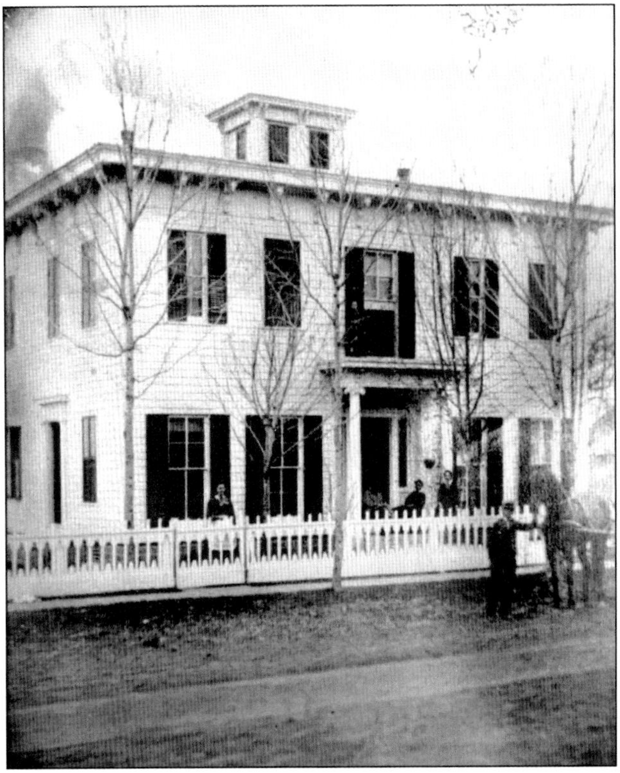

This 1859 tintype shows the home of Harrison North shortly after it was built in the hamlet of Middlefield. Harrison North was a member of one of the oldest and most enduring families in Middlefield. His grandfather had settled not far from this spot on a farm he rented from George Clarke of Springfield. North attended the academic school in the hamlet in the 1820s and became a very wealthy merchant.

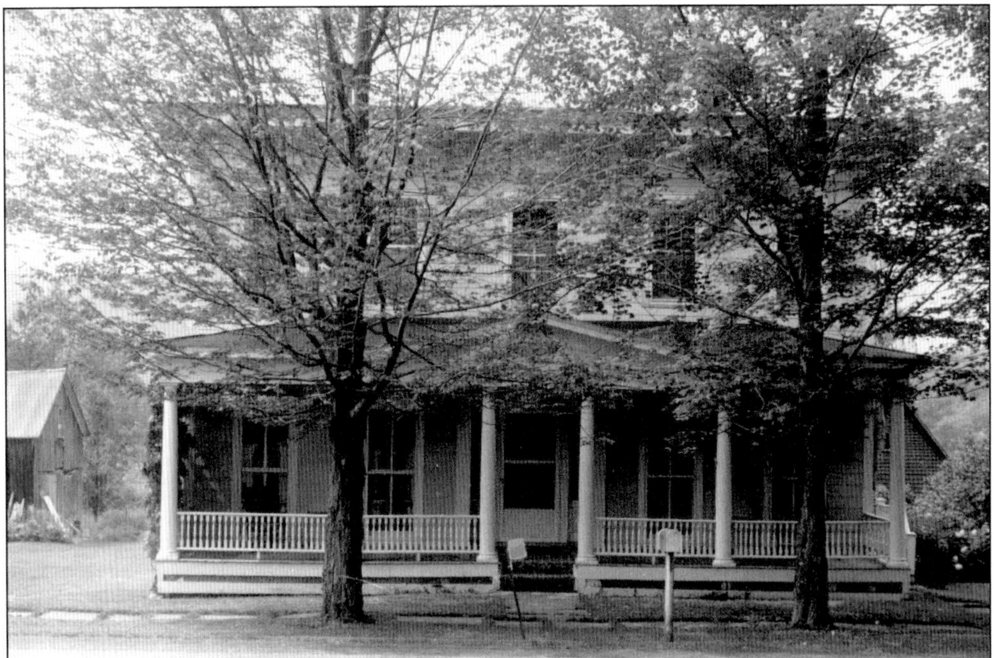

Shown is the Harrison North house after extensive alterations. The house has since been restored to its former beauty. Unfortunately, the cupola, which was lost in a windstorm, has not been rebuilt. The slate sidewalk in front, which still endures, can be seen.

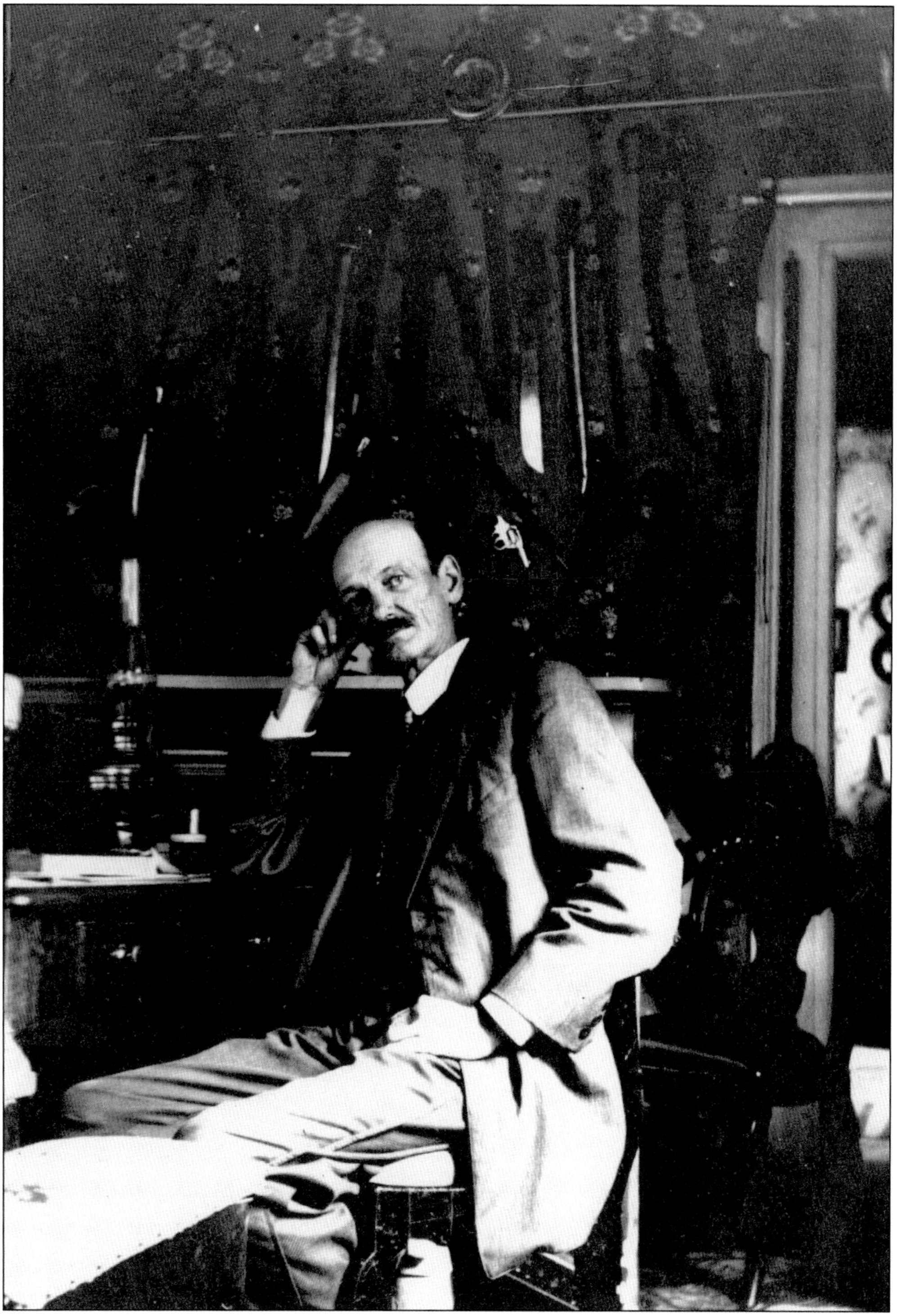

Charles North spent a lifetime assembling a collection of Indian artifacts which he displayed in his family's house. When he died in 1921, the collection was given to the Yager Museum at Hartwick College. (Courtesy TMHA.)

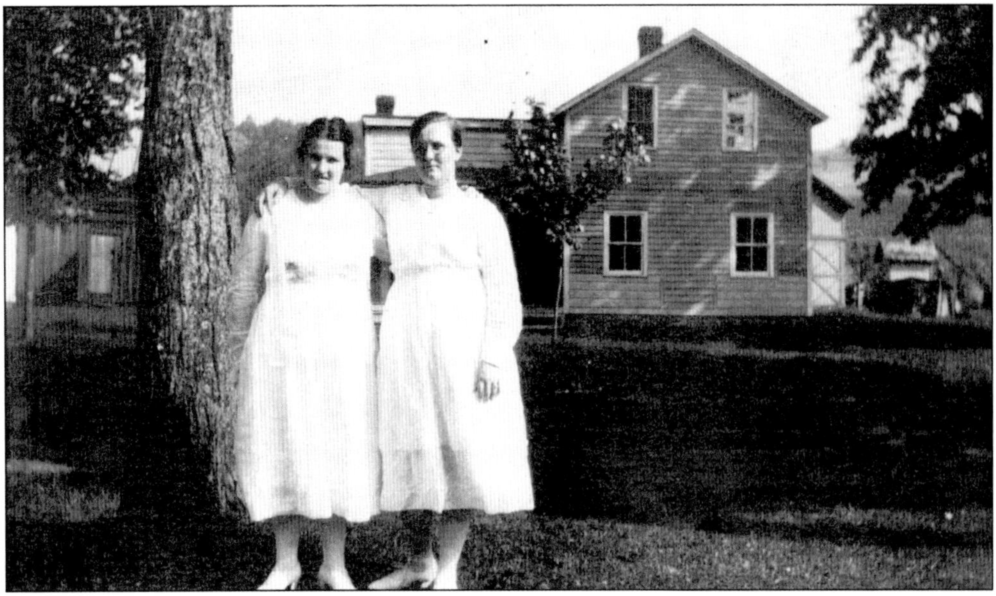

Mabel and Bess Wheeler are pictured on the sidewalk in the hamlet of Middlefield. The house behind them was built in the 1840s to serve as the law office of LeRoy Bowe. Before the side wing was added, the entrance was between the windows of the gabled façade.

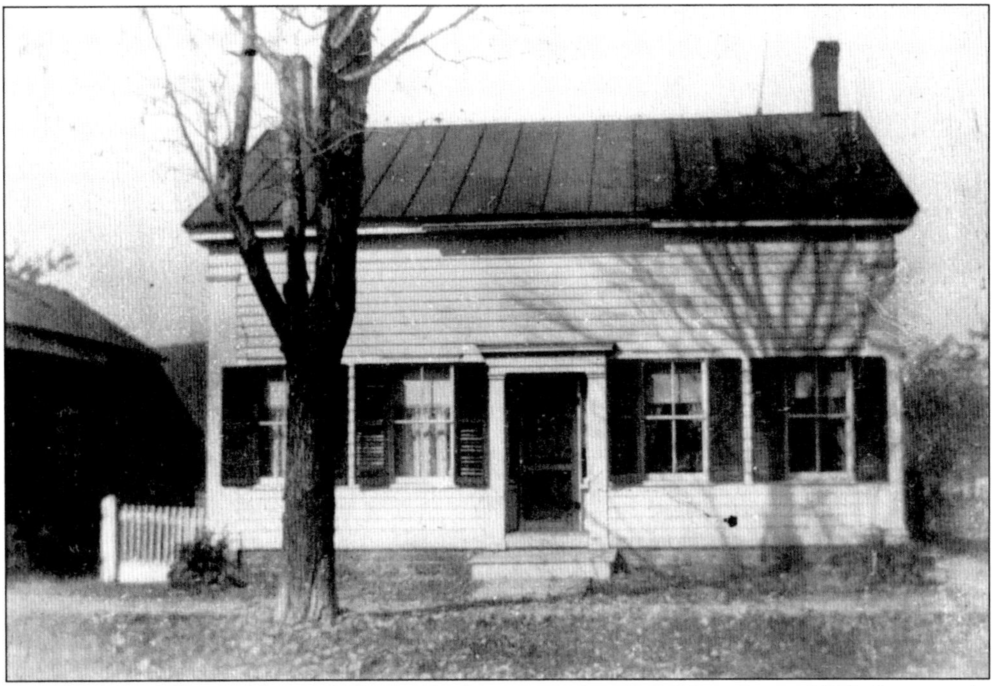

This fine Greek Revival house looks much the same today as it did in this c. 1905 photograph. Certainly its appearance is little changed from when it was built by Levi Crandall. To the left can be seen the wagon shop that was started by Daniel Cummings in the 1820s.

In the spring the Cherry Valley Creek has a tendency to flood in the hamlet of Middlefield. Some years the flooding is worse than others. In 1959, the water level rose precipitously, as these photographs show. The Kanzler house is in the back on the right and the corner of the Snyder house is on the left. The District No. 1 School is in the background. (Courtesy TMHA.)

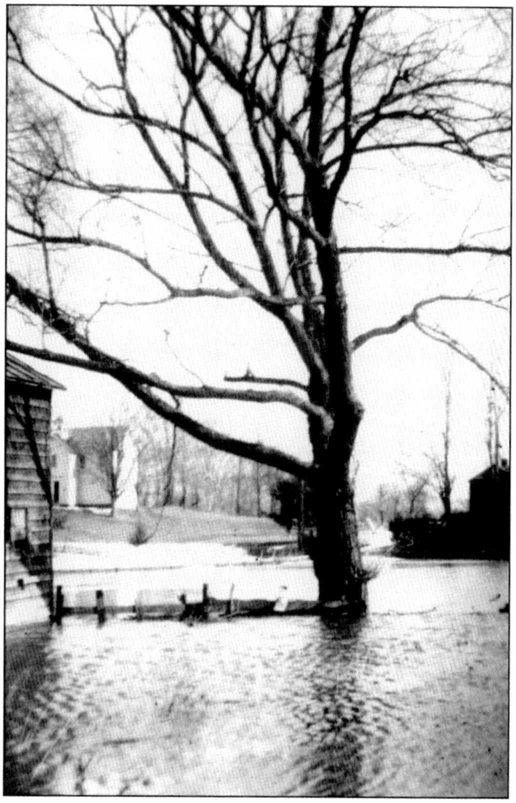

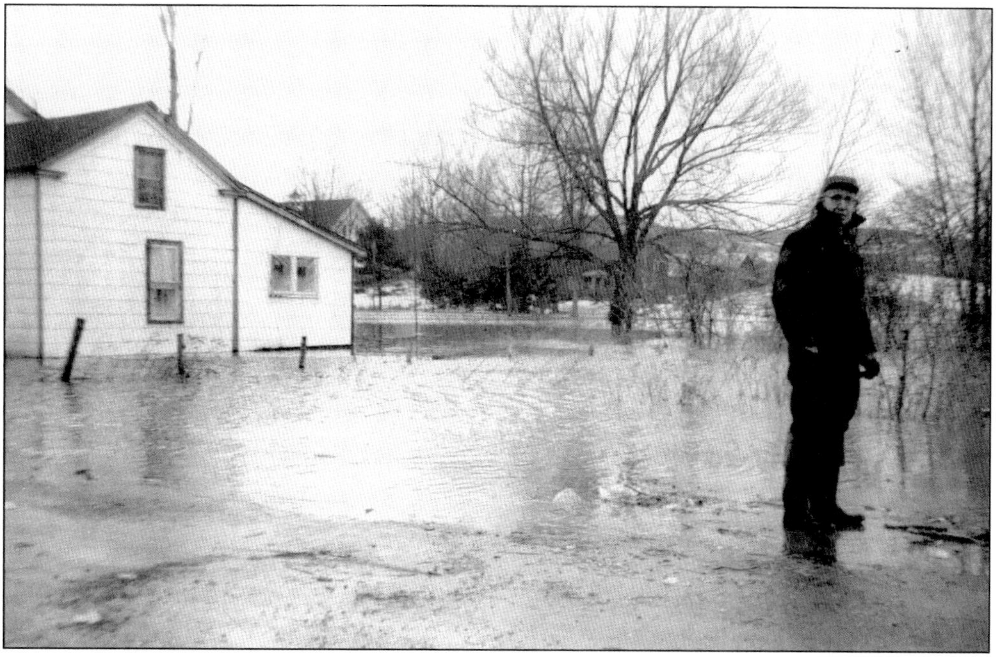

The damage is being surveyed after the flood of 1959. (Courtesy TMHA.)

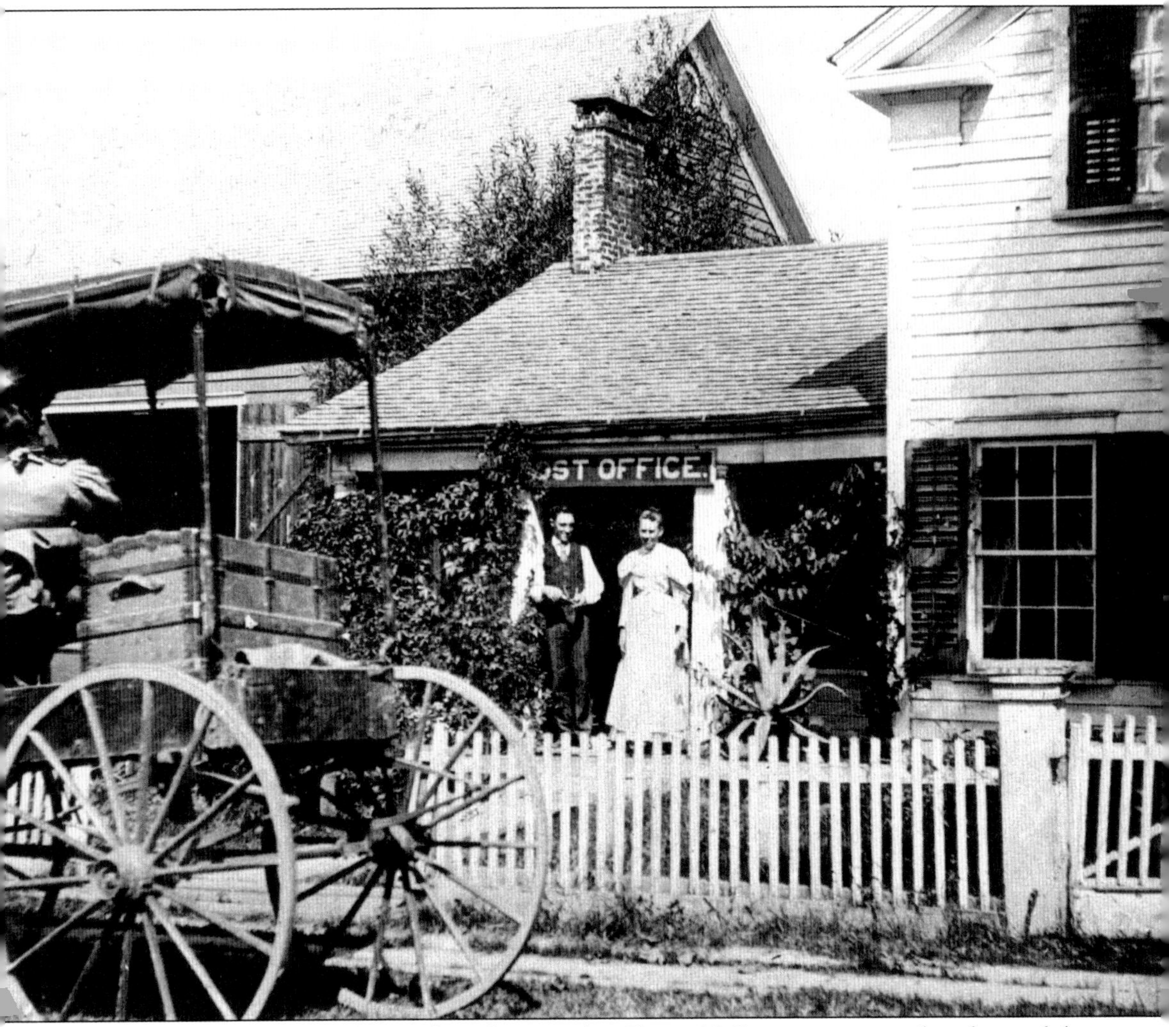

This 1898 photograph shows Ida Calvert in the Cherry Valley stage, stopped in front of the Middlefield Center Post Office. This post office was established in 1826, with Mason Huntington as the first postmaster. On June 20, 1898, Vernie Hanna was appointed postmaster. The post office was closed in 1907. (Courtesy NYSHA.)

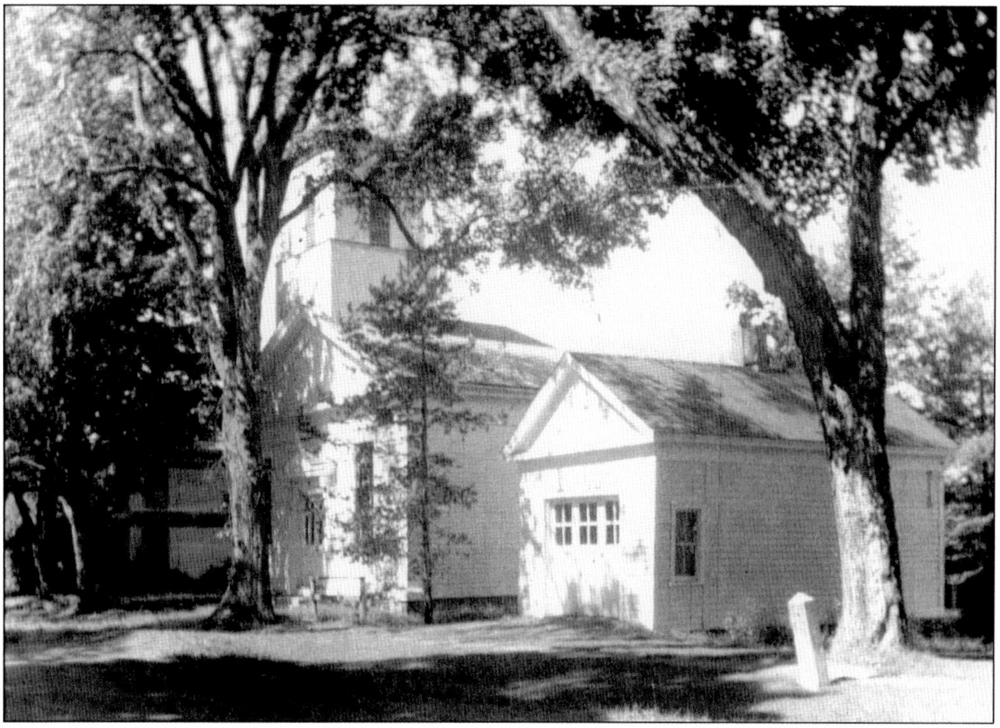

This 1959 photograph shows the main street in the hamlet of Middlefield Center. The Kellar Boot Shop is on the right, and just past it is the Presbyterian church. A close look at the church reveals that the spire has been lost. During a storm, lightning struck the spire and destroyed it. (Courtesy TMHA.)

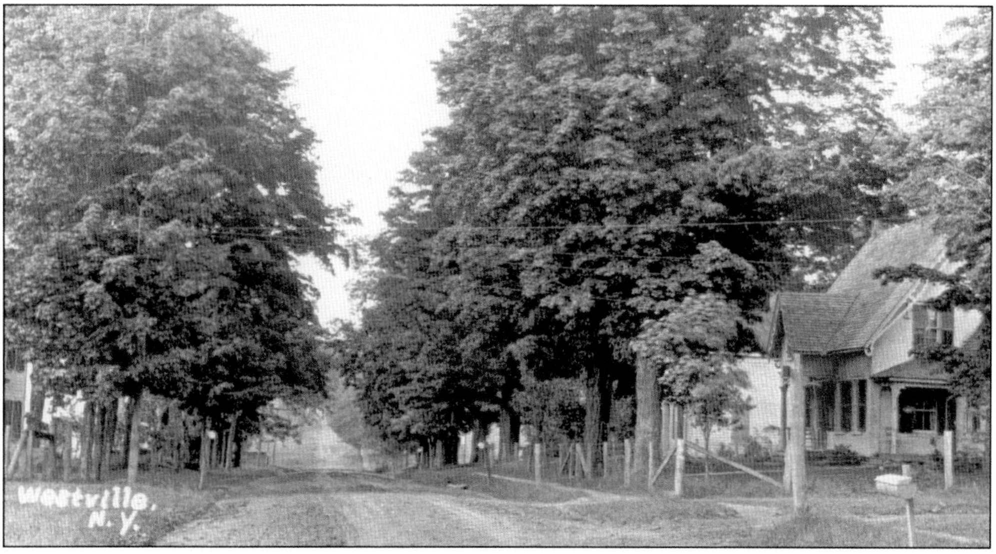

This *c.* 1915 photograph shows the main road heading north out of the hamlet of Westville. The beautiful lines of William Garlock's Gothic Revival house can be seen on the right. (Courtesy TMHA.)

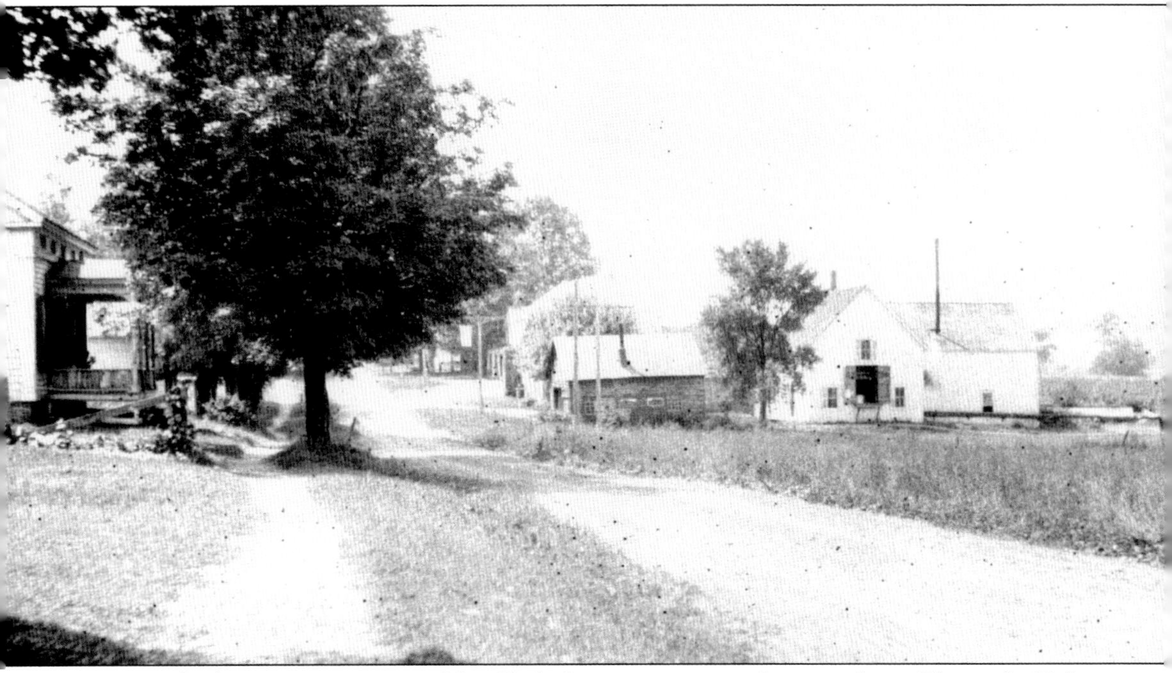

A popular business enterprise in New York dairy country was cheese making. This early-20th-century photograph shows the Westville cheese factory on the right, along with the blacksmith shop in the center and the Methodist parsonage on the left. (Courtesy TMHA.)

Two

Old Schoolhouses

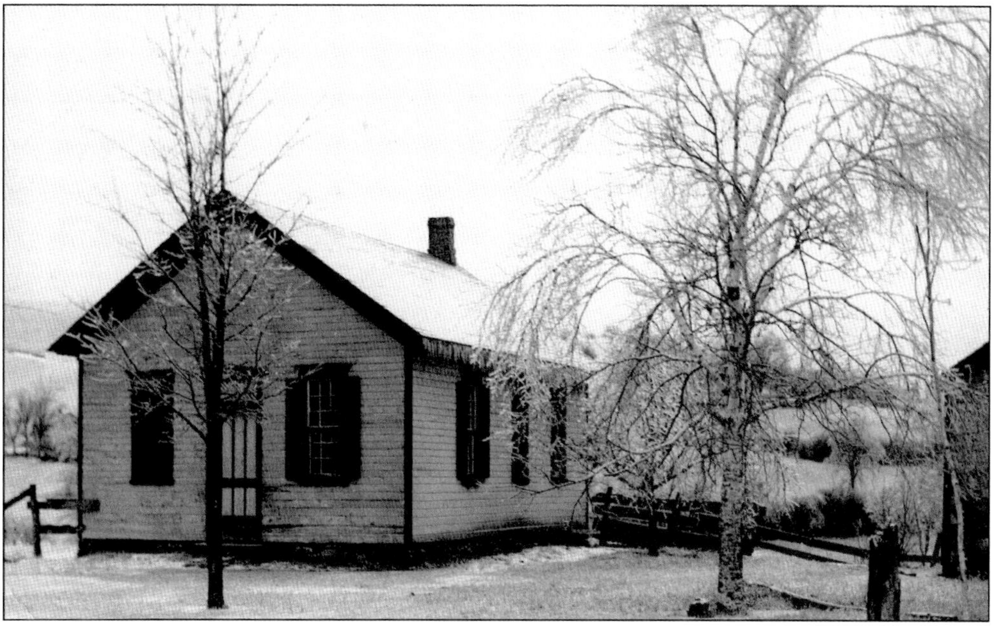

This postcard was sent from Ida in Milford to Mrs. Tipple in Schenevus in 1909; both Milford and Schenevus are neighboring towns of Middlefield. Pictured is the District No. 4 School, known as the Lane School, which has the typical appearance of a rural New York State one-room schoolhouse. (Courtesy TMHA.)

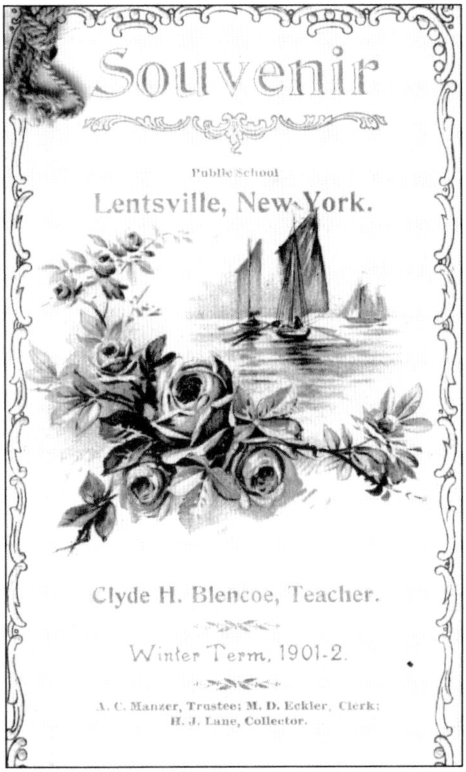
Souvenir

Public School

Lentsville, New York.

Clyde H. Blencoe, Teacher.

Winter Term, 1901-2.

A. C. Manzer, Trustee; M. D. Eckler, Clerk; H. J. Lane, Collector.

During the late 19th and early 20th centuries, schools often printed these "souvenirs." This one of the Lentsville School is for the 1901–1902 winter term. The view hints at the school's proximity to Otsego Lake. (Courtesy TMHA.)

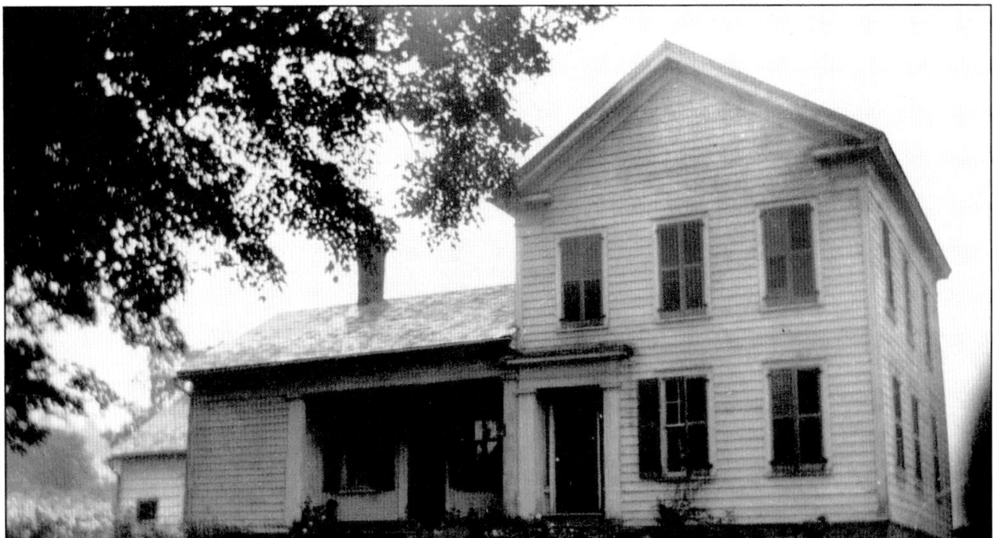

This house in the hamlet of Middlefield has typical Greek Revival features, particularly the front facing gable and the heavy moldings around the front door. The wing shown at the far left once served as a school.

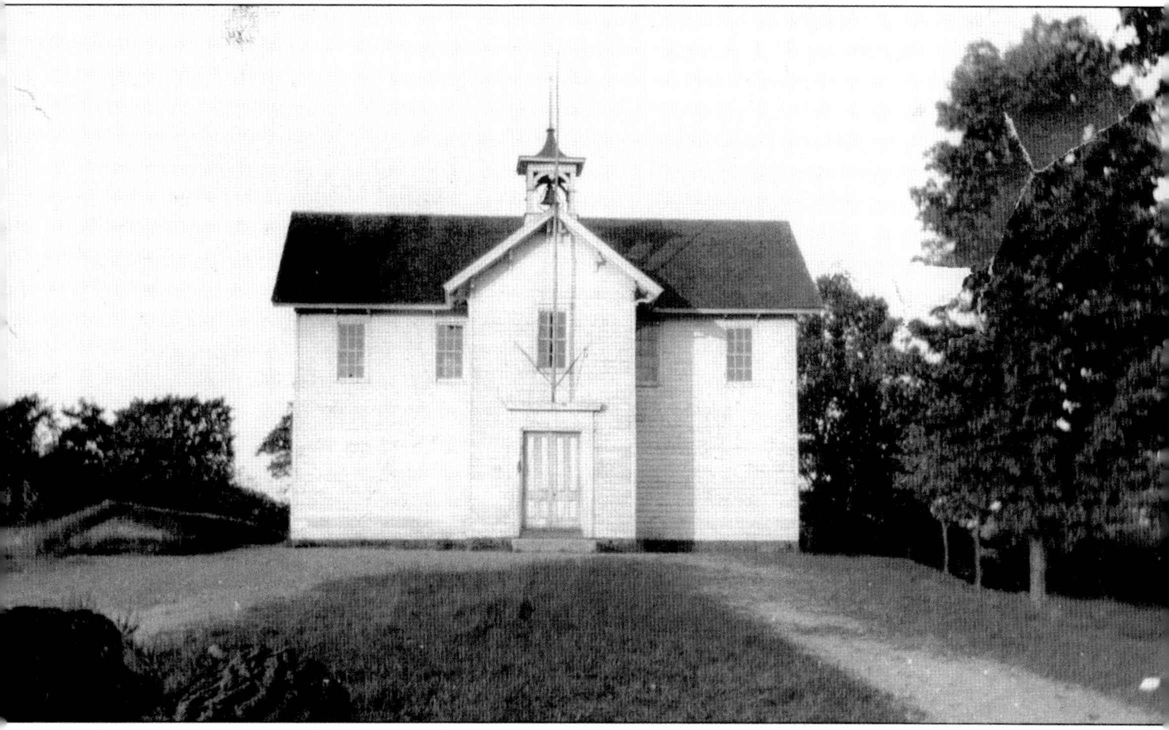

The District No. 1 School in the hamlet of Middlefield was built in 1875 on land donated by George Hyde Clarke of Springfield. This photograph shows the school after the lower front windows were removed but before glass was added to the front doors. This schoolhouse is now headquarters for the Town of Middlefield Historical Association.

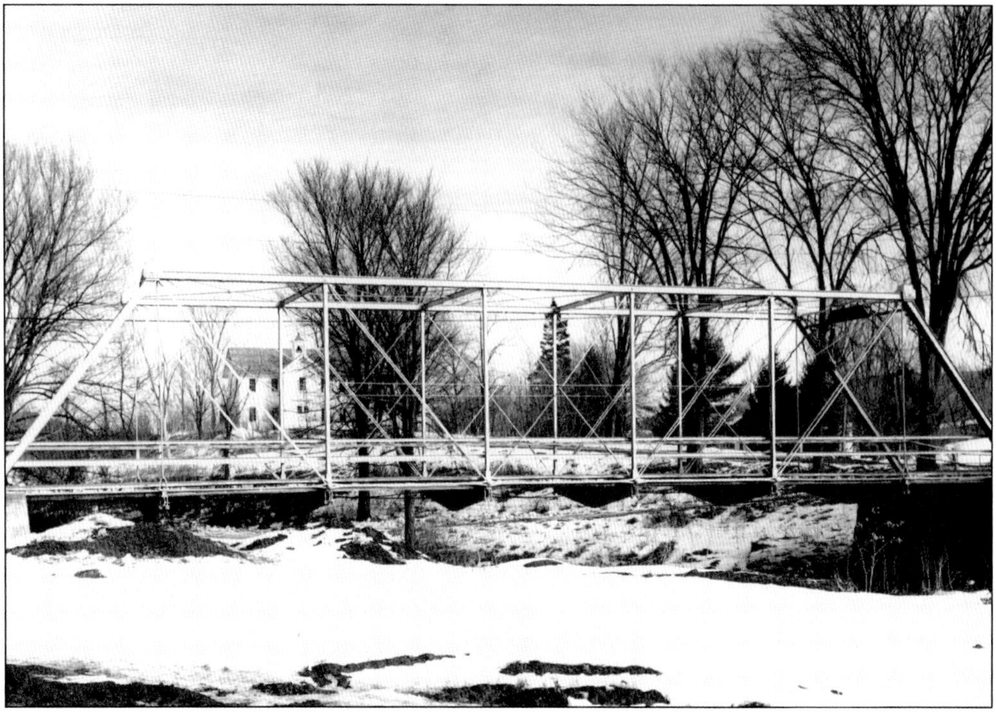

The District No. 1 School is seen through the cold steel of the bridge over the Cherry Valley Creek. The schoolhouse is pictured after undergoing extensive renovations made by the Town of Middlefield Historical Association. Shortly after this photograph was taken, the bridge was replaced with a modern concrete and steel bridge. (Courtesy TMHA.)

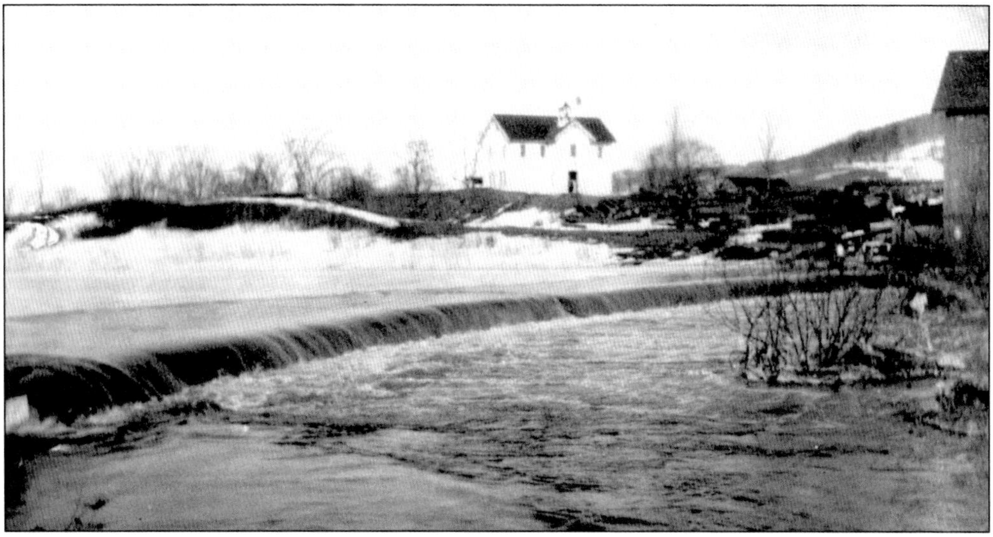

In 1921, the trustees changed the windows in the front of the schoolhouse, removing the front lower-story windows and moving them to the side of the building. This photograph, taken later the same year, shows the school from across the sawmill dam. The water level is exceptionally high due to the spring snowmelt. (Courtesy NYSHA.)

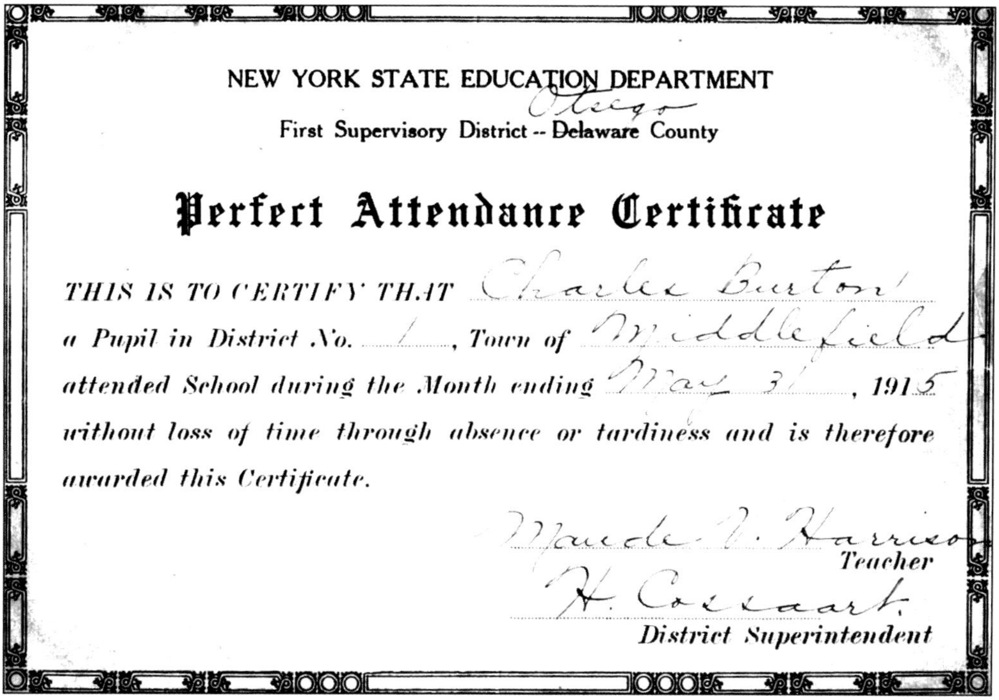

NEW YORK STATE EDUCATION DEPARTMENT

First Supervisory District -- ~~Delaware~~ Otsego County

Perfect Attendance Certificate

THIS IS TO CERTIFY THAT Charles Burton

a Pupil in District No. 1, *Town of* Middlefield

attended School during the Month ending May 31, 1915

without loss of time through absence or tardiness and is therefore awarded this Certificate.

Maude V. Harrison
Teacher

H. Cossaart.
District Superintendent

This certificate would indicate that attending a whole month of school without missing any time was quite a feat in 1915. The parents of Charles must have been proud.

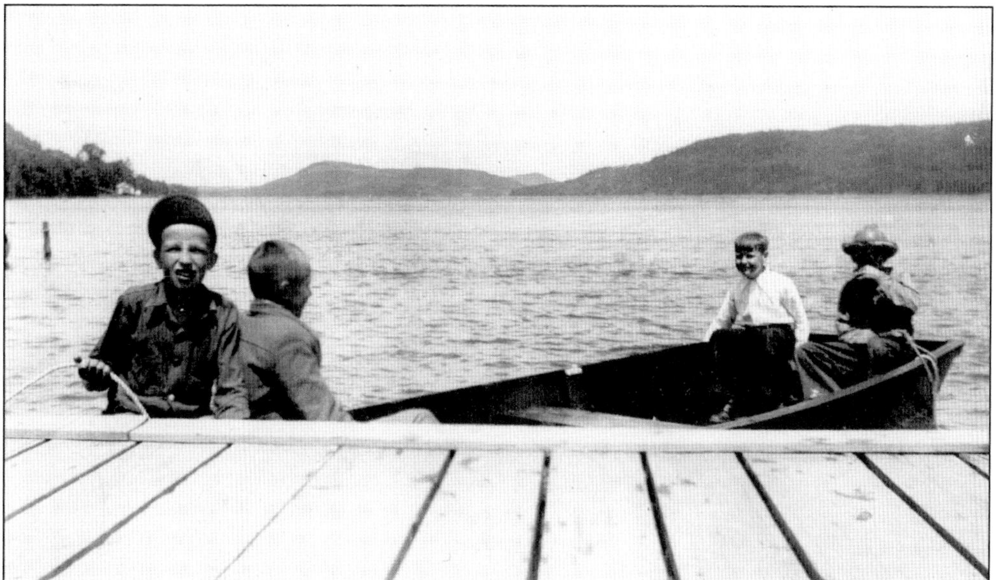

Children from the District No. 1 School are off for a picnic at Otsego Lake's Three Mile Point in 1940. The point has been a popular picnic area since the village of Cooperstown was founded by Judge William Cooper, the father of famous novelist James Fenimore Cooper. (Courtesy TMHA.)

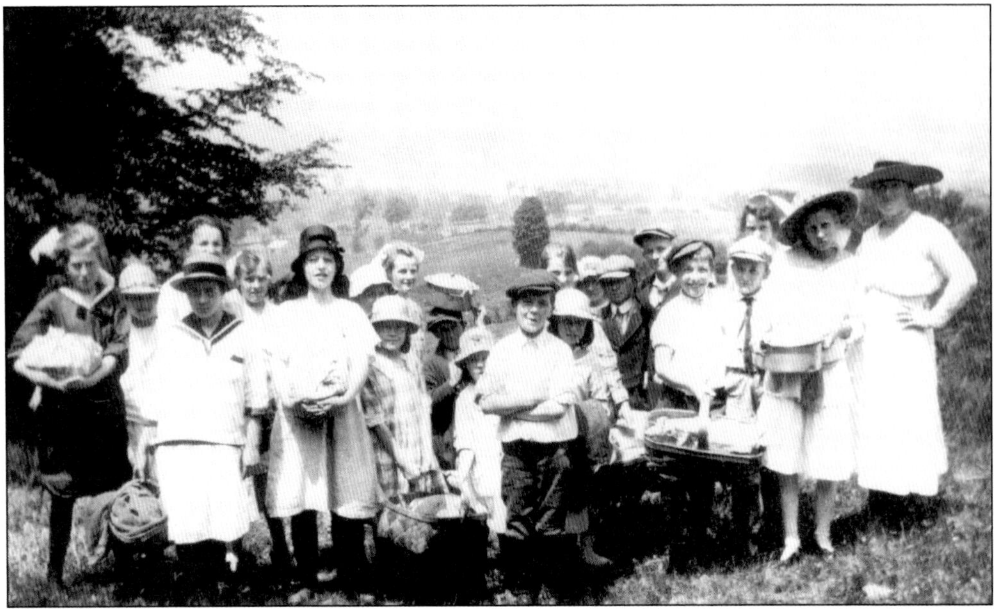

Other popular picnic areas were only a short walk from the schoolhouse. (Courtesy TMHA.)

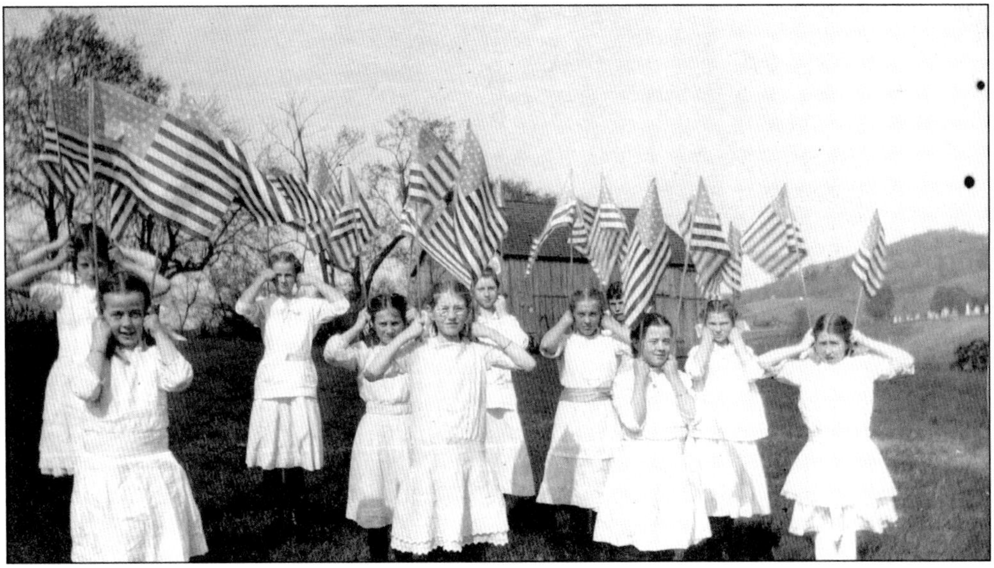

The U.S. entry into World War I was greeted with an outpouring of patriotic fervor. These girls from the District No. 1 School are practicing for the 1918 Field Days. (Courtesy TMHA.)

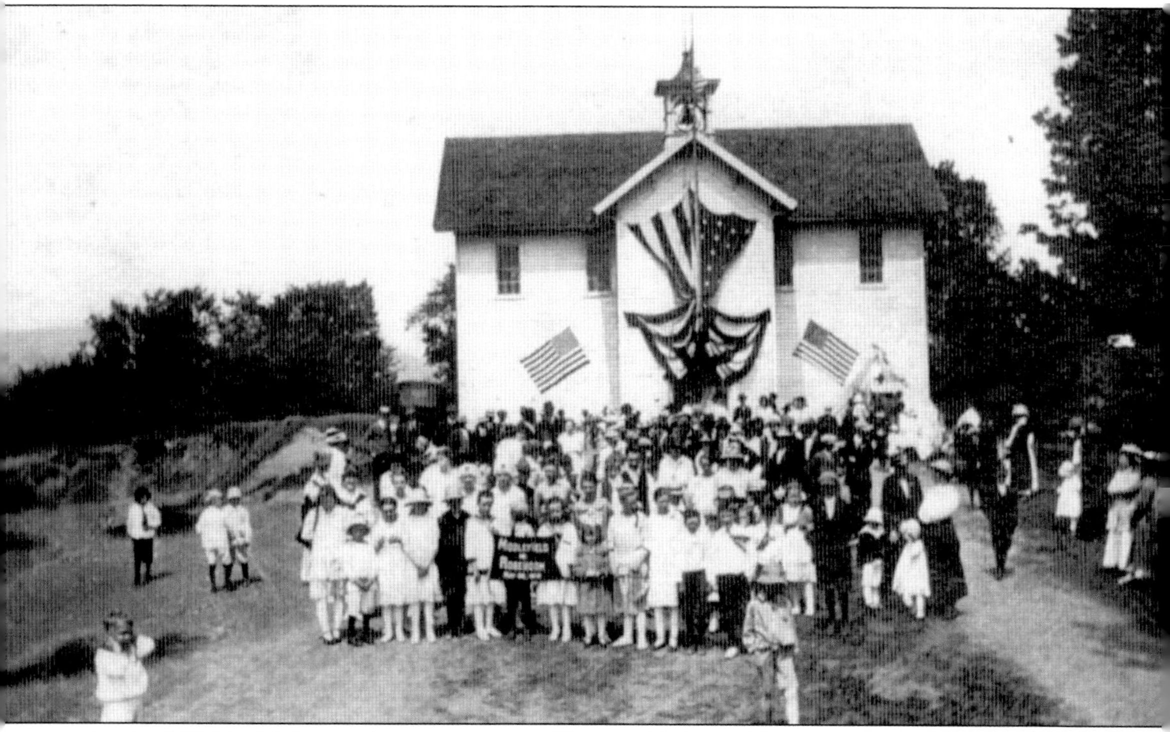

For the 1918 Field Days celebration, the children of Middlefield District No. 1 are joined by children from the neighboring town of Roseboom. (Courtesy TMHA.)

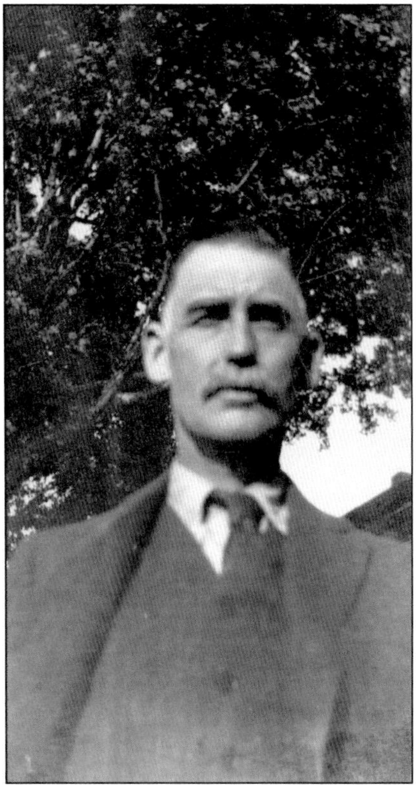

Not all children had to make the proverbially walk to school. George Garlock was responsible for driving first the wagon and then the bus that brought children to the District No. 1 School.

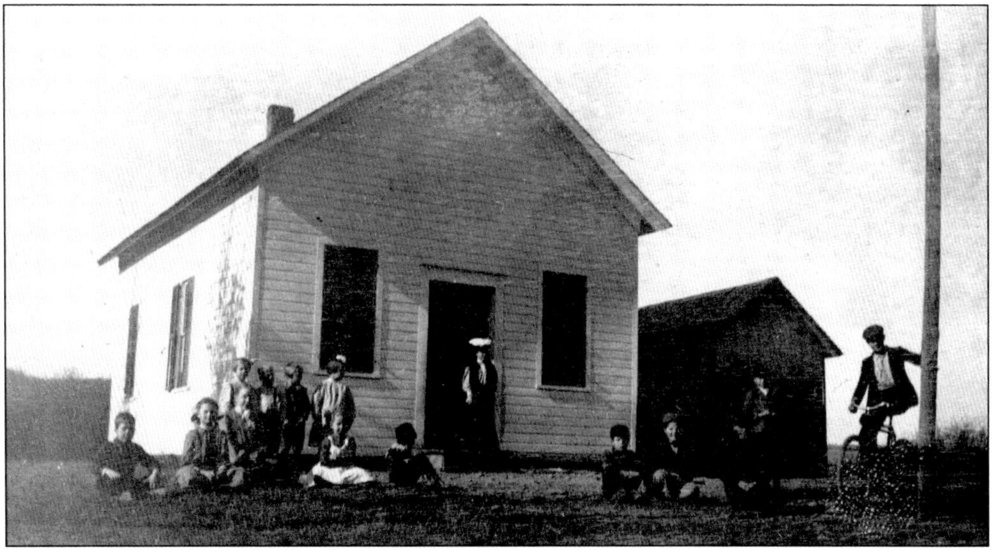

Children gather outside the District No. 12 School in the hamlet of Middlefield Center. This c. 1908 postcard shows how unadorned and utilitarian some of the one-room schoolhouses were. (Courtesy TMHA.)

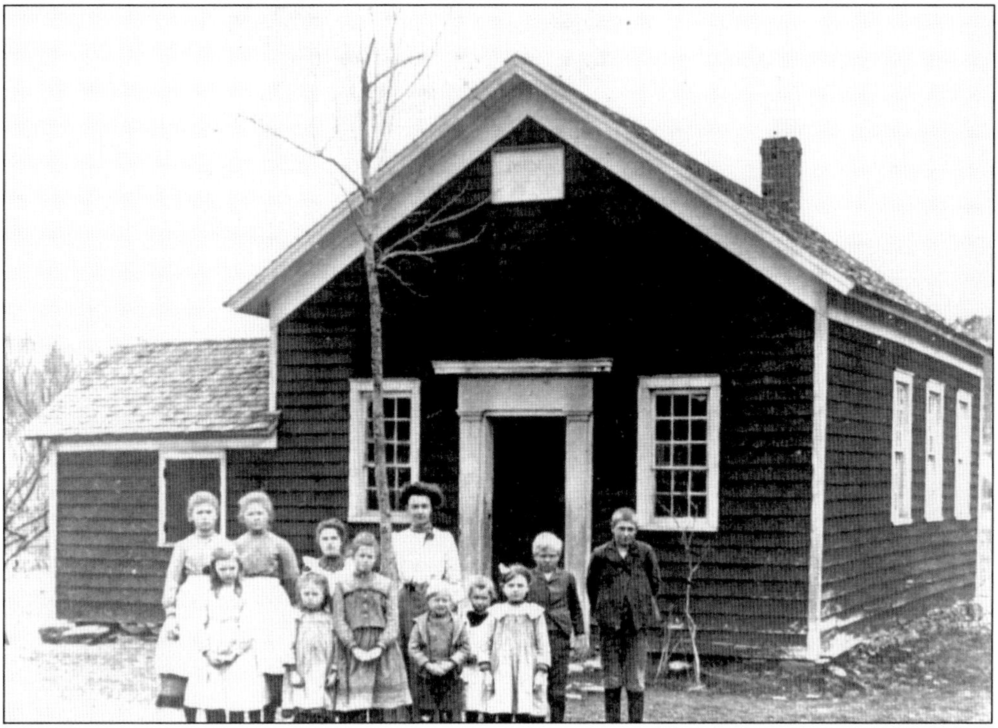

The District No. 16 School, known as the Pitts School, was built in the Greek Revival style, as evidenced by the heavy pilasters and wide entablature of the doorway, as well as by the front facing gable. This style was ubiquitous in rural New York throughout the 19th century. (Courtesy TMHA.)

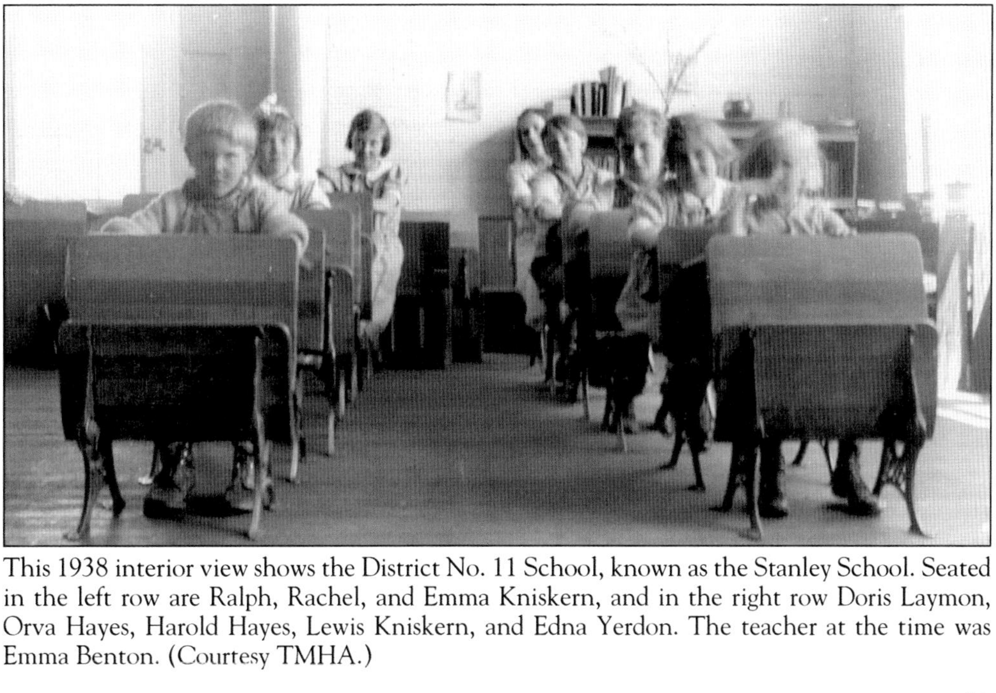

This 1938 interior view shows the District No. 11 School, known as the Stanley School. Seated in the left row are Ralph, Rachel, and Emma Kniskern, and in the right row Doris Laymon, Orva Hayes, Harold Hayes, Lewis Kniskern, and Edna Yerdon. The teacher at the time was Emma Benton. (Courtesy TMHA.)

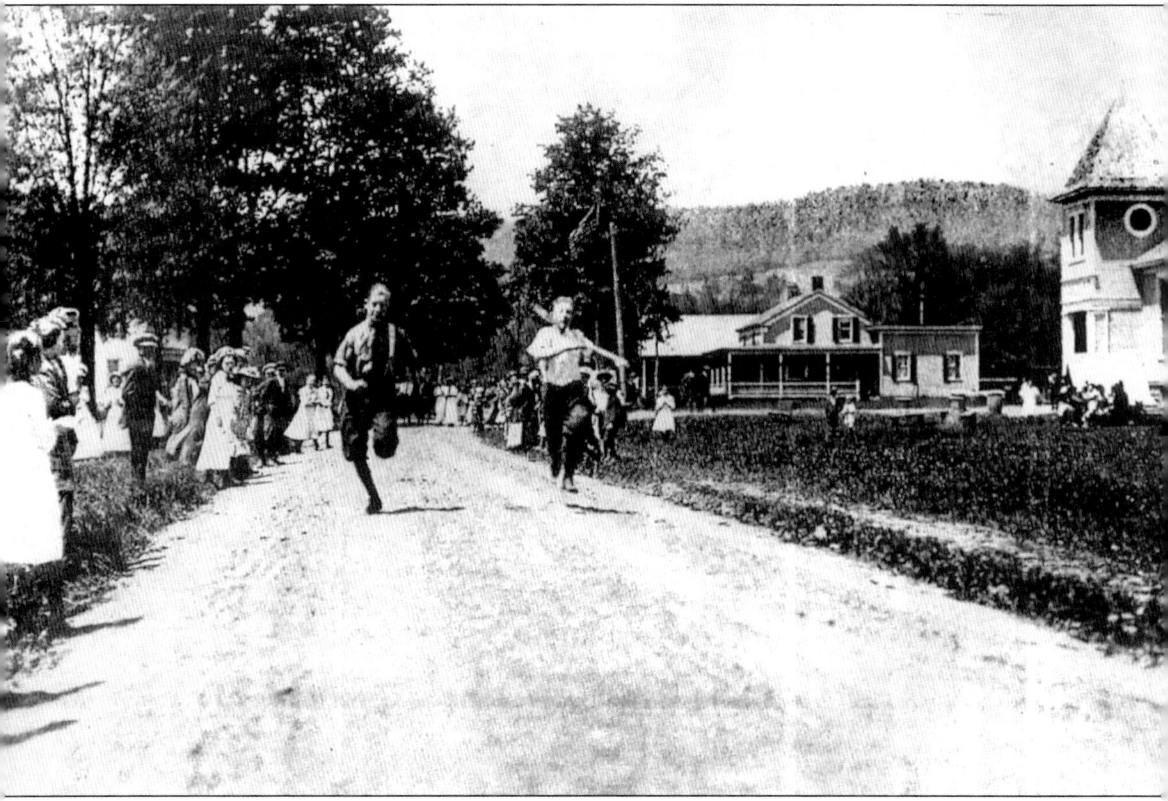

A racing competition is under way during the 1915 Field Days at the Westville School. (Courtesy TMHA.)

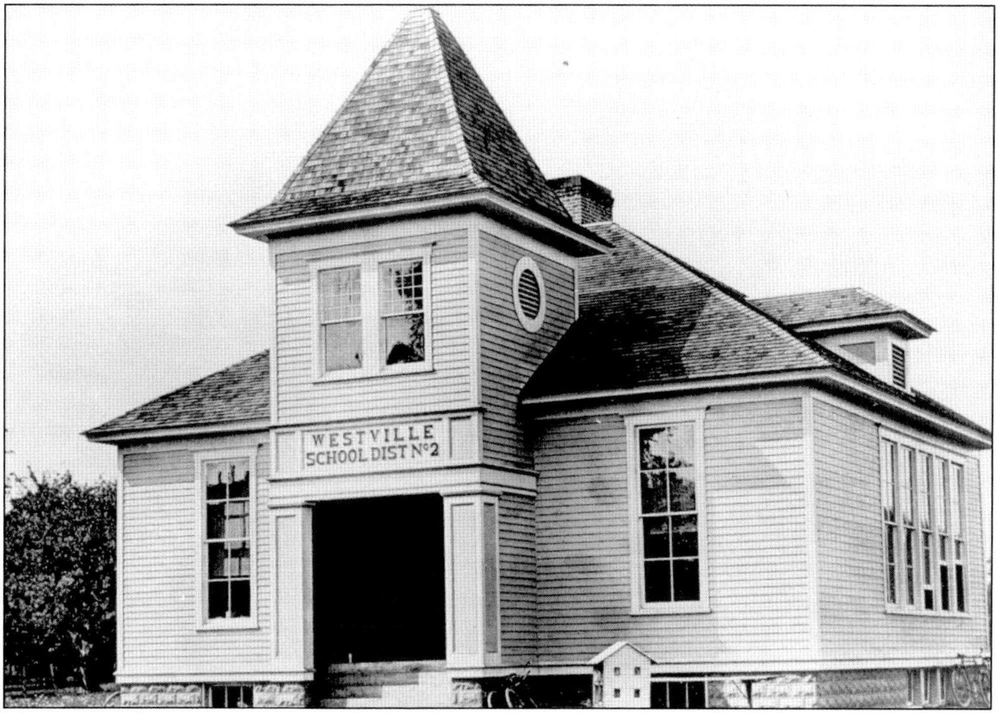

The Westville District No. 2 School is shown in 1914. This building combined several one-room schoolhouses into a modern model school. (Courtesy TMHA.)

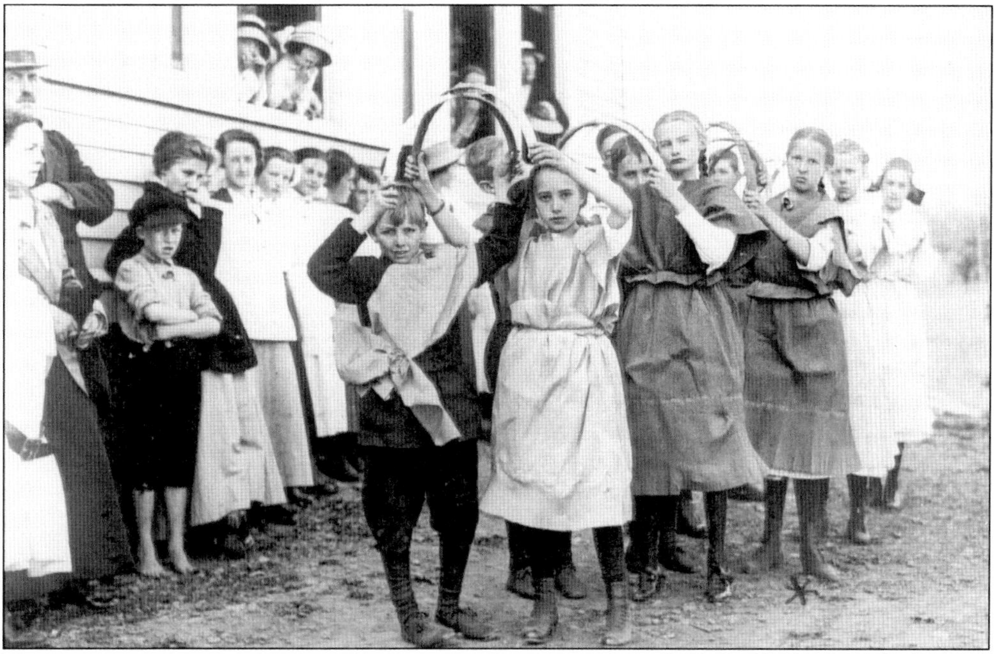

Children march past the school in the hoop drill during the 1915 Field Days in Westville. (Courtesy TMHA.)

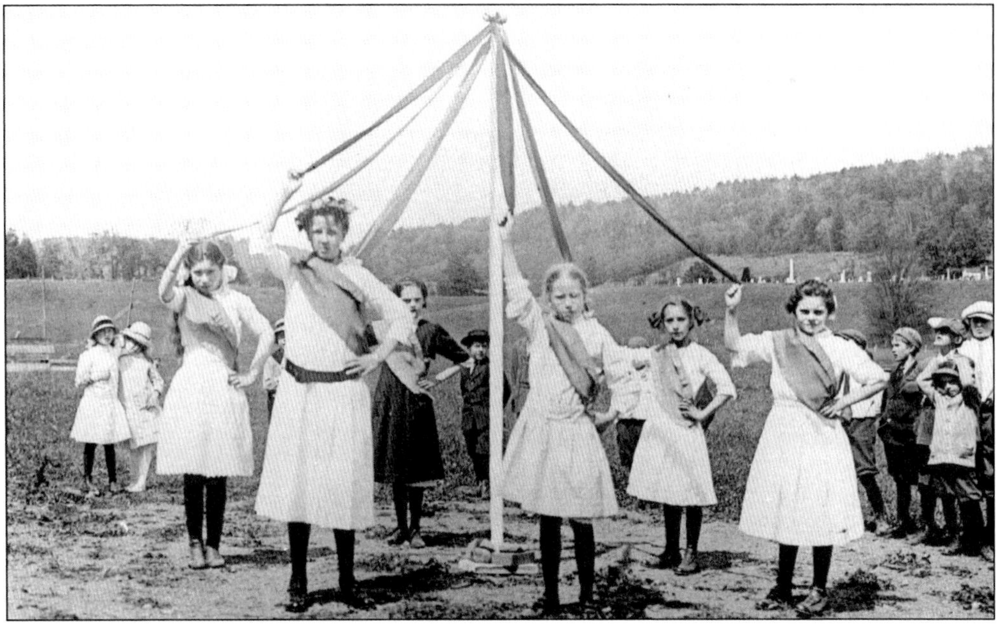

A Maypole dance is performed at the Westville School in 1915. (Courtesy TMHA.)

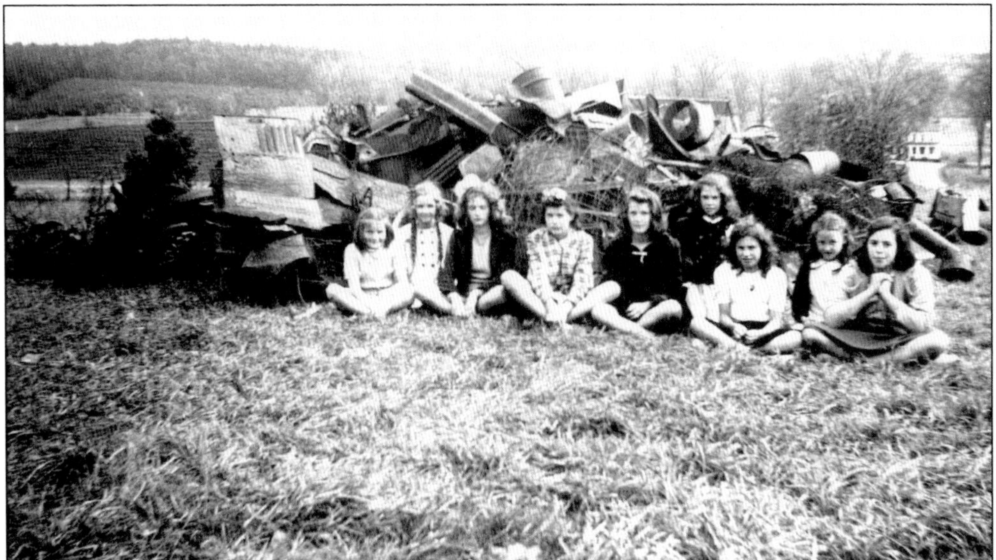

During World War II, children from the District No. 2 School collected scrap metal to aid in the war effort. (Courtesy TMHA.)

Three

Faiths and Churches

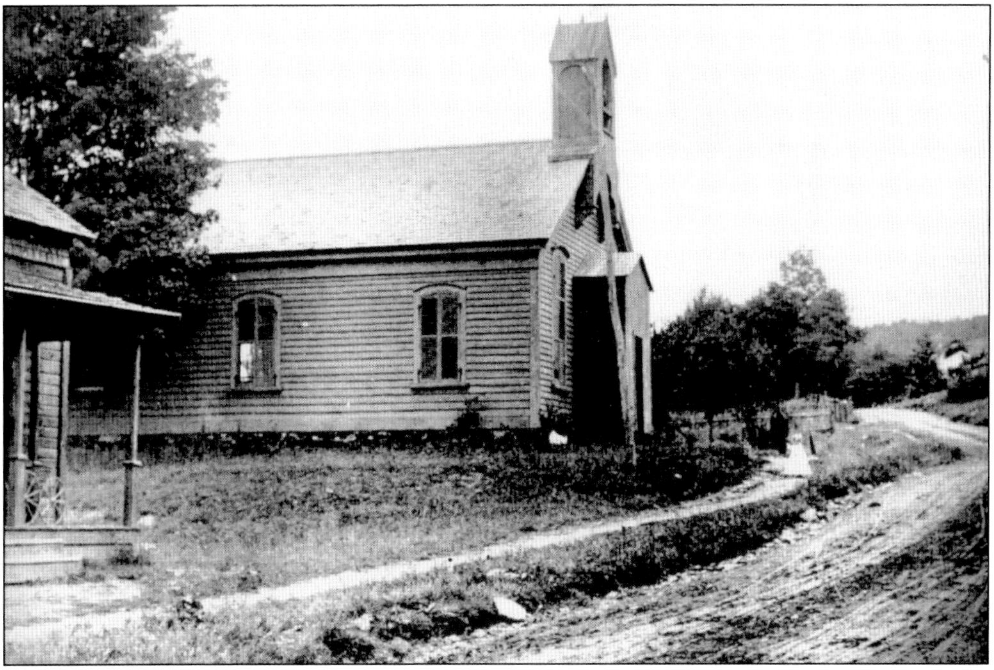

Shown *c.* 1890 is the Presbyterian chapel in Bowerstown, a hamlet named for John Bowers, who purchased the land patent in the late 18th century. The road winds around to Murphy Hill. The chapel is now a residence. (Courtesy TMHA.)

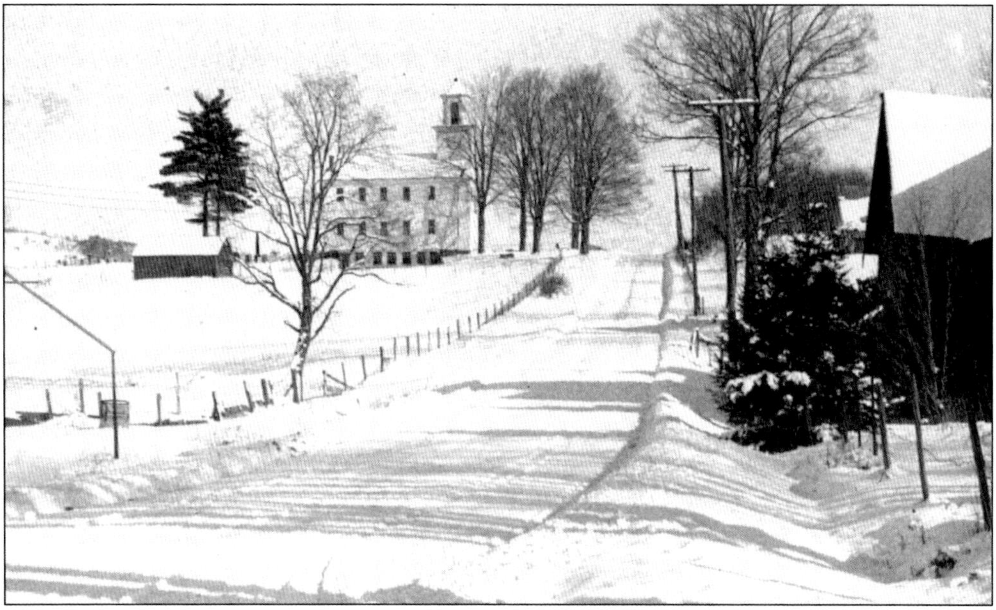

These pictures show the Baptist church perched on the hill overlooking the hamlet of Middlefield. The tower clock still tolls the hours, as it has for the past 150 years.

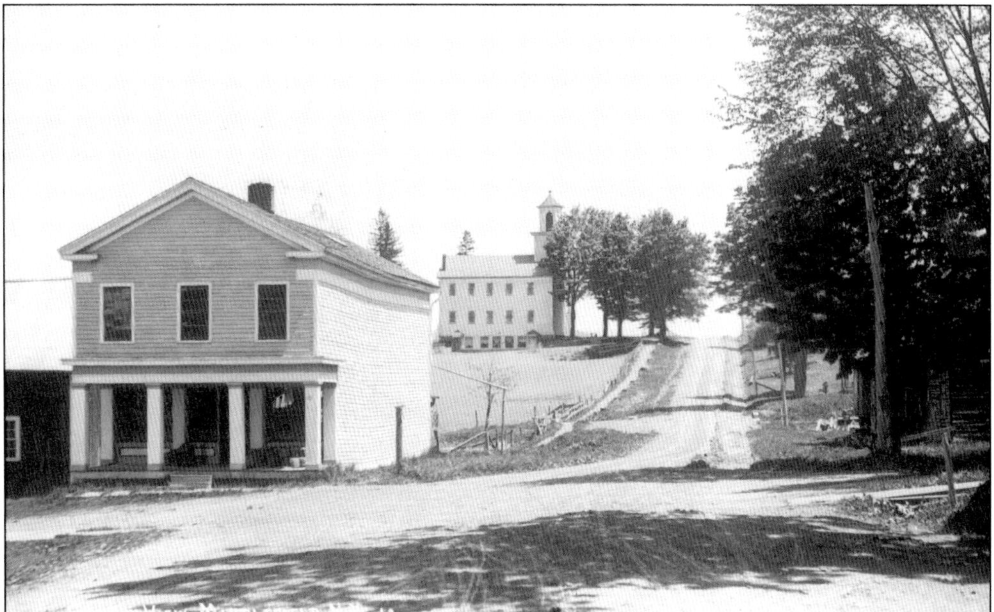

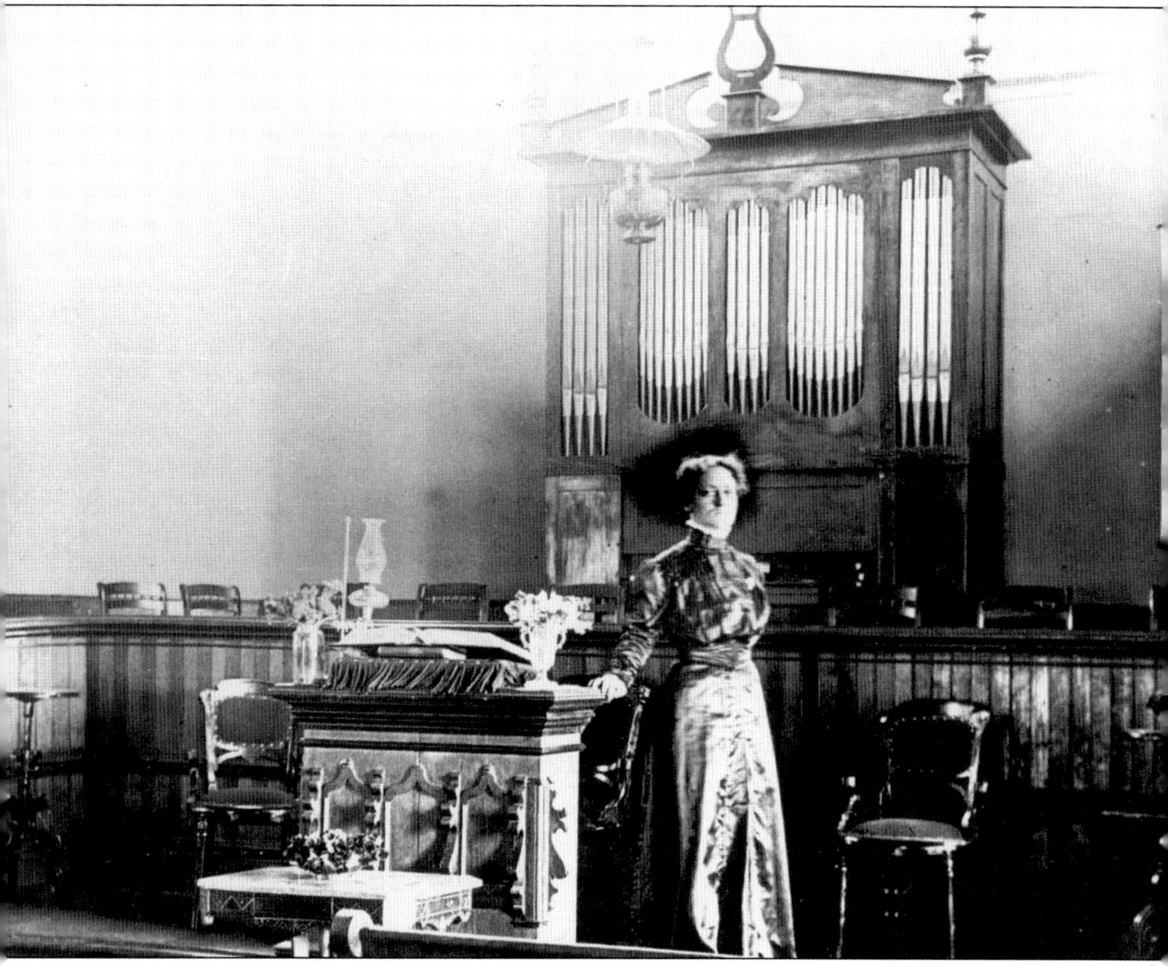

Ordained on July 8, 1909, Victoria Ingalls served as the minister of the Middlefield Baptist Church from 1908 to 1910. The furnishings of the church are little changed since this photograph was taken. The organ in the back is the oldest pipe organ in Otsego County. (Courtesy NYSHA.)

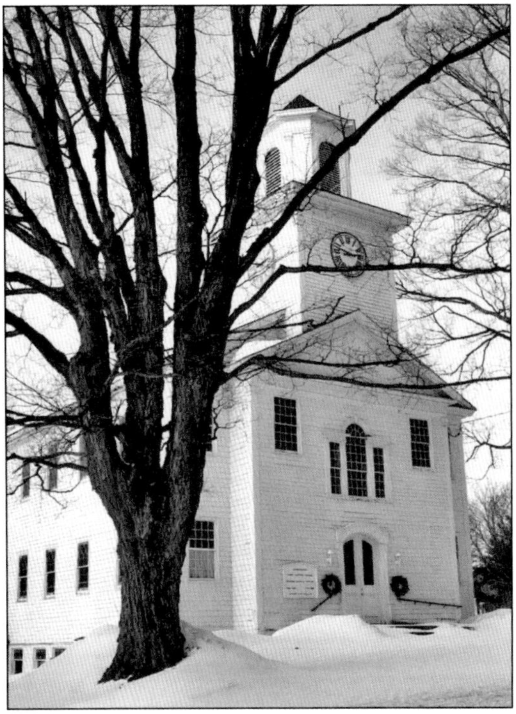

Built in 1826, the Baptist church was based on the design in plate 27 of Asher Benjamin's *The Country Builder's Assistant*, first published in 1797. Asher Benjamin's design was largely copied in New England. The Middlefield example is a particularly fine rendering. The clock was added *c.* 1852.

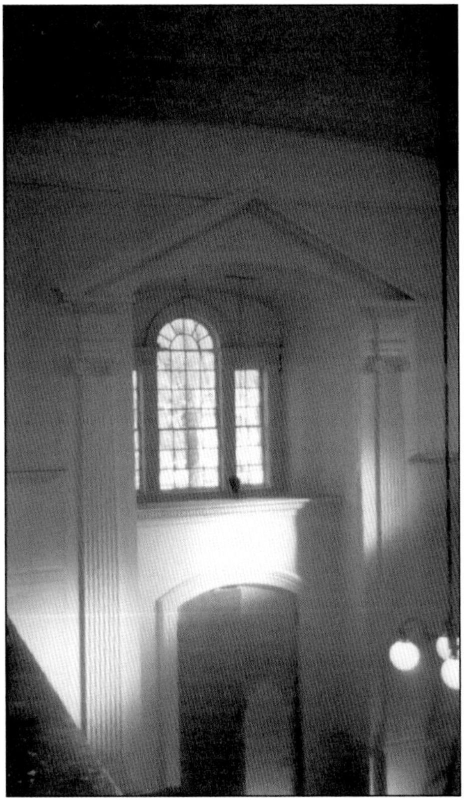

The interior of the Baptist church is a marvel of country architecture. Evening light accentuates the fine pilasters and surround of the Palladian window.

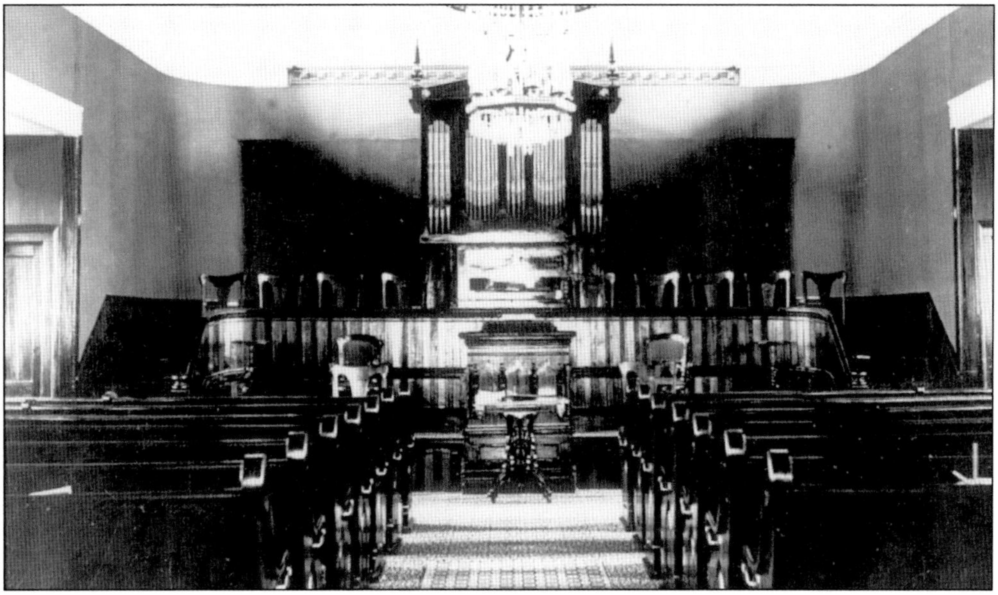

This photograph taken inside the Baptist church shows the pipe organ and a delicate chandelier. (Courtesy NYSHA.)

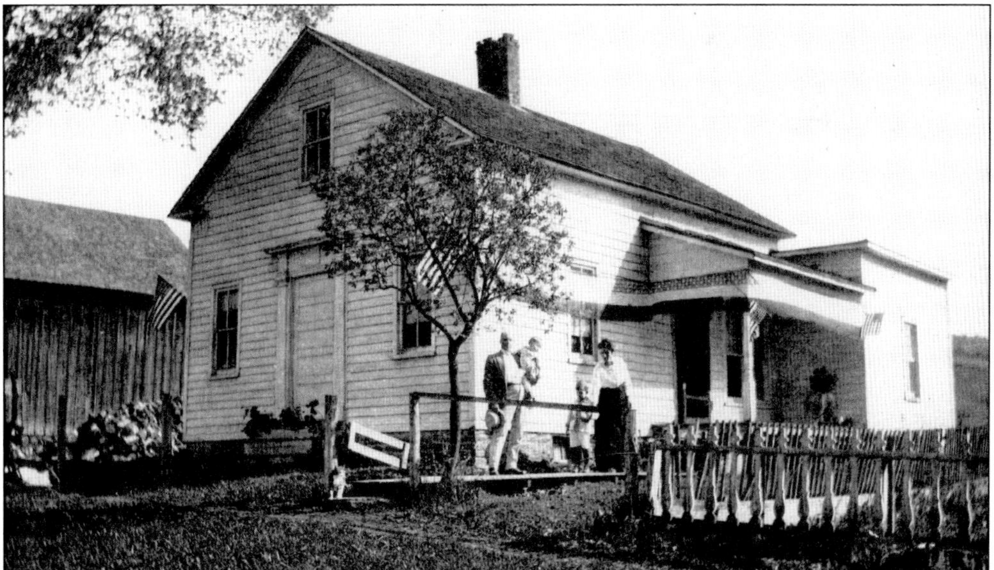

The Baptist parsonage stands on Whiteman Hill Road leading out of the hamlet of Middlefield. The beautiful Federal-style pilasters and entablature around the front door are now obscured by a porch.

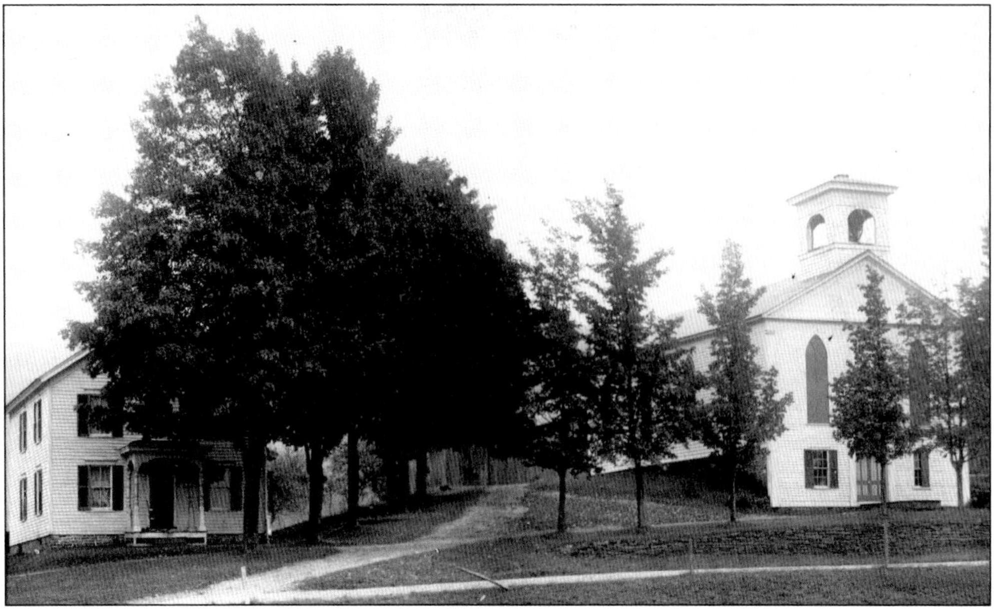

The Methodist church in the hamlet of Middlefield was built in 1832. It sits on lands donated by George Clarke of Springfield. On the left is the parsonage. The road between the church and the parsonage leads to the horse stables behind the church.

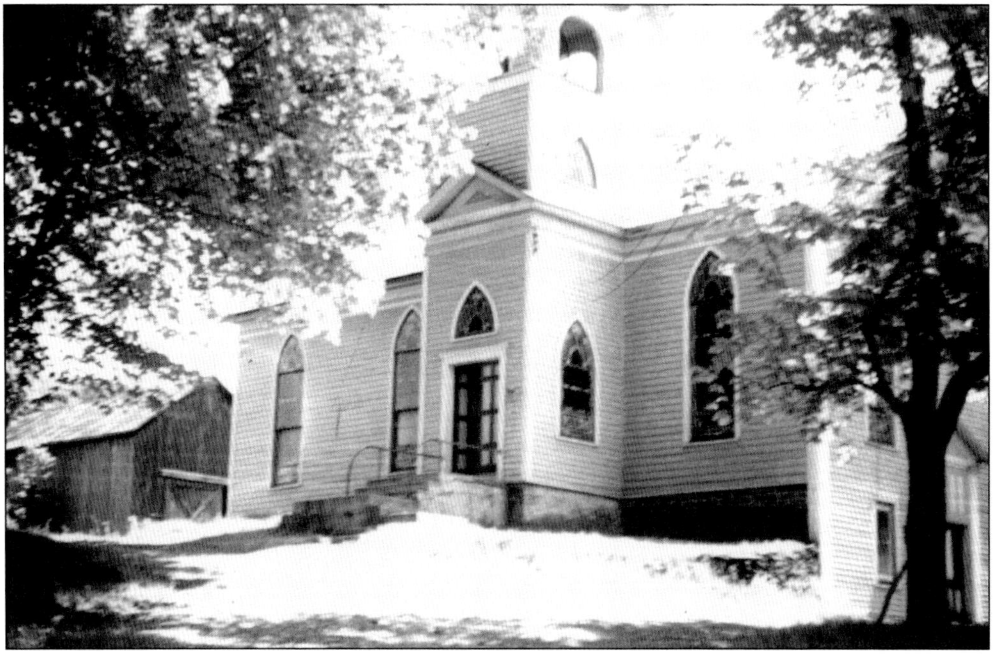

The Methodist church is shown after the extensive renovations of 1910. The belfry and entrance were moved to be more convenient as wagons unloaded on their way to the stables behind the church. The interior was also changed: the altar was placed in the corner, as prescribed in the Akron plan. (Courtesy TMHA.)

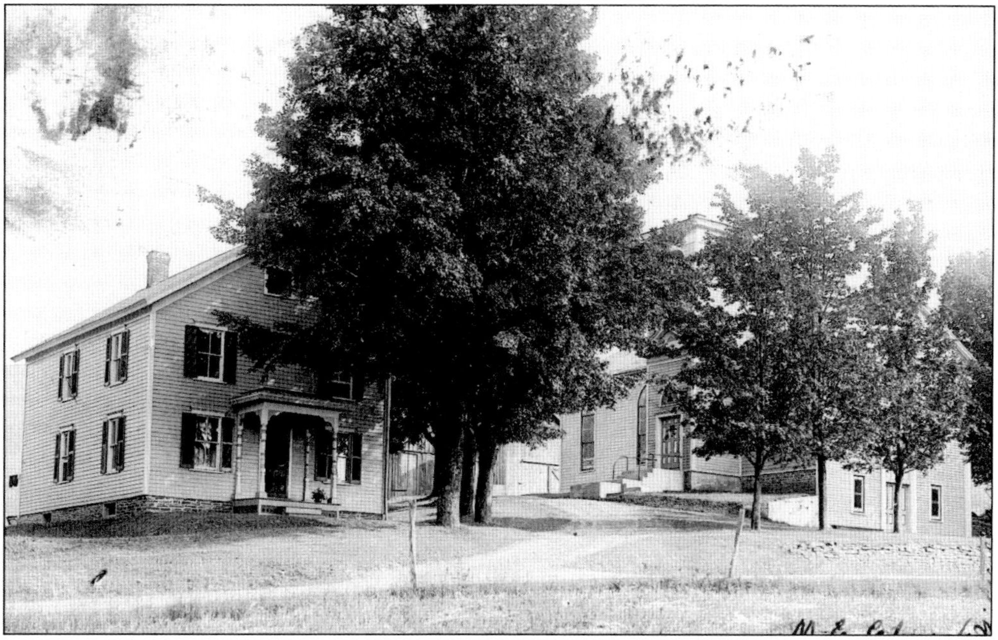

This is another view of the renovated Methodist church in the hamlet of Middlefield.

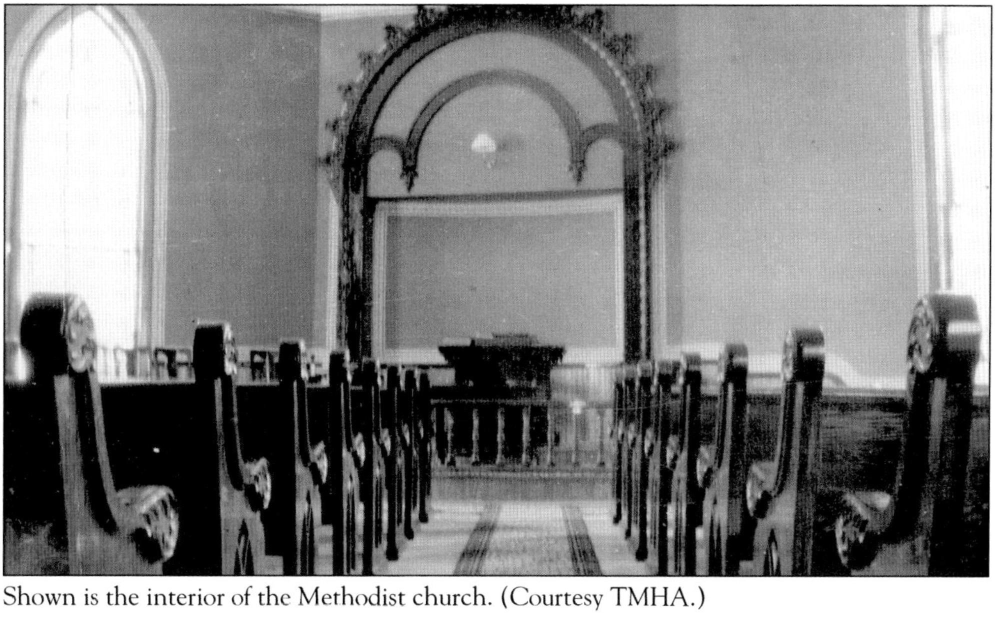

Shown is the interior of the Methodist church. (Courtesy TMHA.)

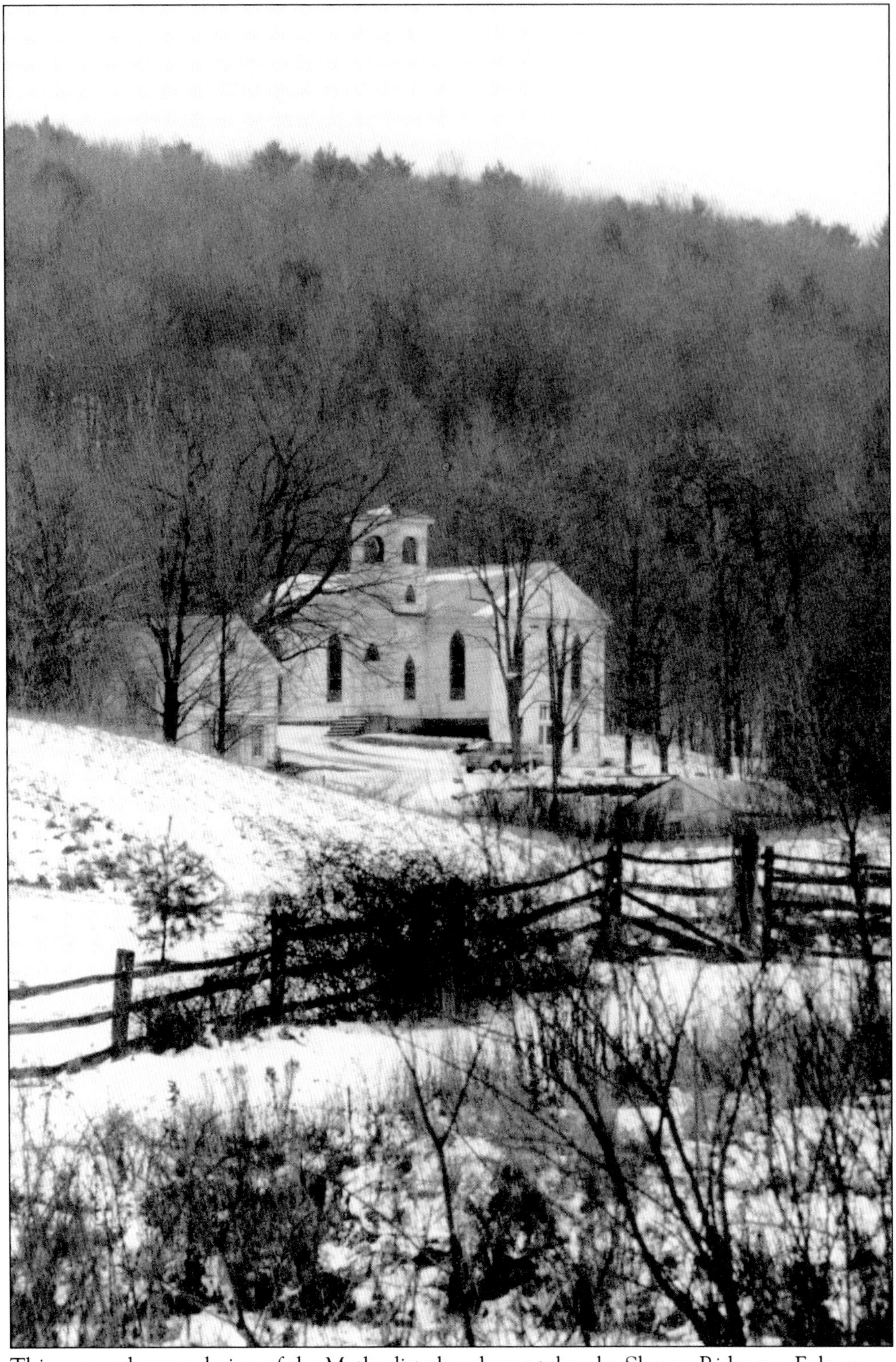

This rare and unusual view of the Methodist church was taken by Sharon Ridgeway Folmer.

This photograph of the Presbyterian church in Middlefield Center was taken by N.F. Blencoe during the time that he taught school in Middlefield Center. The church still has its spire, which was later removed after being hit by lightning. (Courtesy TMHA.)

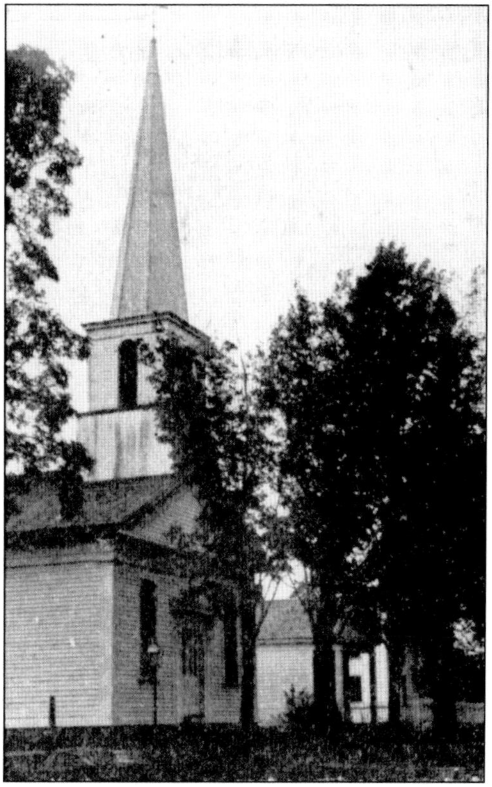

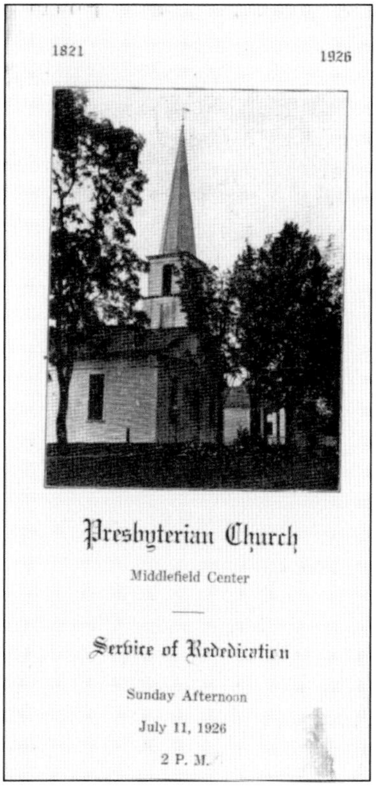

1821 1926

Presbyterian Church

Middlefield Center

Service of Rededication

Sunday Afternoon

July 11, 1926

2 P. M.

In 1926, the Presbyterian church was rededicated. The Reverend Petrie gave the sermon, and Mr. Barnum gave a historical sketch. Organized in 1821, the Presbyterians built this church in 1843.

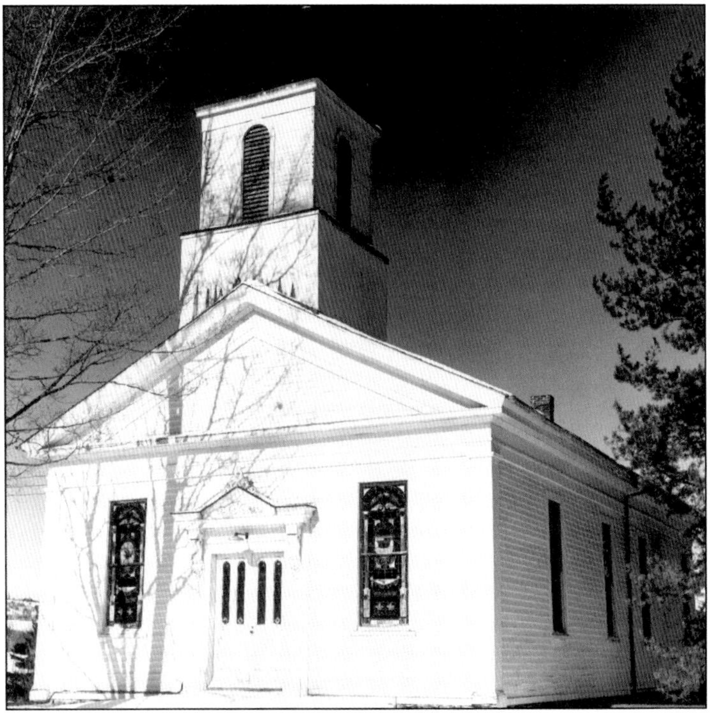

After its spire was struck by lightning, the Presbyterian church took on a much squattier appearance. The heaviness of the molding and the front facing gable show this church to be a fine example of Greek Revival architecture, consistent with its 1843 construction date. (Courtesy TMHA.)

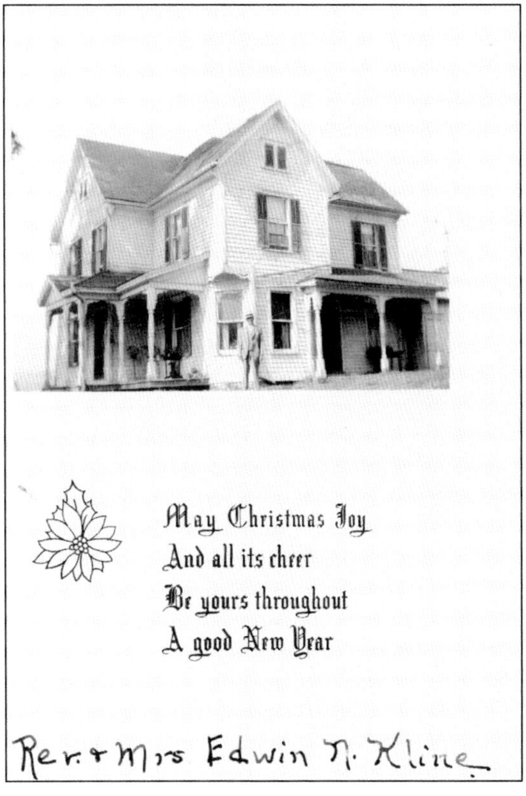

Christmas wishes come from the Reverend and Mrs. Edwin Kline. Pictured is the Presbyterian manse in Middlefield Center. (Courtesy TMHA.)

Four

Commerce and Business

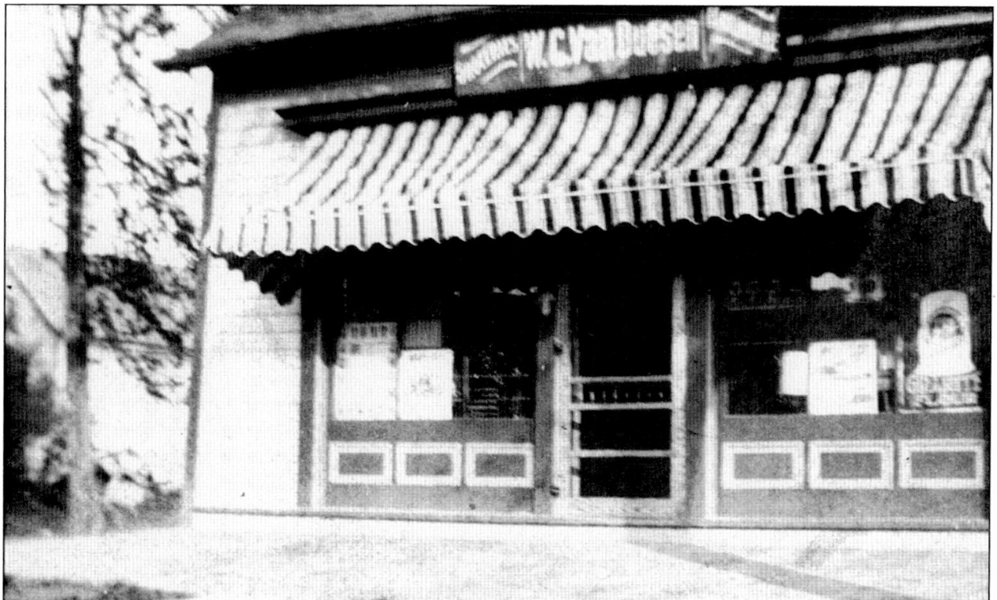

W.C. VanDeusen operated this grocery store in Middlefield Center before it burned. The front awning certainly gives this store a less rural feel. After the fire the site was used as Harbison's Garage. (Courtesy TMHA.)

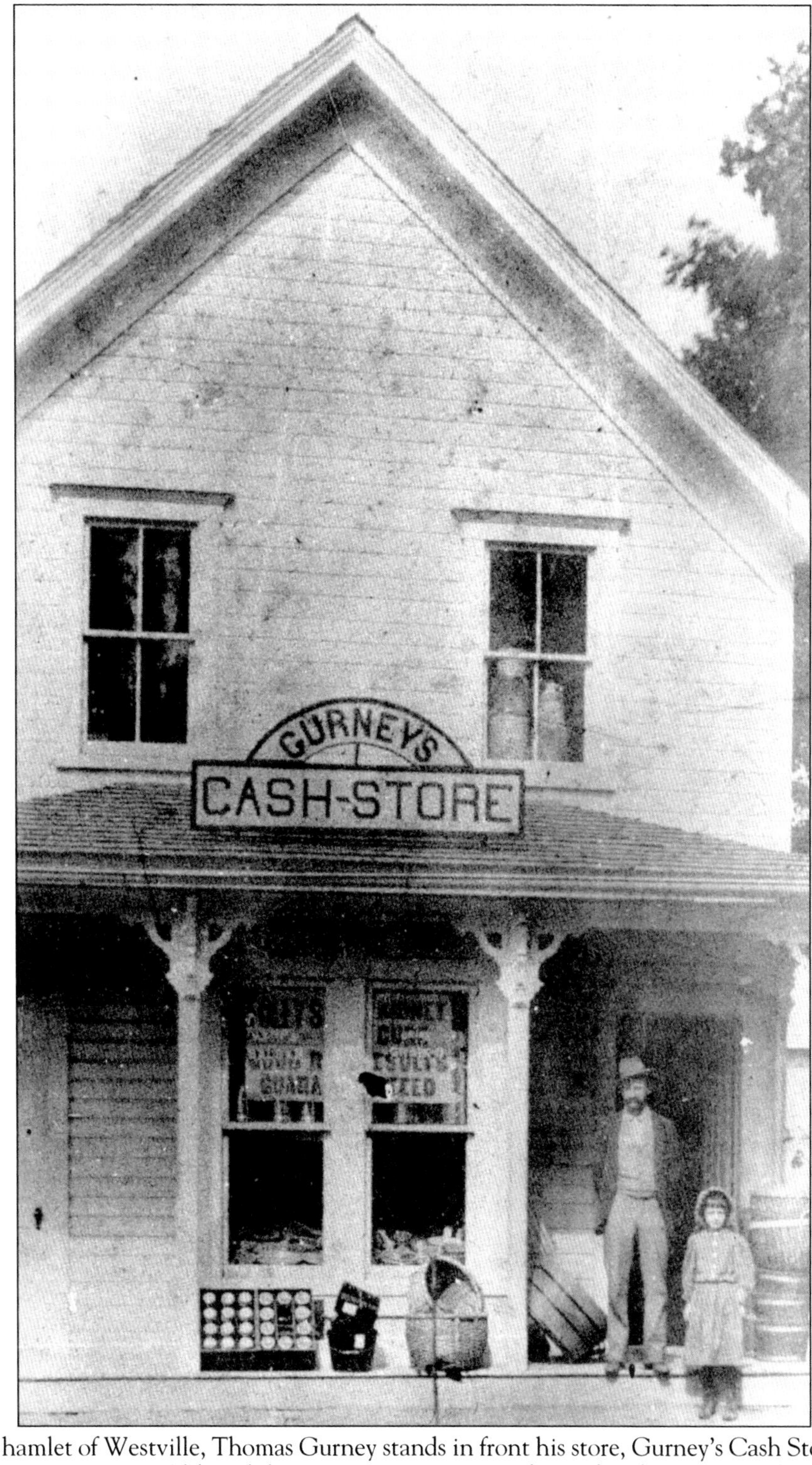

In the hamlet of Westville, Thomas Gurney stands in front his store, Gurney's Cash Store, with Edith Saxton c. 1898. Although bartering was a common form of exchange in rural New York, as the store name implies, Gurney was not fond of the practice. (Courtesy TMHA.)

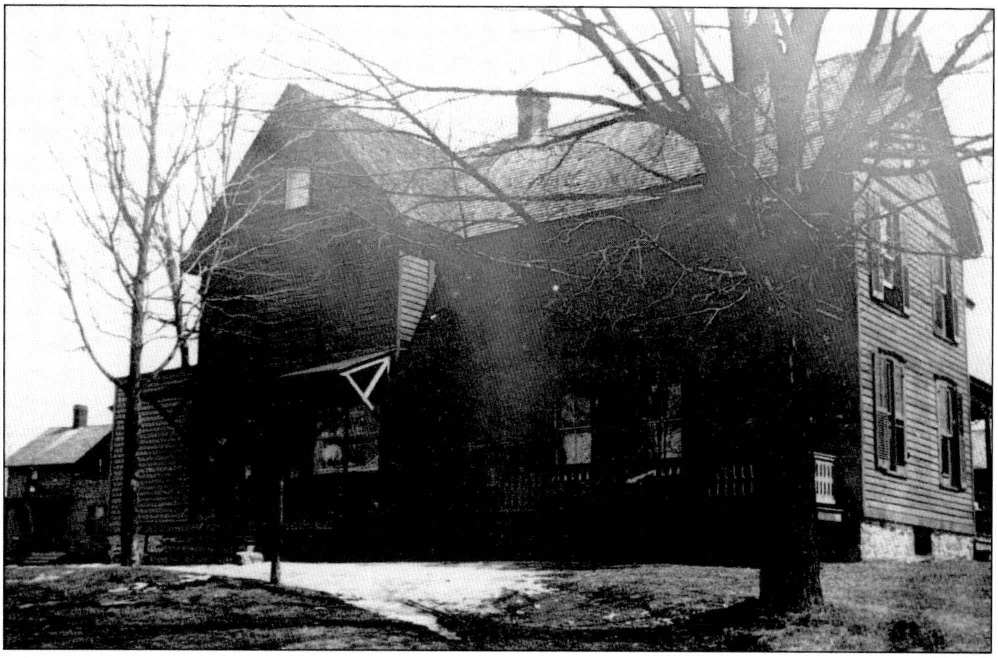

This c. 1917 photograph shows the store in the hamlet of Bowerstown during the time it was being operated by Dorothy K. Varney. (Courtesy TMHA.)

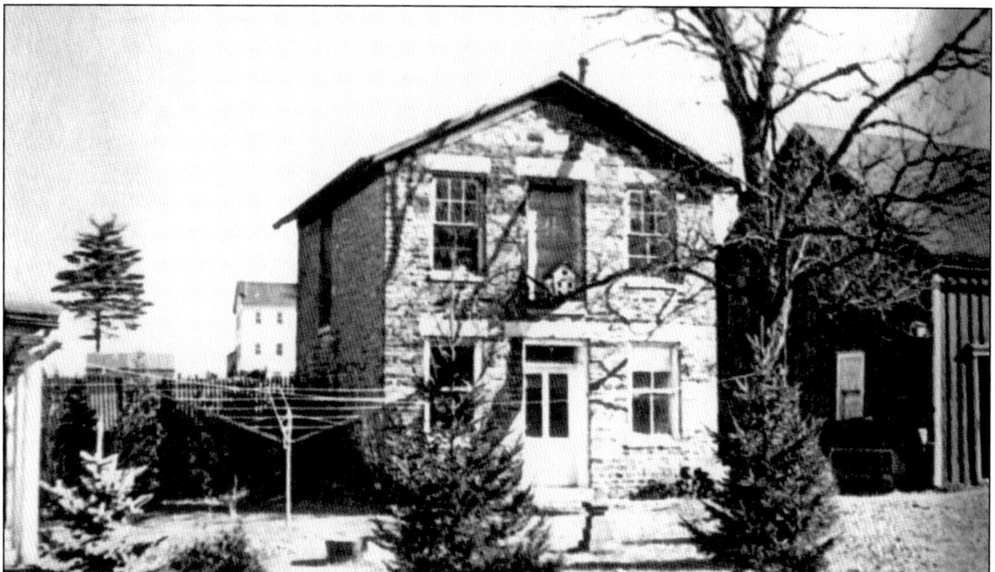

Probably the earliest commercial building in the hamlet of Middlefield, this stone structure was moved to the Farmer's Museum in Cooperstown in 1951. It started as a store and may have been used as early as 1816 by Joshua Pinney, who also ran a tavern. The stone in the gable reads "BDN 1829," which must refer to Benjamin D. North. However, it is a bit of a mystery since Benjamin North did not purchase the building from Joshua Pinney until 1833. To the left is the side porch for the Central Hotel, and behind the store is the back of the Baptist church. (Courtesy TMHA.)

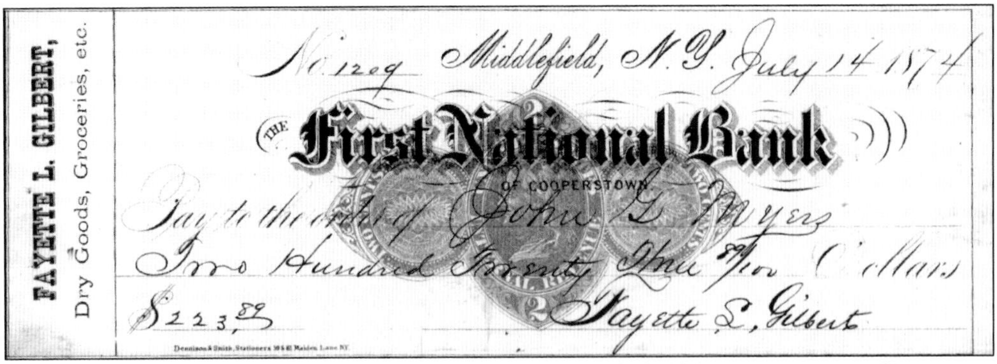

Fayette L. Gilbert took over the store in the hamlet of Middlefield from Manning and Mortimer Gilbert. It was one of the three stores in the hamlet in the late 19th century that bounded the crossroads. When Gilbert was elected Otsego County Clerk, he hired Thomas Hearn to run the store.

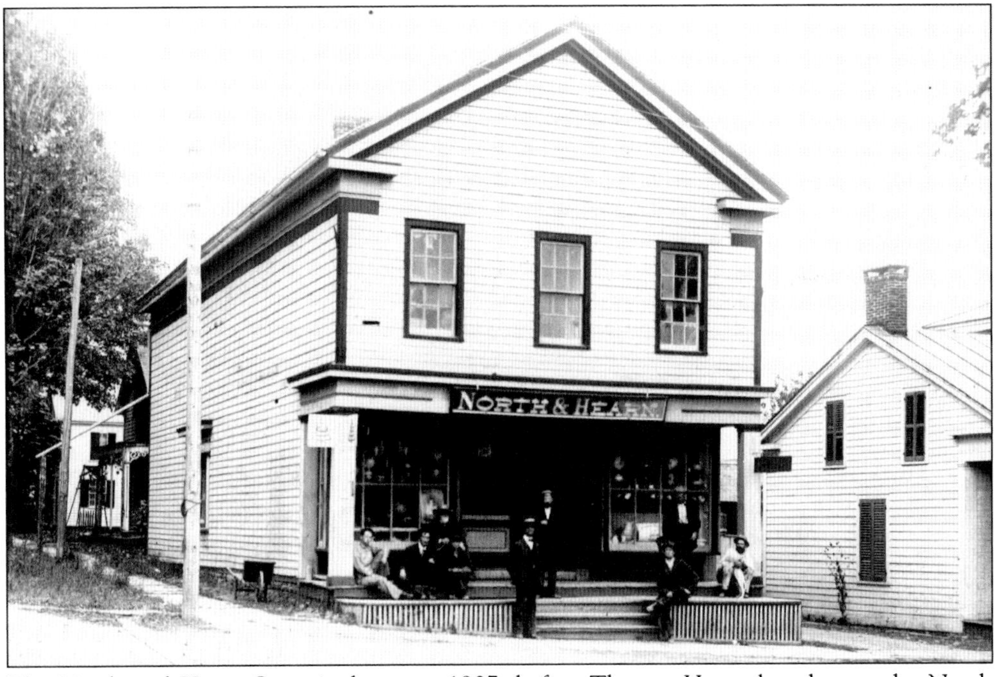

The North and Hearn Store is shown c. 1907, before Thomas Hearn bought out the North interest. From left to right are the following: (front row) Homer Mumford, Ralph ?, Edward Boorn, and Charles North; (back row) Rev. T. E. Jones, Thomas Hearn, and Charles Hearn. (Courtesy TMHA.)

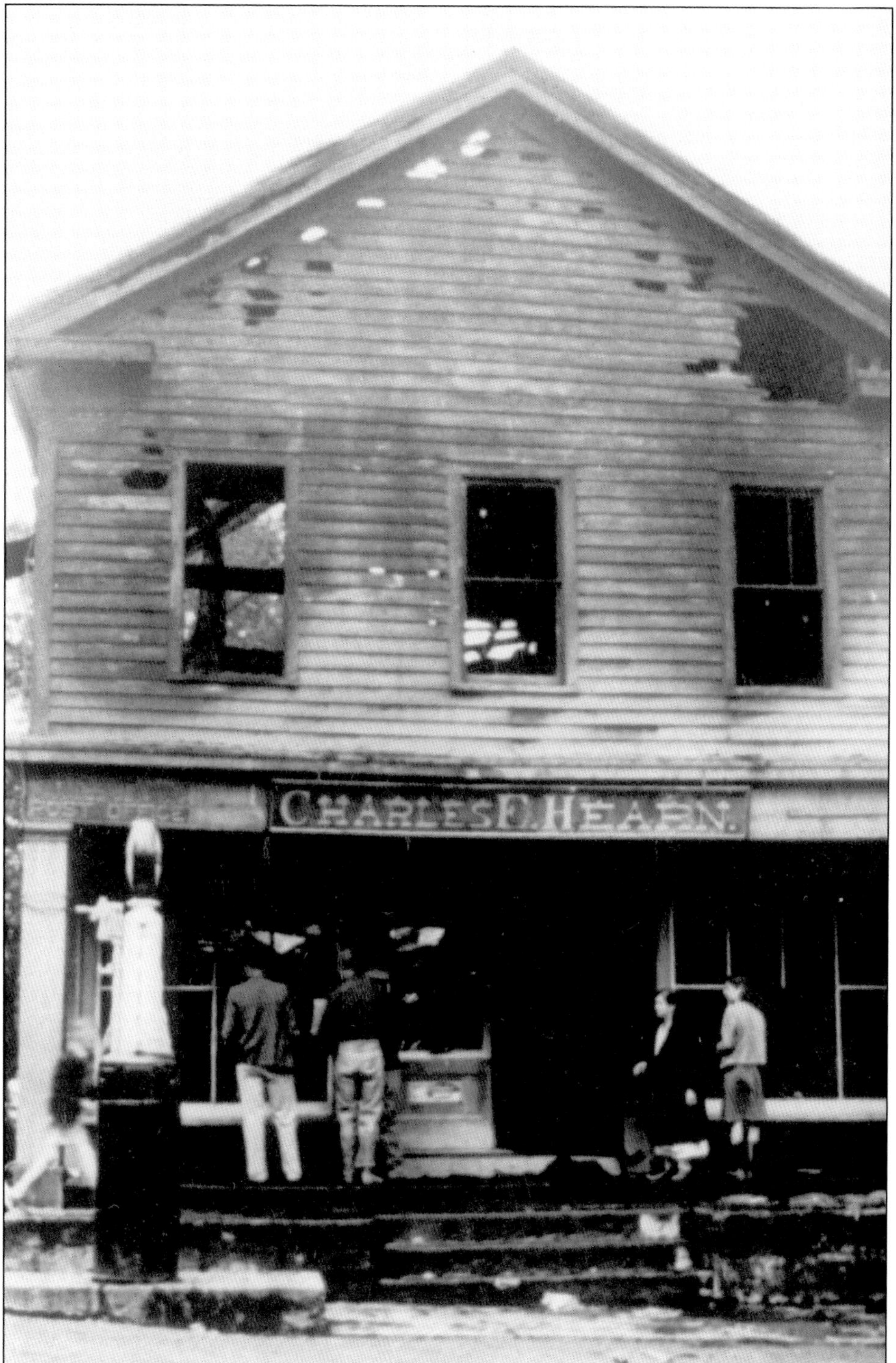

Shown is the façade of the Hearn Store after the 1942 fire. The post office boxes were in this store as Charles Hearn was postmaster. They were saved and moved to the store across the street, as was the sign above the door.

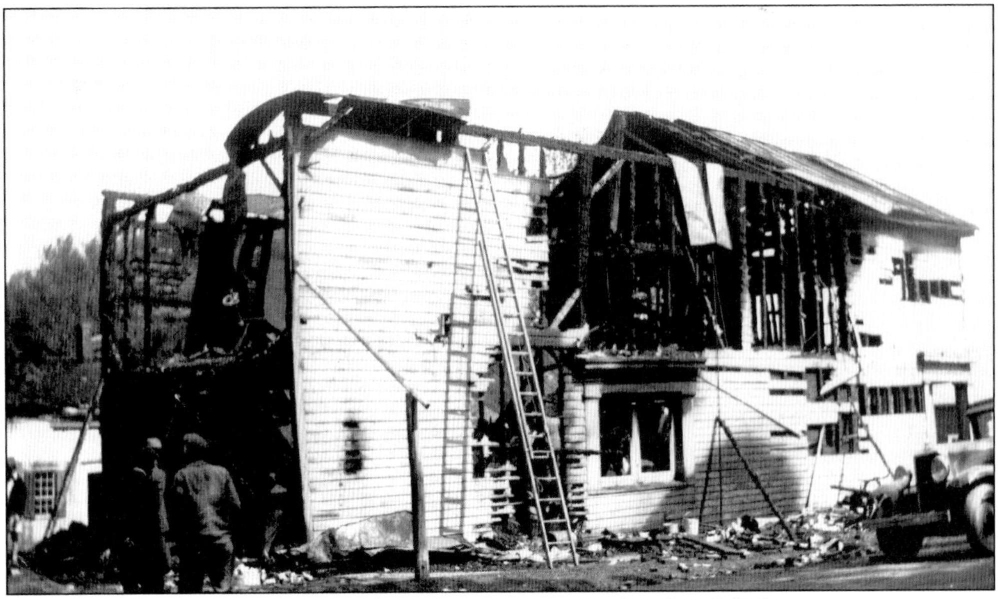

The two photographs on this page show the Hearn Store after the 1942 fire.

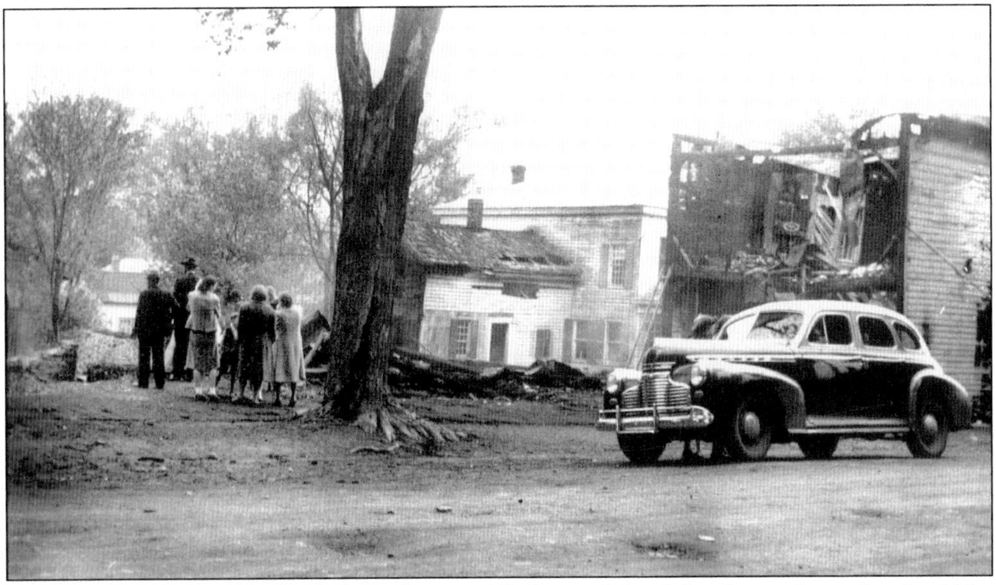

The 1942 fire started in the Roberts house. All that is left of that house is a pile of rubble. Frances Roberts was lucky to get out alive after reentering the house to retrieve her purse.

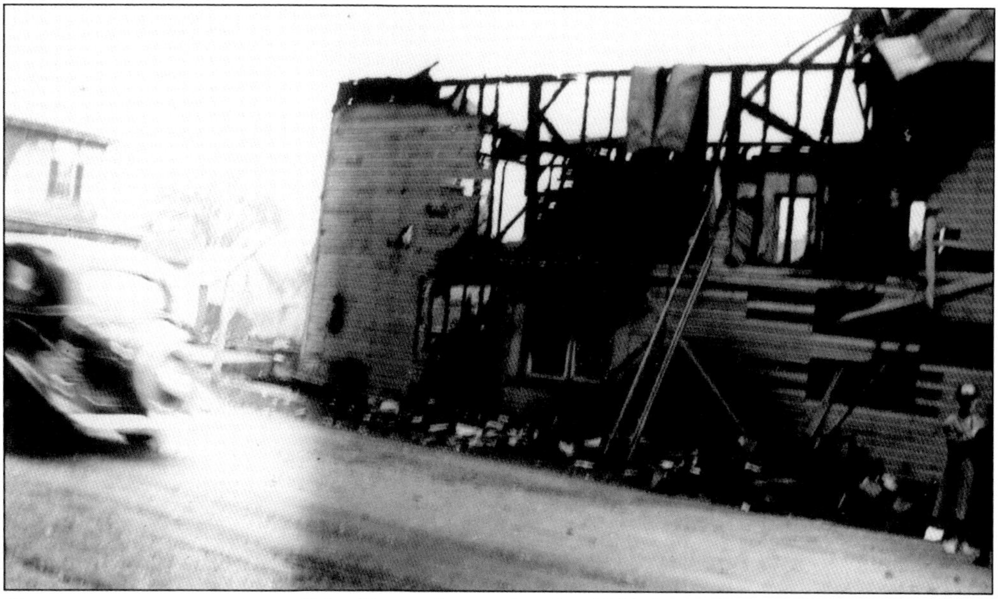

Shown are two more views of the Hearn Store after the 1942 fire.

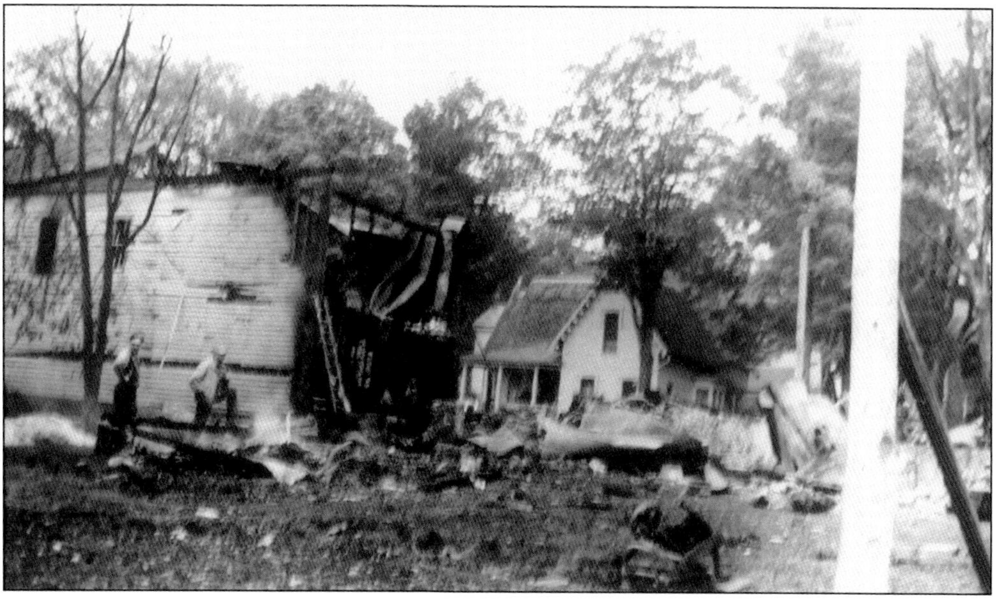

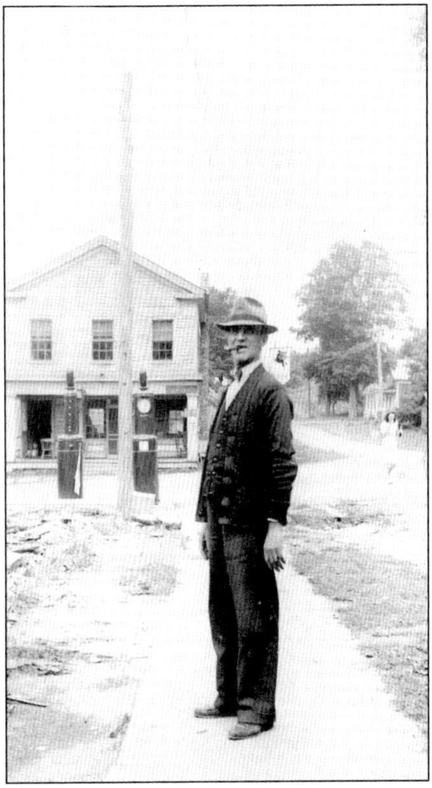

Charles Hearn, storekeeper and postmaster, surveys the damage to his store after the 1942 fire. (Courtesy TMHA.)

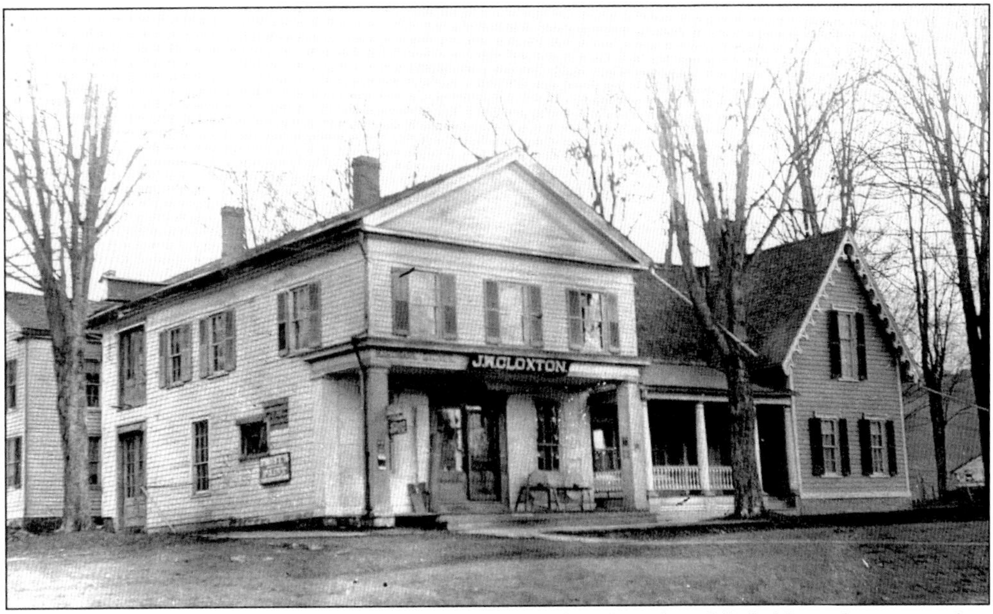

Projecting from the side of the Cloxton Store in the hamlet of Middlefield is a hoist to aid in loading merchandise to the upper floor. On the right is a fine Gothic Revival house, built in the 1850s. It is only one of two such houses in the hamlet. The Cloxton Store was later moved from this site.

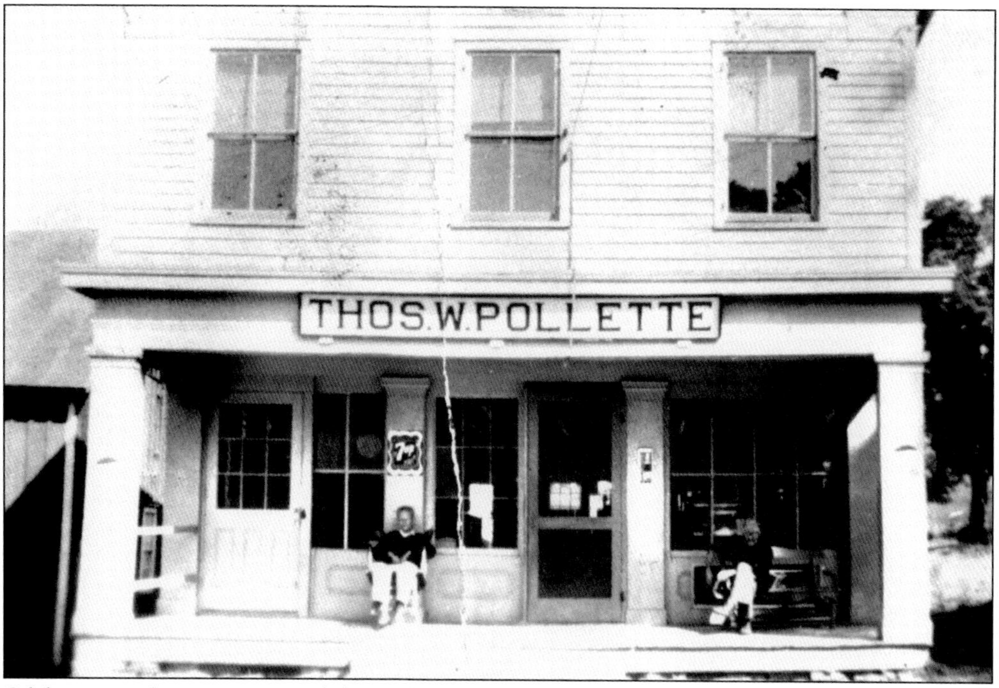

Of the stores that once covered three of the four corners in the hamlet of Middlefield, this is the only one left. This photograph was taken in 1948. It is interesting to note that the two center columns have been removed. (Courtesy TMHA.)

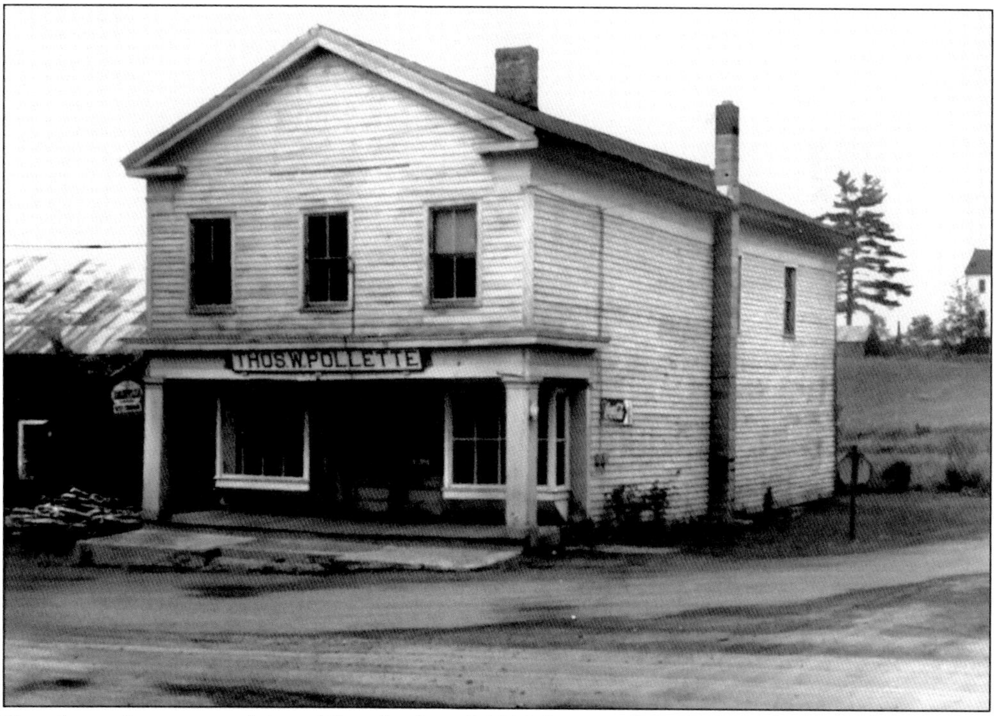

Frugal people waste nothing. After the fire of 1942 destroyed the Roberts home and the Hearn Store, the sign above the door of the store was reused on this store across the street.

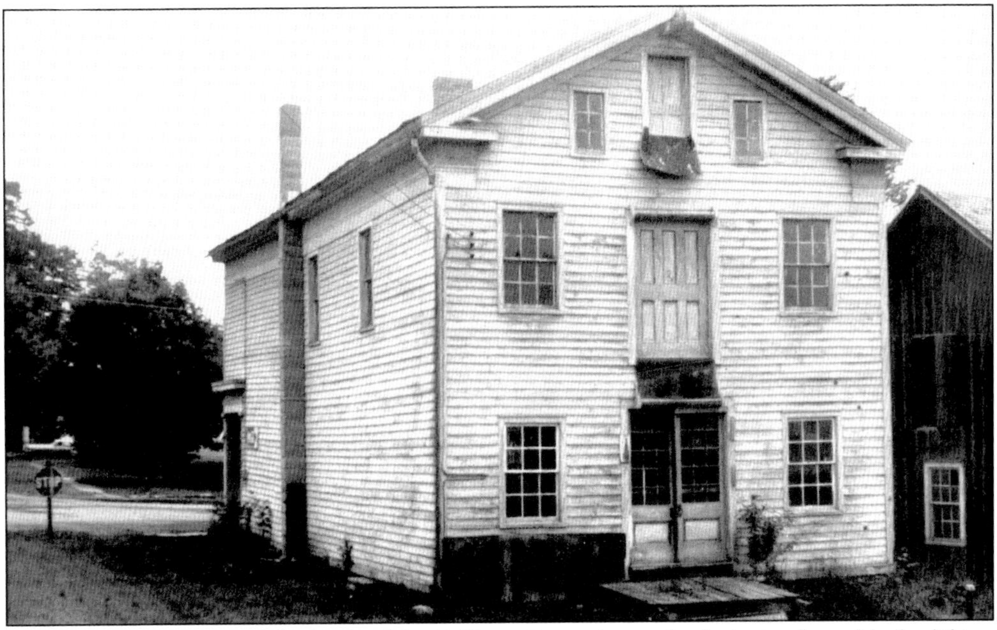

This uncommon view of the back of the Pollette Store shows the hoist in the gable for lifting dry goods to the upper floors.

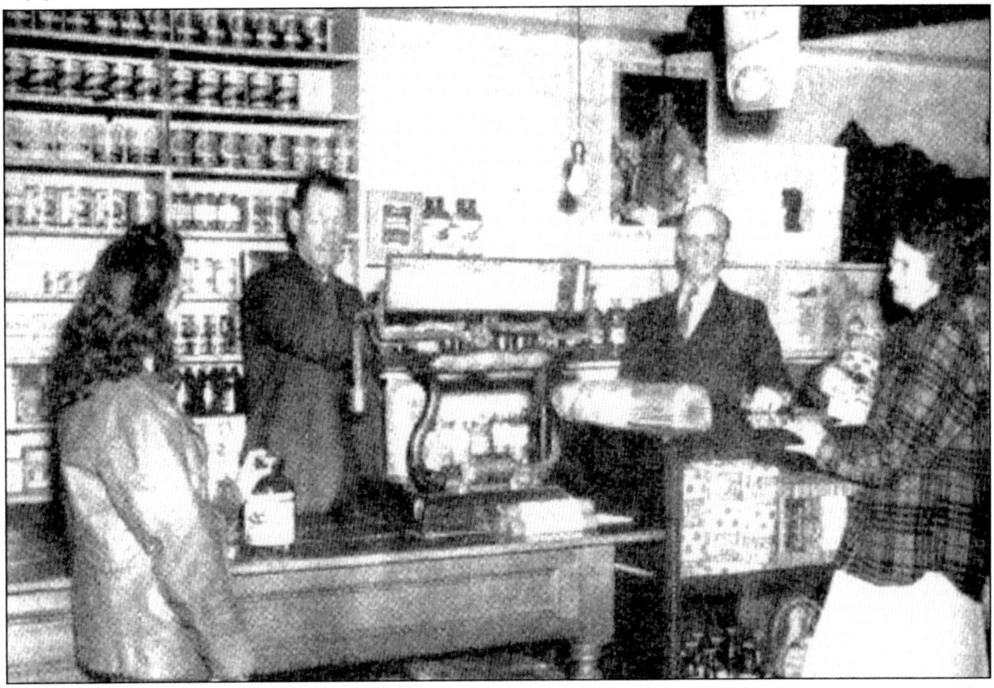

This photograph was taken for the Freeman's Journal in 1944 when Charles Hearn announced he was retiring as Middlefield postmaster. From left to right are Marian Barnum, Lee Roberts, Charles E. Hearn, and Marie Hayden. In 1812, Hearn bought out the Charles North share in the store, thus ending the North and Hearn partnership. After the 1942 fire, Hearn reopened in the vacant building across the street, which later became the Thomas Pollette Store. Thomas Pollette was Hearn's son-in-law. (Reproduced with permission from the *Freeman's Journal*.)

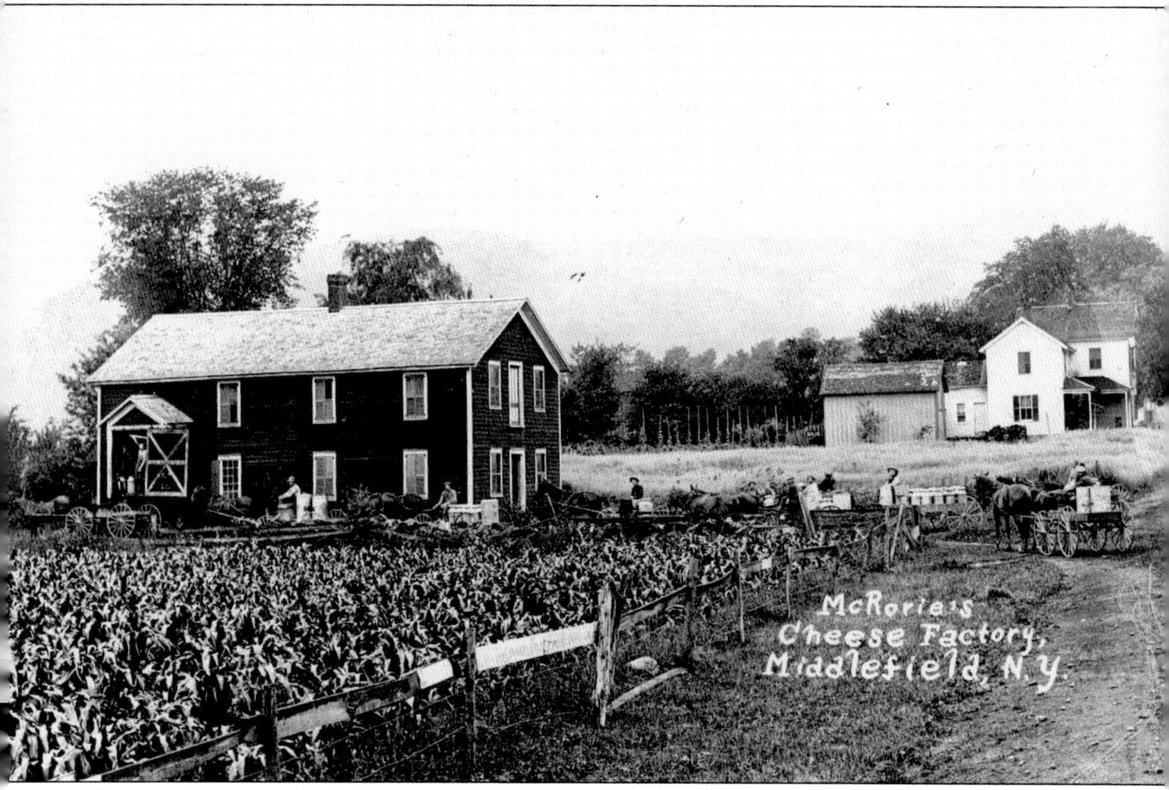

This excellent view shows farmers lining up to sell their milk at the McRorie Cheese Factory in the hamlet of Middlefield. This is the present site of the Middlefield town offices.

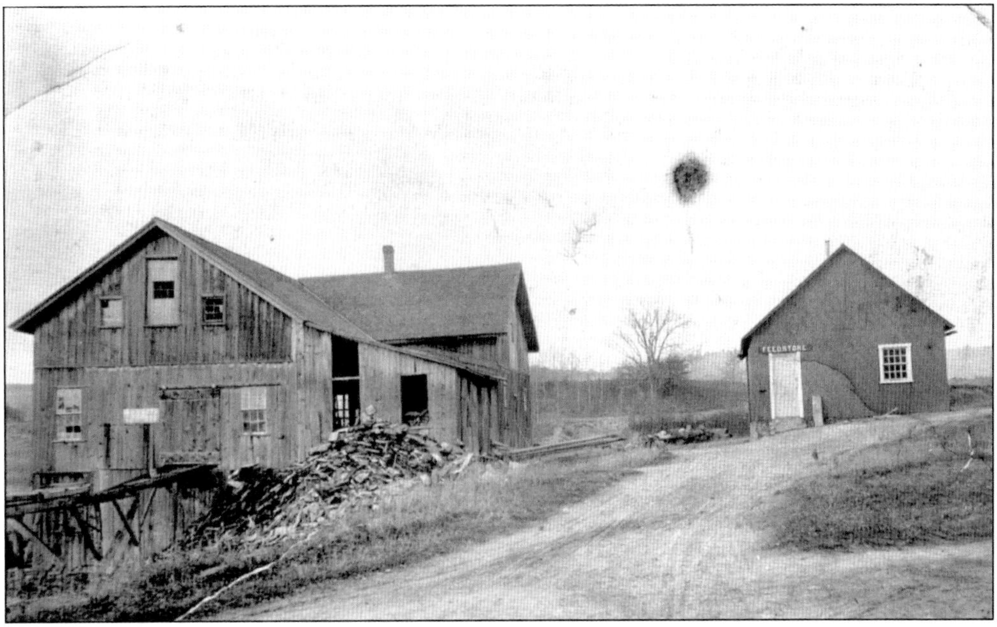

A sawmill has been documented on this site as early as 1817, when it was owned by Moses Rich Jr. This early-20th-century photograph shows the sawmill in the center and the feed store on the right. The road that bends past the feed store leads to the District No. 1 School.

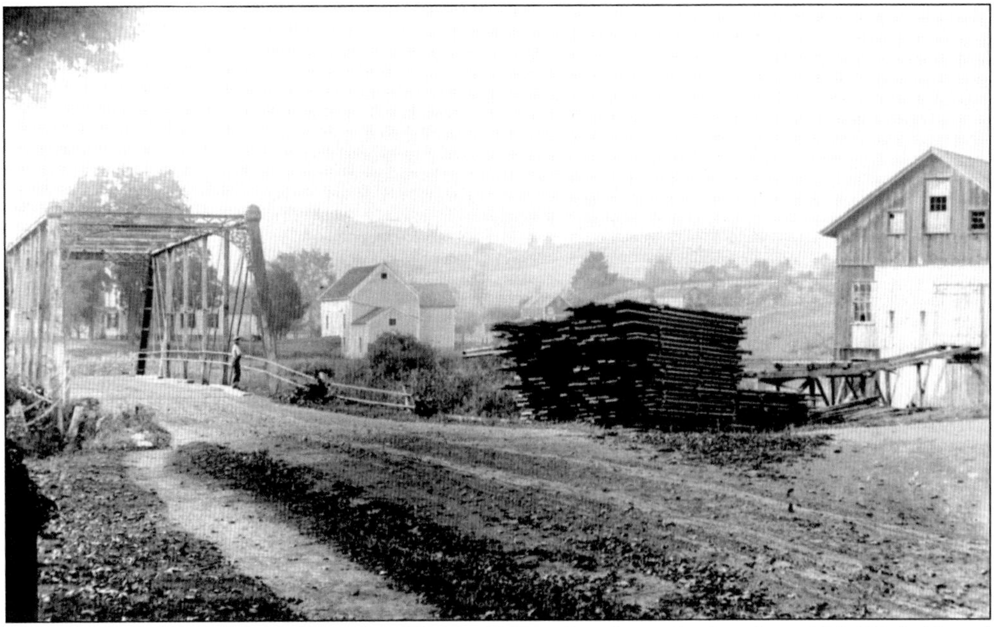

This view shows the sawmill on the Cherry Valley Creek in the hamlet of Middlefield and Shipman Hill in the background. The house on the left was owned by Lucian Coleman. (Courtesy TMHA.)

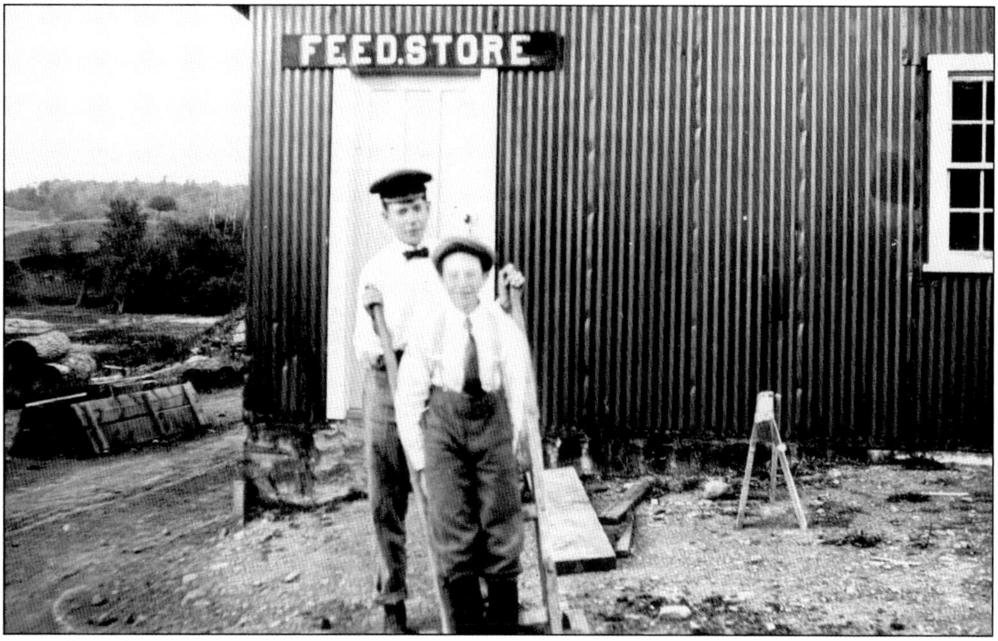

Some boys horse around on a hand truck in front of the feed store.

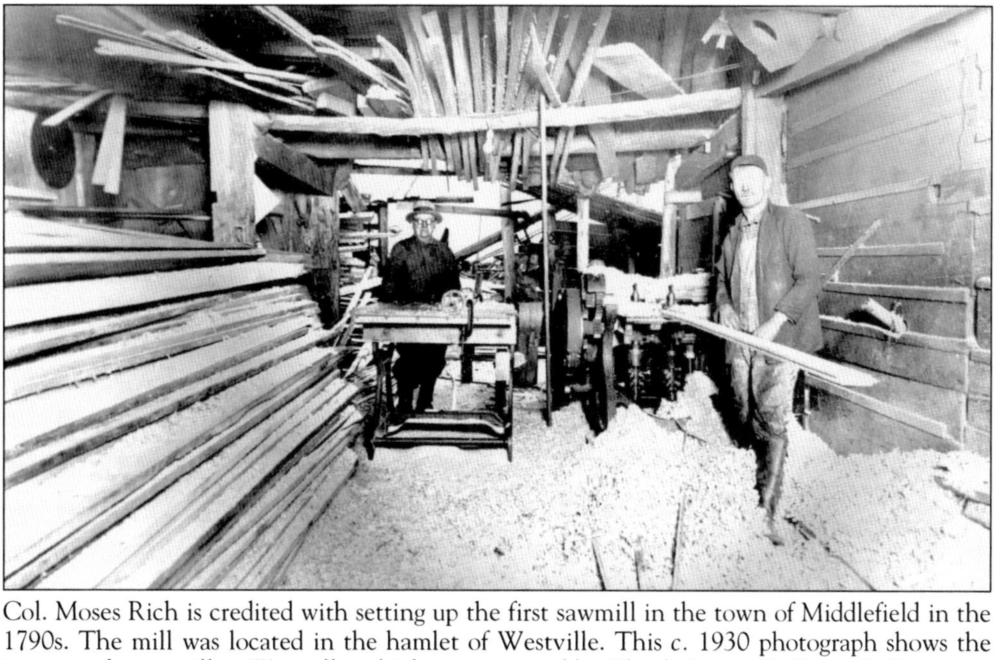

Col. Moses Rich is credited with setting up the first sawmill in the town of Middlefield in the 1790s. The mill was located in the hamlet of Westville. This c. 1930 photograph shows the interior of a sawmill in Westville, which was operated by Claude Jay McCollister (left) and his assistant Herbert Herdman (right). (Courtesy TMHA.)

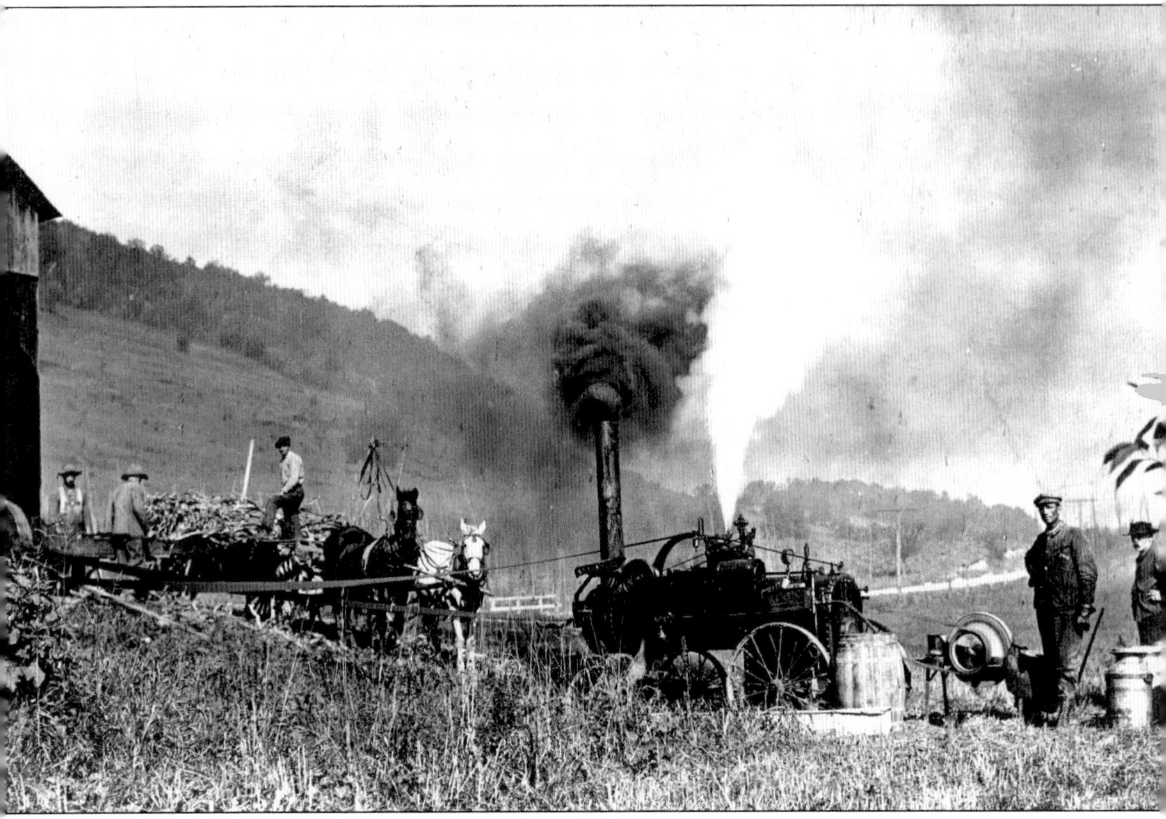

An early steam engine powers a sawmill in Westville. Among those pictured is Art Wood, second from the right.

Five

Down on the Farm

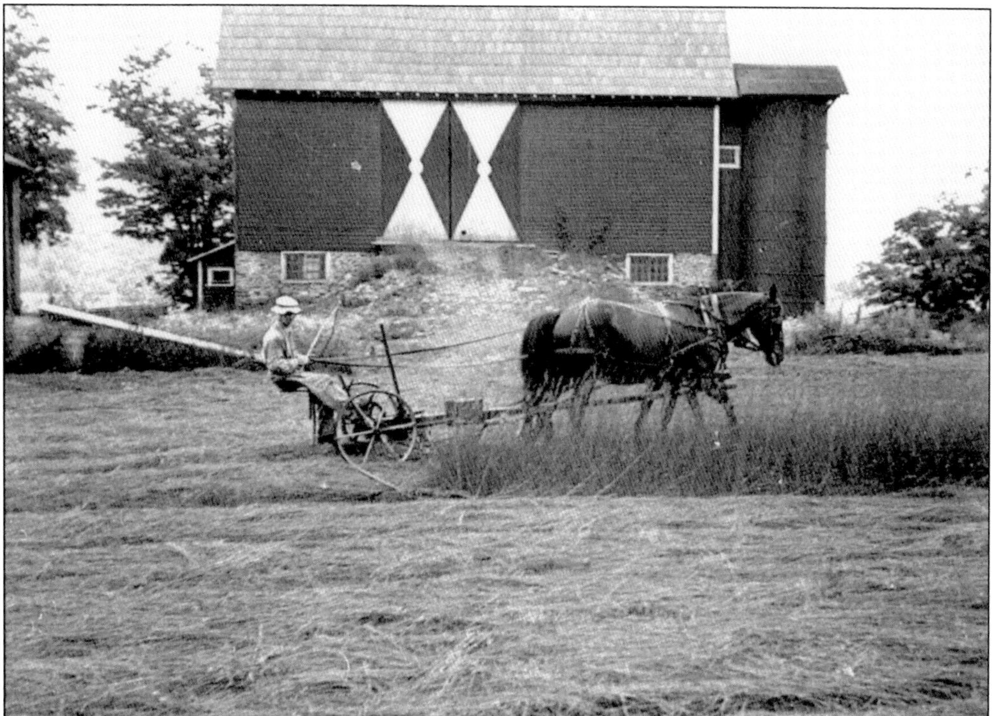

One of the Wilson boys cuts hay on the Wilson farm, on Long Patent Road outside of the hamlet of Middlefield, in the early 20th century.

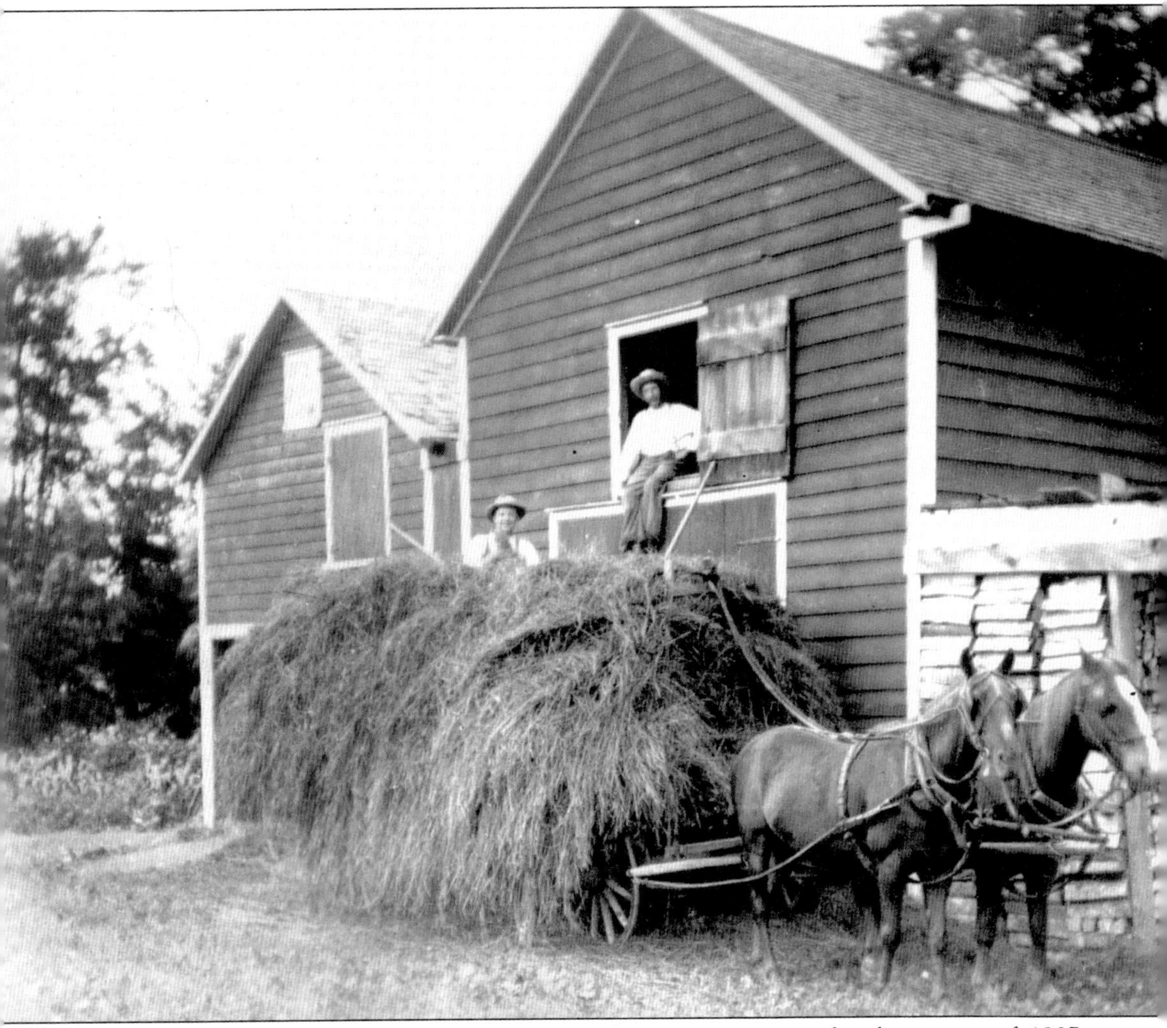

Orville Gayler (left) and Bill Gayler bring in hay in preparation for the winter of 1907. (Courtesy TMHA.)

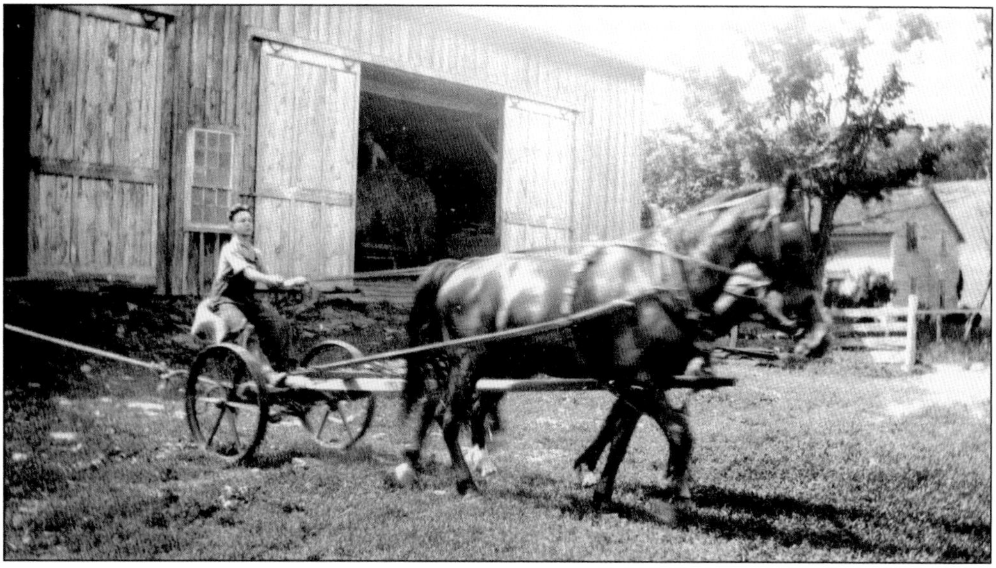

Chauncey M. Hearn works at Ellery Thompson's farm in 1920. (Courtesy TMHA.)

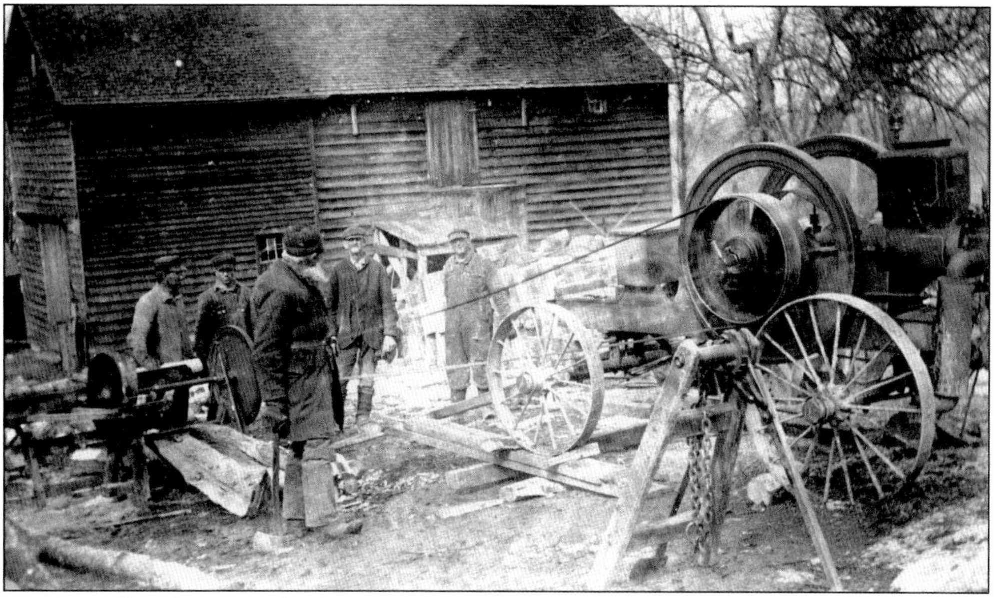

On the Gillett farm, wood is being cut behind the hop house. David Gillett, with the white beard, is in the foreground. (Courtesy TMHA.)

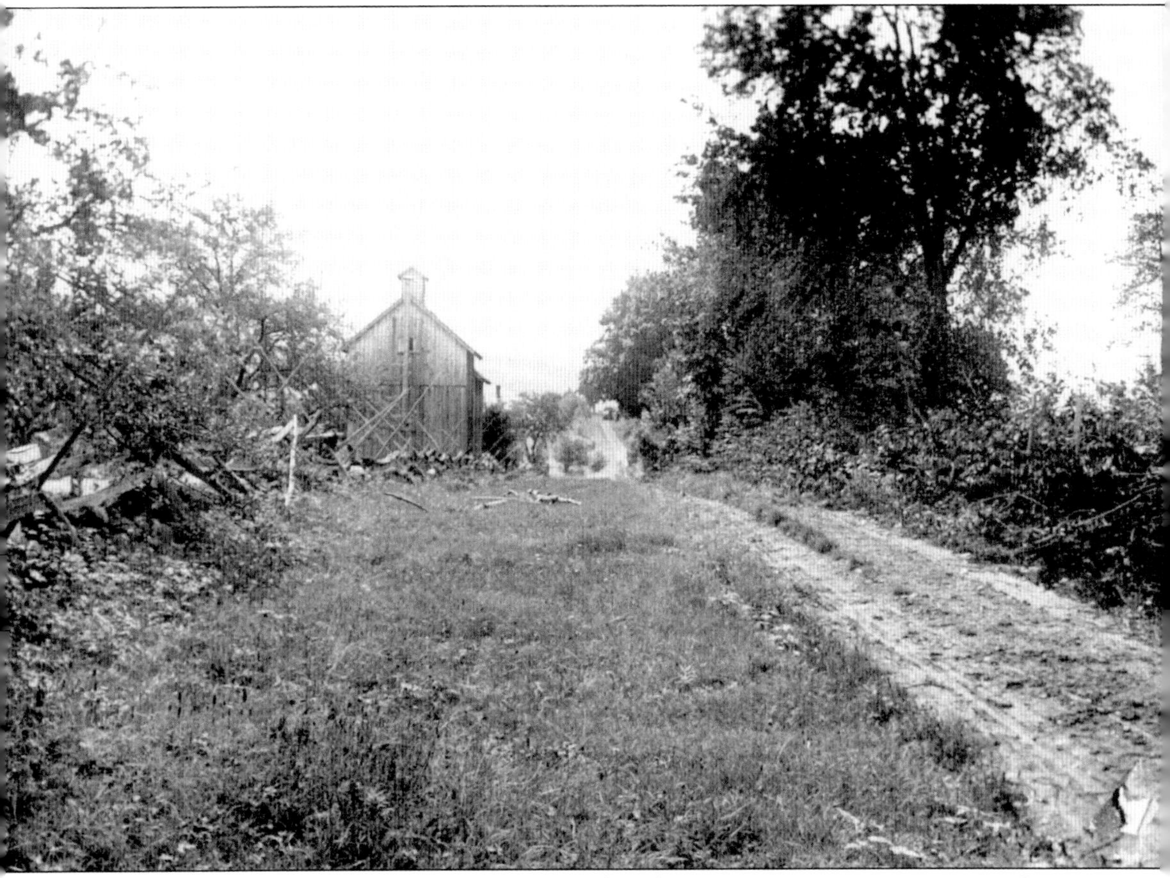

Throughout the 19th and early 20th centuries, hop farming was a major enterprise in Otsego County. In 1874, a total of 790 acres in Middlefield were devoted to this crop, producing a total of 323,303 pounds of hops. The hops were used in the making of beer. Many growers set up hop kilns like this one located on Pink Street above Whig Corners. The street got its name, so the story goes, because a man who lived on this road frequently dressed his three girls in pink. (Courtesy NYSHA.)

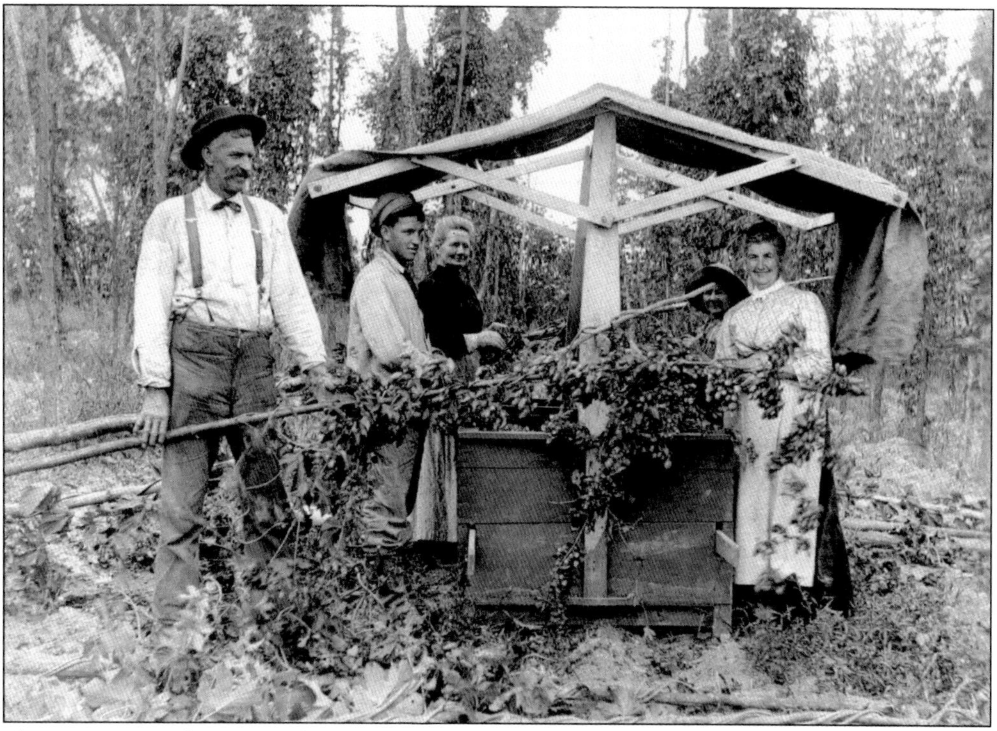

Shown is a typical scene in Otsego County during hop-picking time. (Courtesy TMHA.)

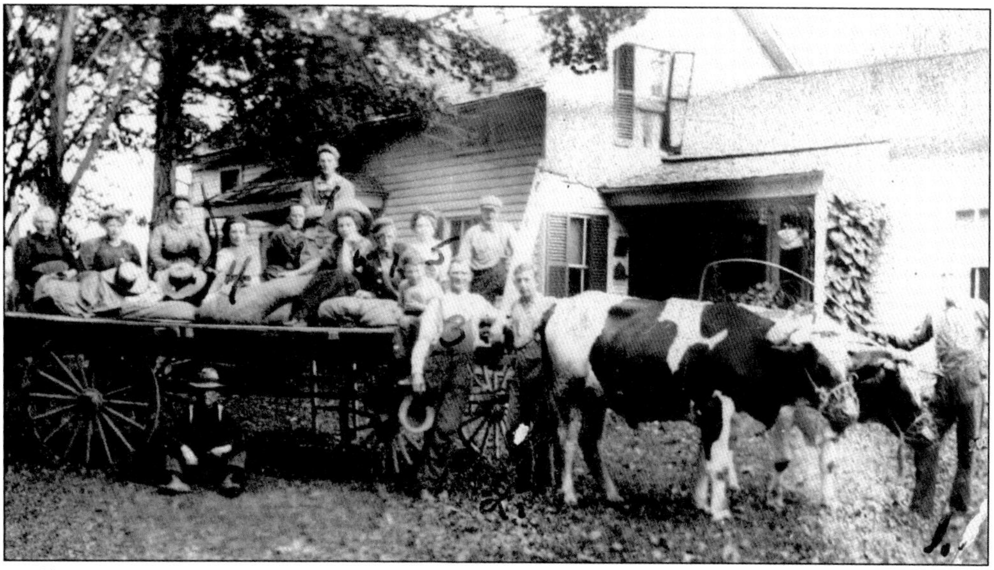

Wallace Ferguson stands in front of the oxen, with the wagon full of hop pickers ready to head out into the fields c. 1912. This photograph was taken in front of the Ferguson farm. (Courtesy TMHA.)

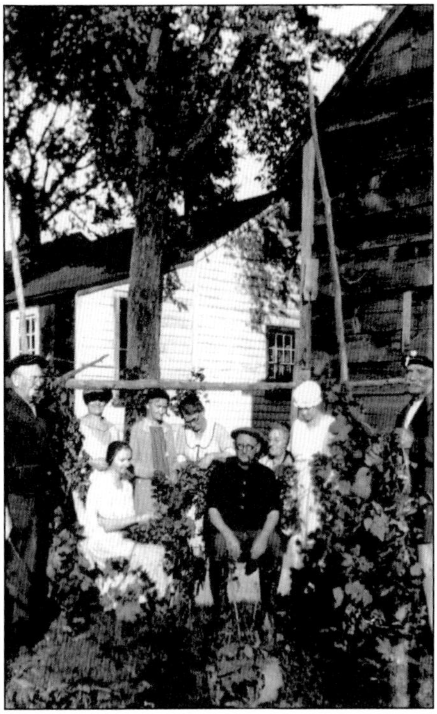

Pausing for a moment behind the American Hotel in the hamlet of Middlefield are Charles Flint, seated with a pipe, and some hop pickers. Flint was the proprietor of the American Hotel.

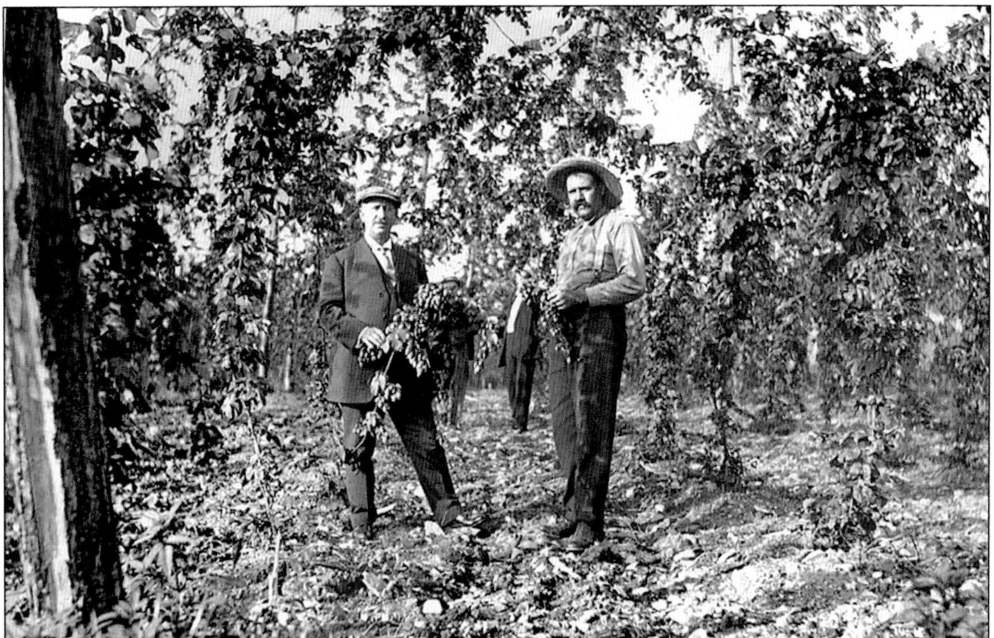

Fortunes were made and lost in the volatile hop market. Hop Dealers like this well-dressed man would often purchase hops from farmers in advance of planting and hope for a rise in prices by the time the hops made it to market. (Courtesy TMHA.)

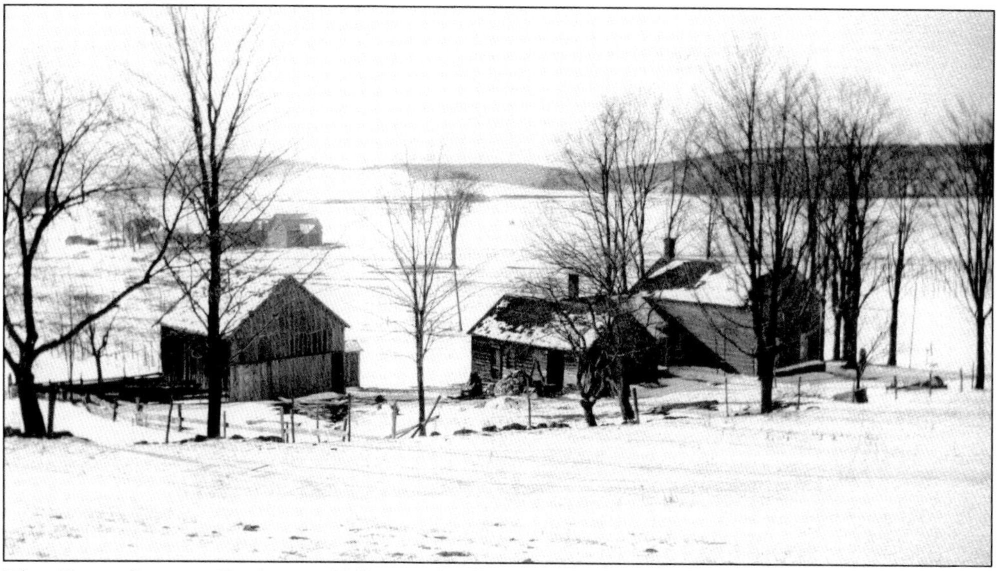

The Camp farm on Eggleston Hill reveals the isolation a rural farm faced during the winter months. Ira Holmes took this photograph in 1919. Note how sparsely populated some parts of the town were. (Courtesy TMHA.)

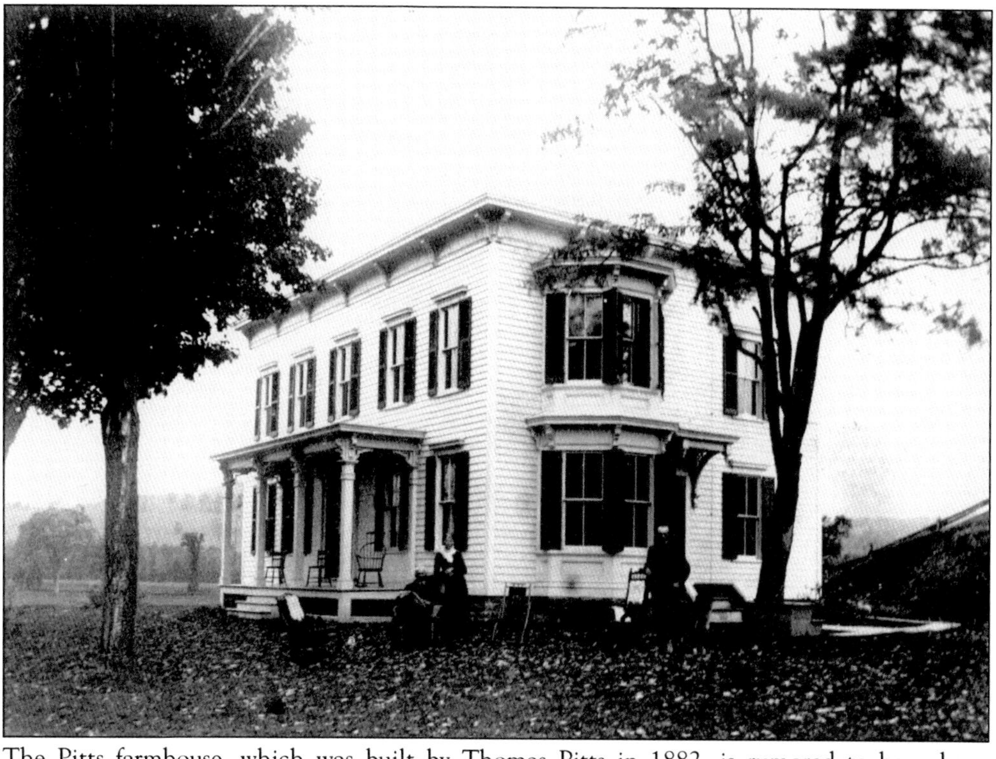

The Pitts farmhouse, which was built by Thomas Pitts in 1882, is rumored to have been designed by his wife, Ann Pitts. The small porch next to the bay windows was later removed and replaced with the fine portico from the house built by Harrison North in the hamlet of Middlefield. (Courtesy TMHA.)

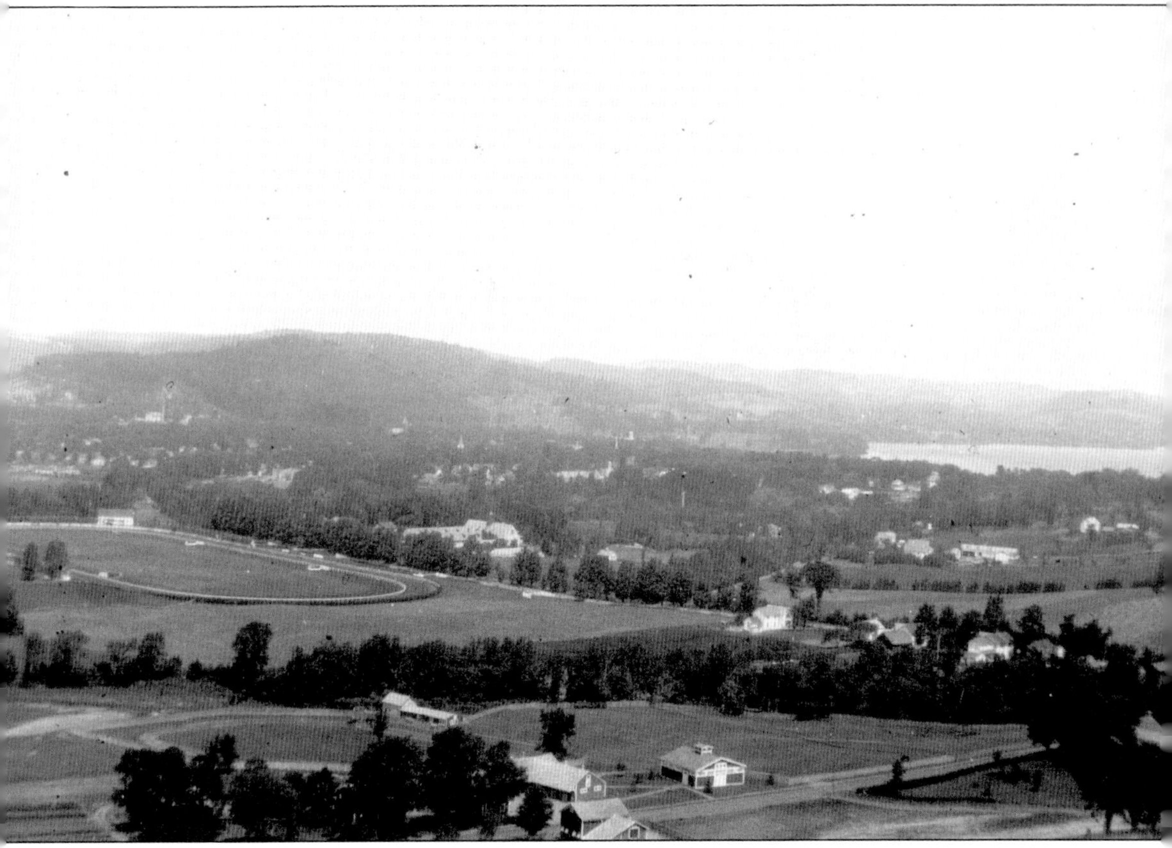

Iroquois Farm, which sprawled along River Road, is an example of one of the large and very prosperous farms that dotted Middlefield. This photograph shows the farm as Ambrose Clark had it, complete with its riding ring and polo field. Clark was very fond of his horses. The Clark Sports Center is now on the site of the riding ring. Part of the farm is still used for the Junior Livestock Show. To the right is the foot of Otsego Lake. (Courtesy TMHA.)

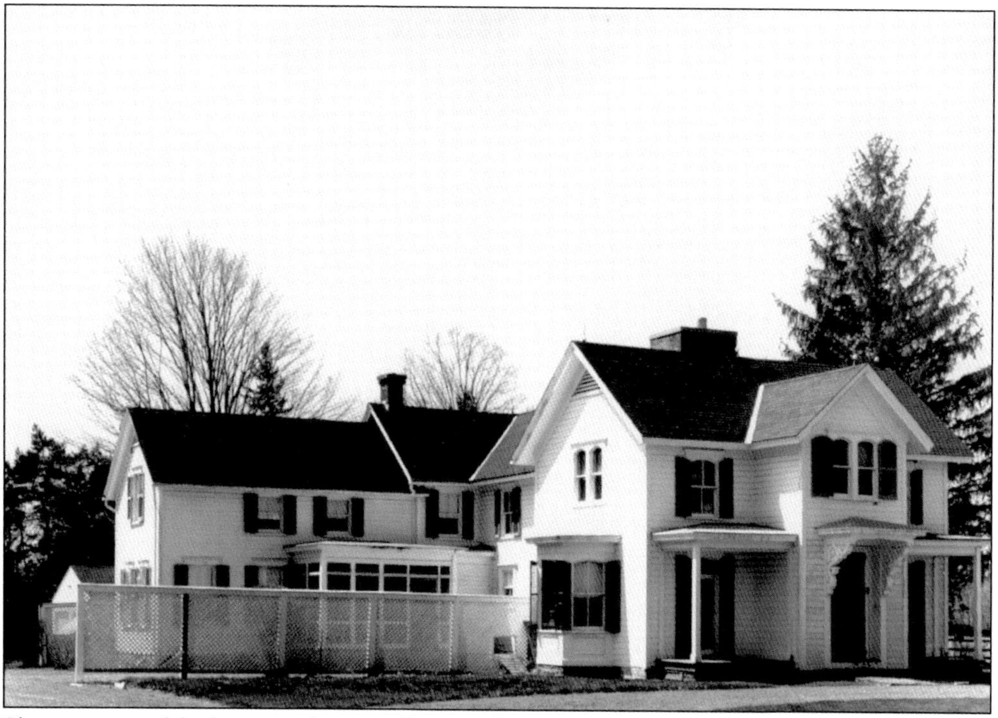

Shown is one of the houses at Iroquois Farm. When this house was later demolished, the kitchen cabinets were salvaged and preserved in the kitchen of the Town of Middlefield Historical Association headquarters, at the District No. 1 School. (Courtesy TMHA.)

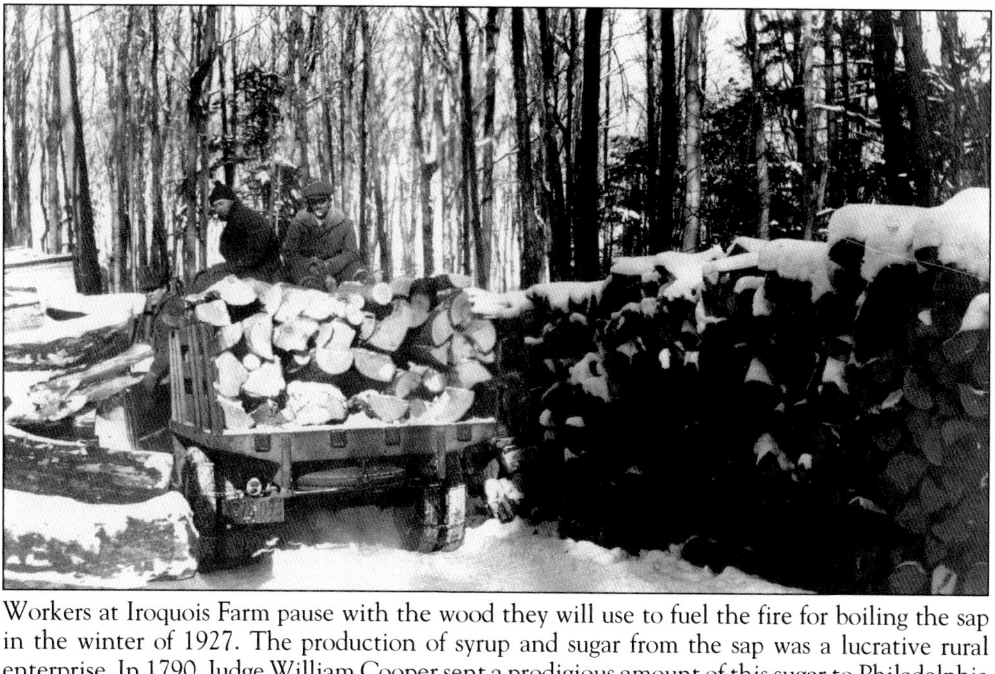

Workers at Iroquois Farm pause with the wood they will use to fuel the fire for boiling the sap in the winter of 1927. The production of syrup and sugar from the sap was a lucrative rural enterprise. In 1790, Judge William Cooper sent a prodigious amount of this sugar to Philadelphia as part of a grand marketing scheme to compete with sugars from the Indies. Cooper's grand idea failed, but the practice endured. (Courtesy TMHA.)

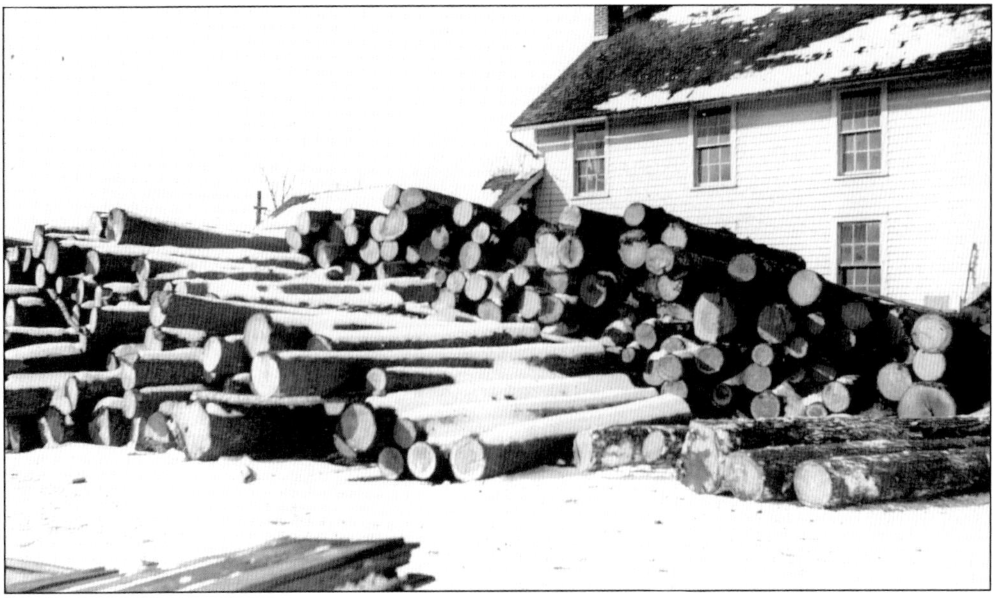

Logs are stacked and ready for the sawmill at Iroquois Farm. This photograph was taken in 1927. (Courtesy TMHA.)

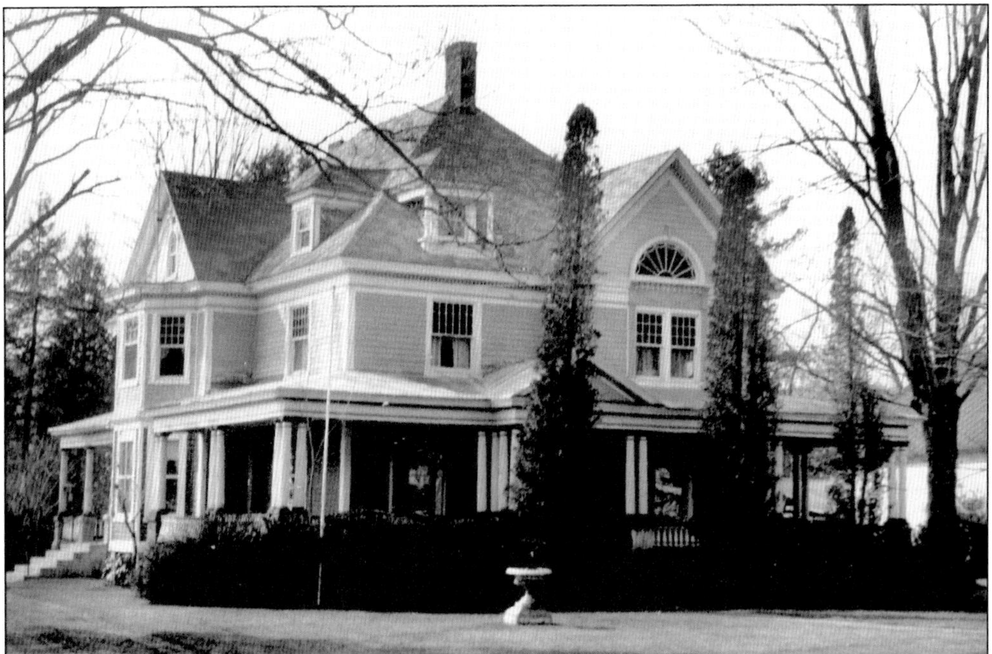

The Green Mansion was built in 1900 for Frank and Jane Green, owners of the Oak Hill Stock Farm, outside of the hamlet of Westville. (Courtesy TMHA.)

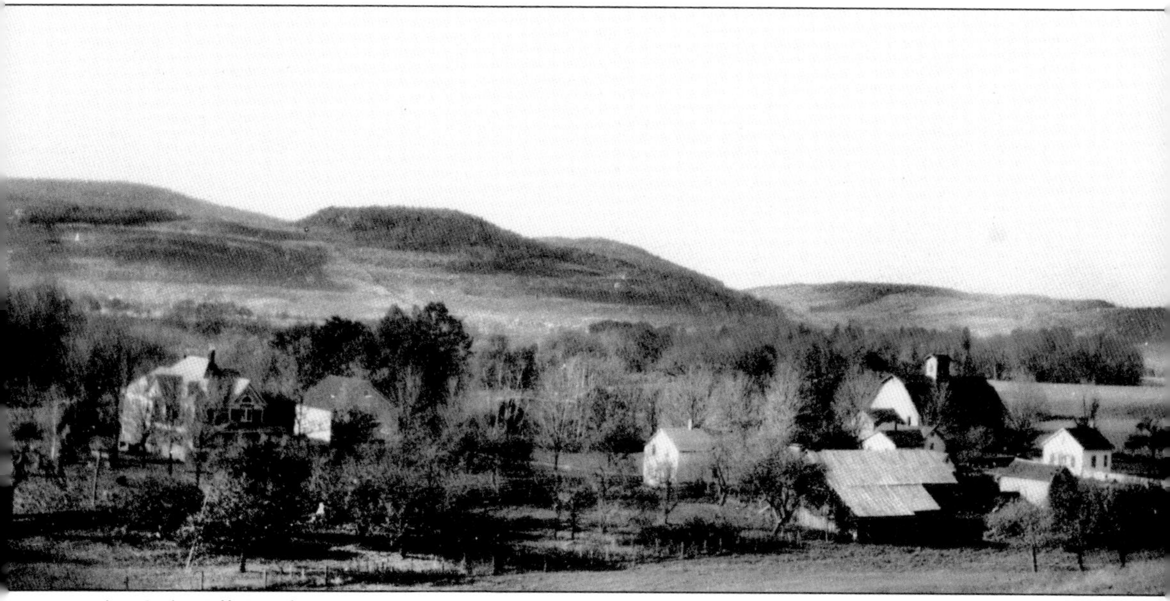

The Oak Hill Stock Farm was another of those very large and prosperous farms spread across Middlefield. Looking northeast, this view shows the expanse of the farm. (Courtesy TMHA.)

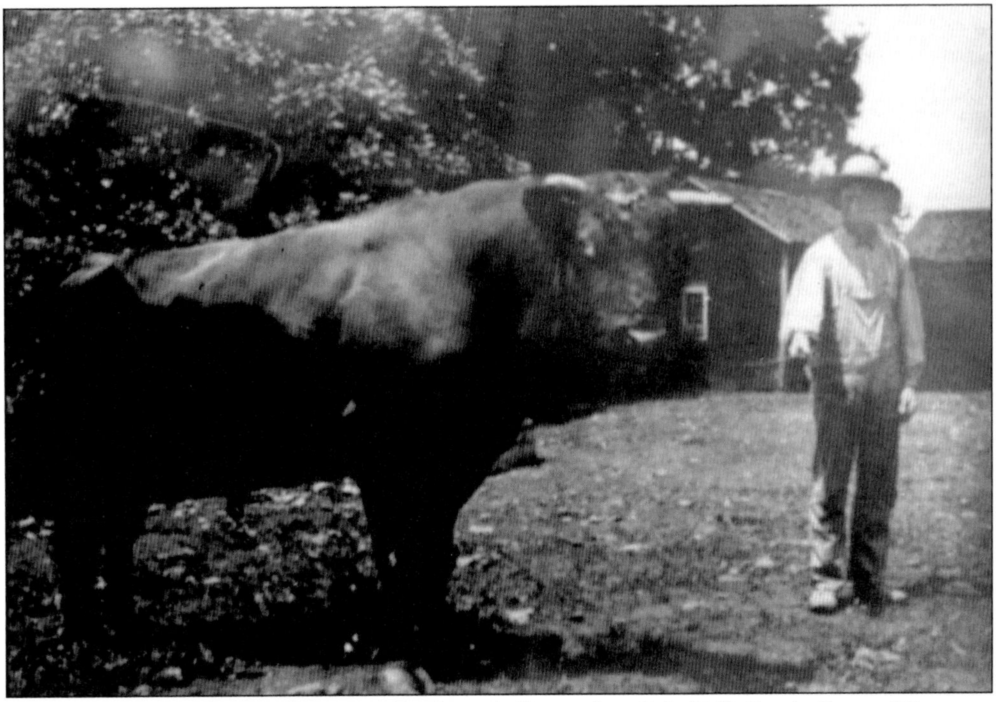

Howard Garlock shows off a prize Durham bull on the Oak Hill Stock Farm. (Courtesy TMHA.)

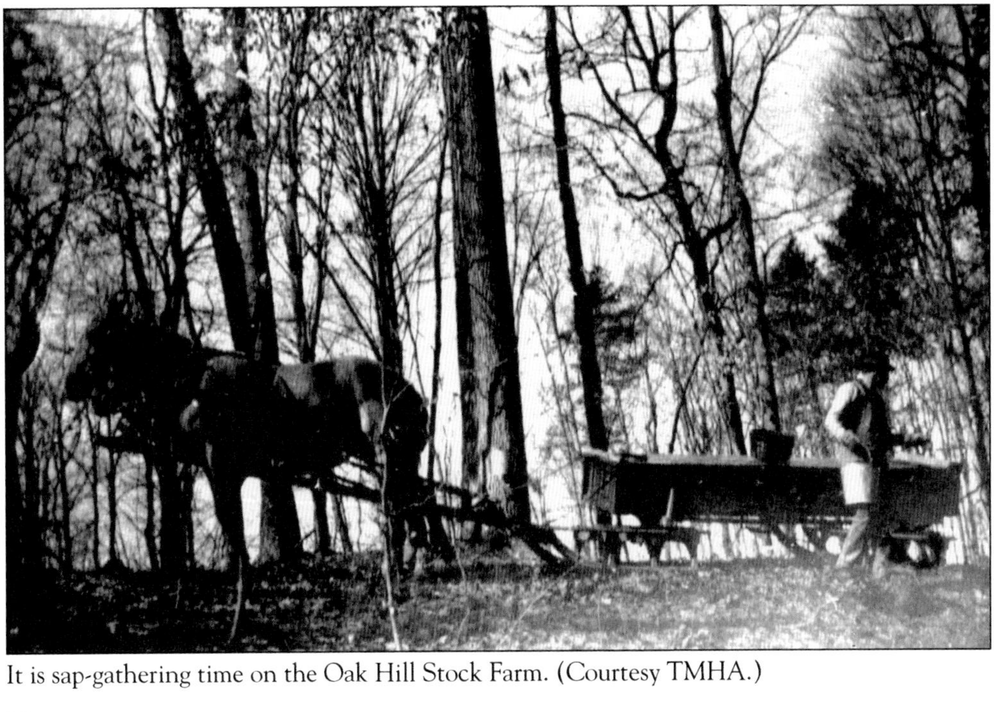

It is sap-gathering time on the Oak Hill Stock Farm. (Courtesy TMHA.)

Seven

MILES TO GO

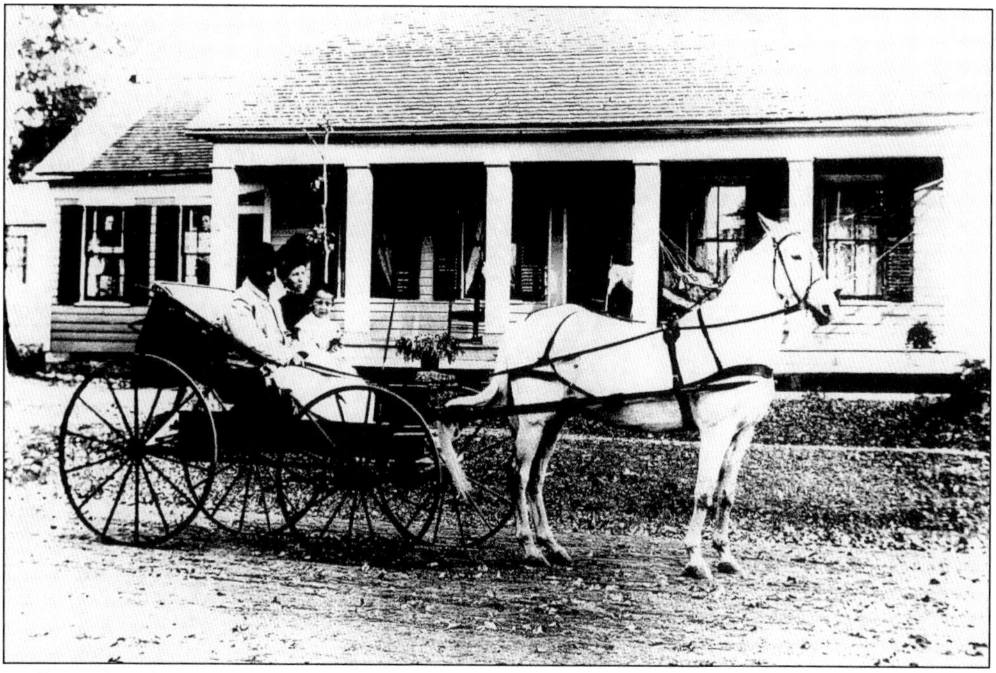

Willis and Helen Haskins pose with their grandson Bertram Boorn in 1908. They were renting this house in the hamlet of Middlefield from John H. Shafer. The house was constructed by Elijah Rich *c.* 1816 on property he acquired in a sheriff's sale, which was precipitated by landowner Reuben Rich's inability to pay a debt to Joshua Pinney for dry goods. The house remains little changed from its appearance in this photograph.

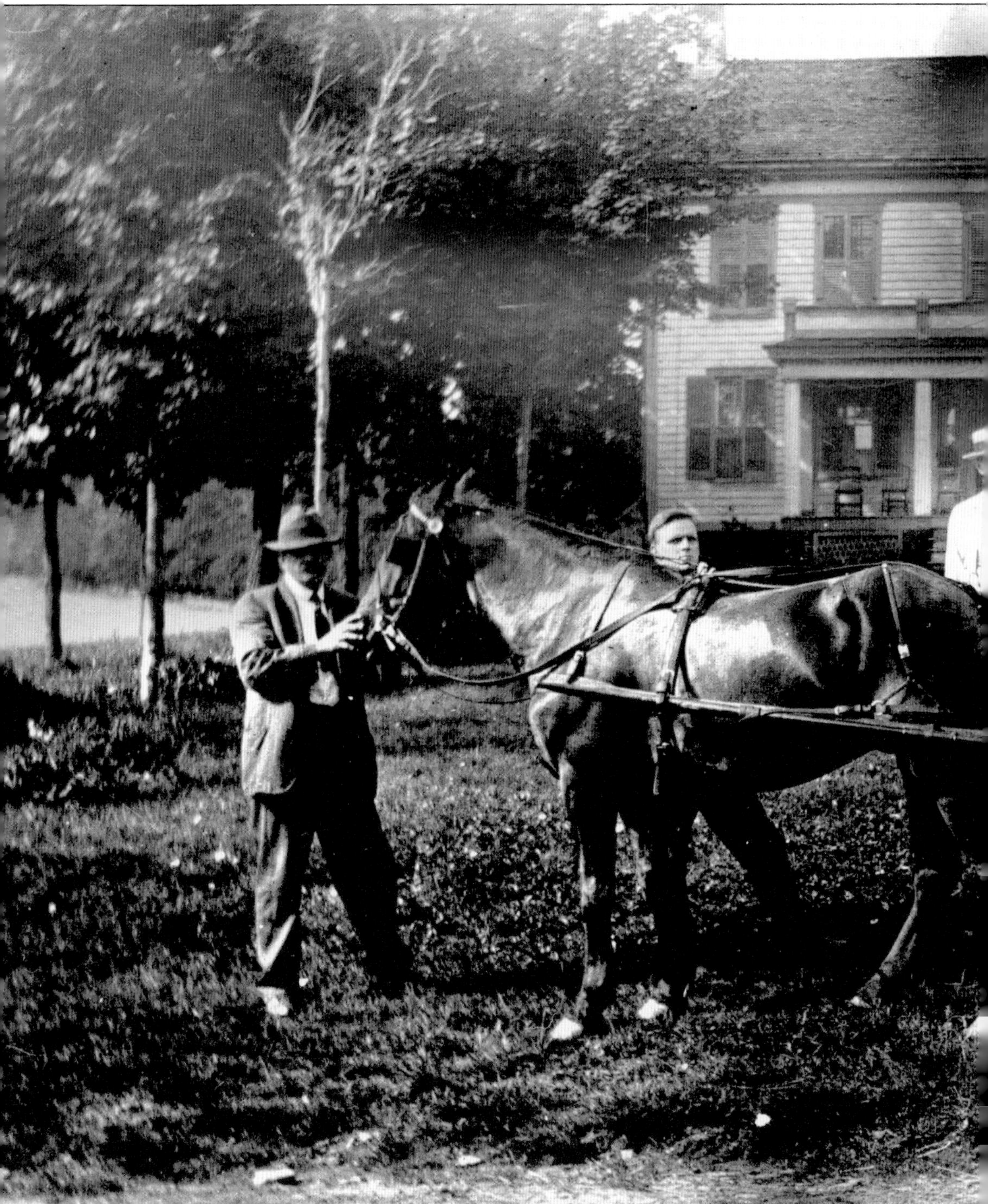

Members of the Eckler family pose in front of their house on Ricetown Road. As the name implies, this road winds down to the area known as Ricetown, presumably deriving its name

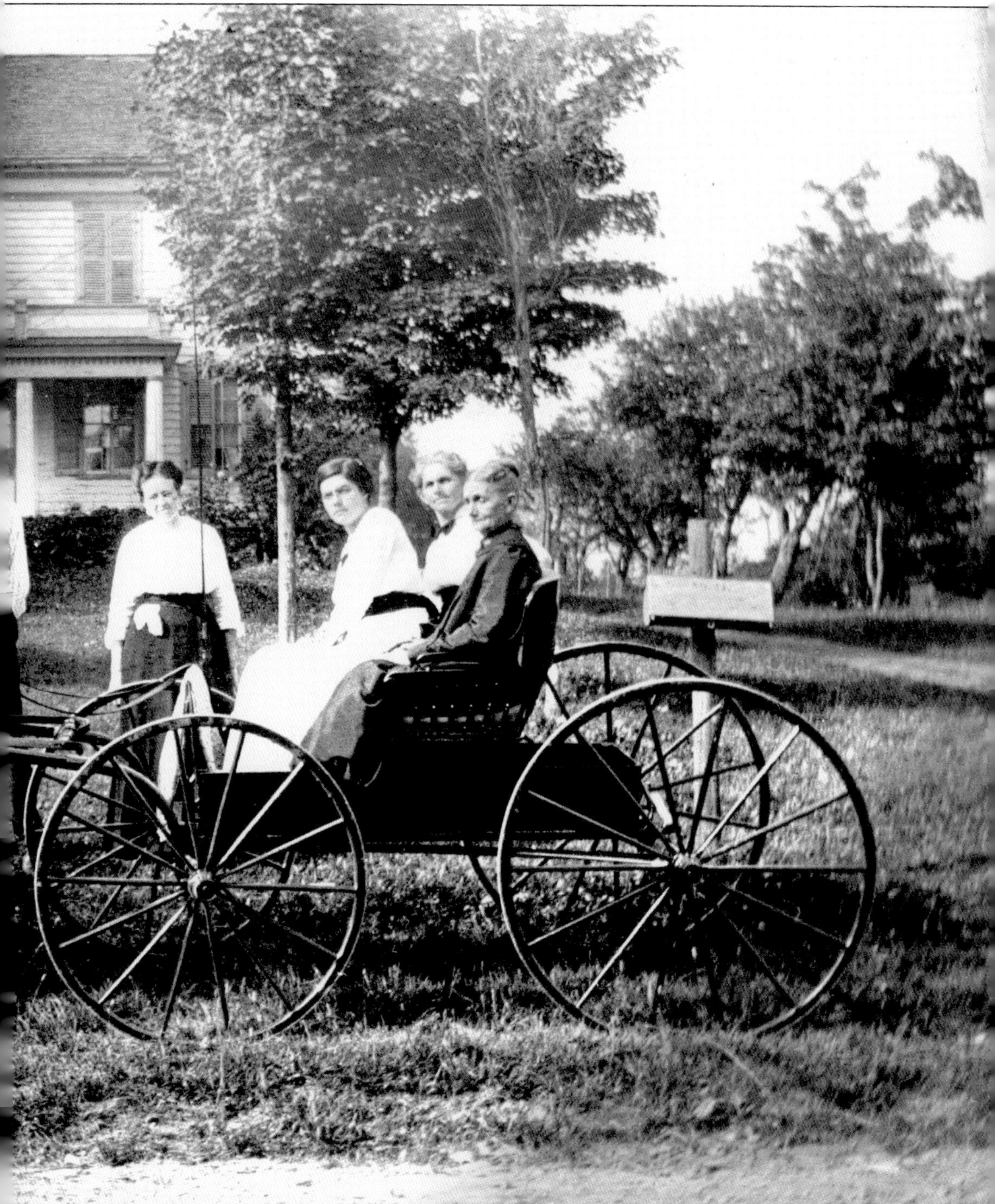

from a man named Rice. The Eckler house is a fine Federal-style house. The portico has delicate fluted columns.

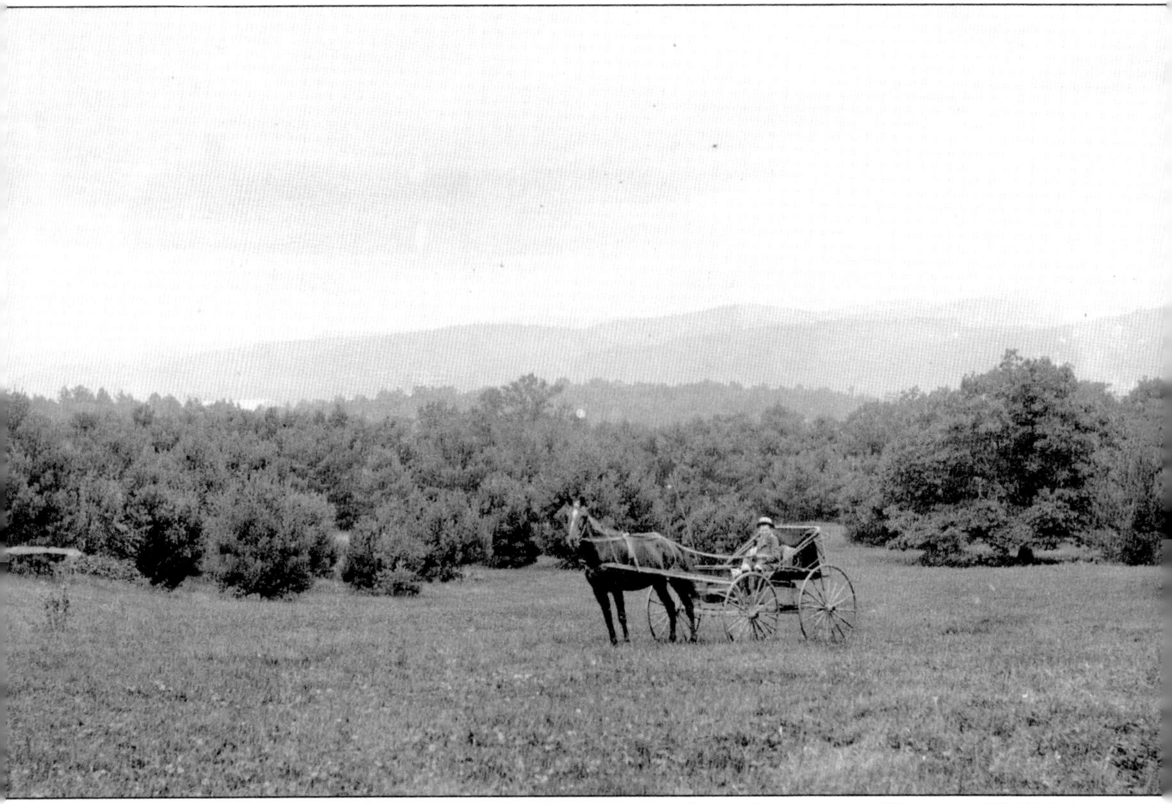

Howard Cunningham is shown in the family carriage at Stony Lonesome. (Courtesy TMHA.)

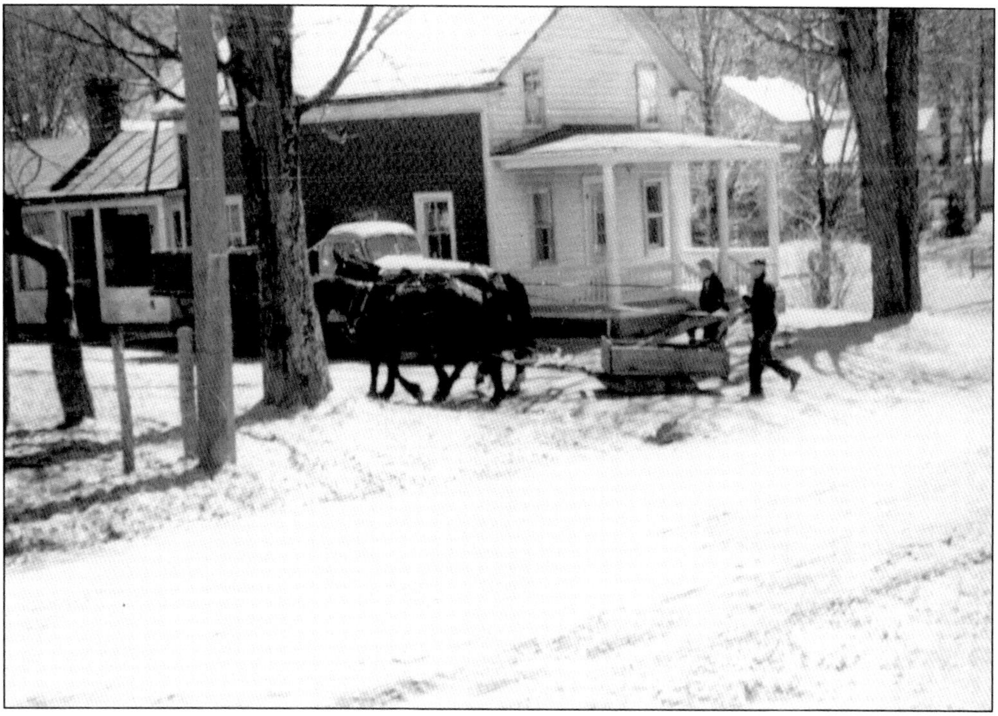

Well into the 20th century, horses were used to drag sleds in winter and to perform other work. This house is one of several that served as the Baptist parsonage in the hamlet of Middlefield. (Courtesy TMHA.)

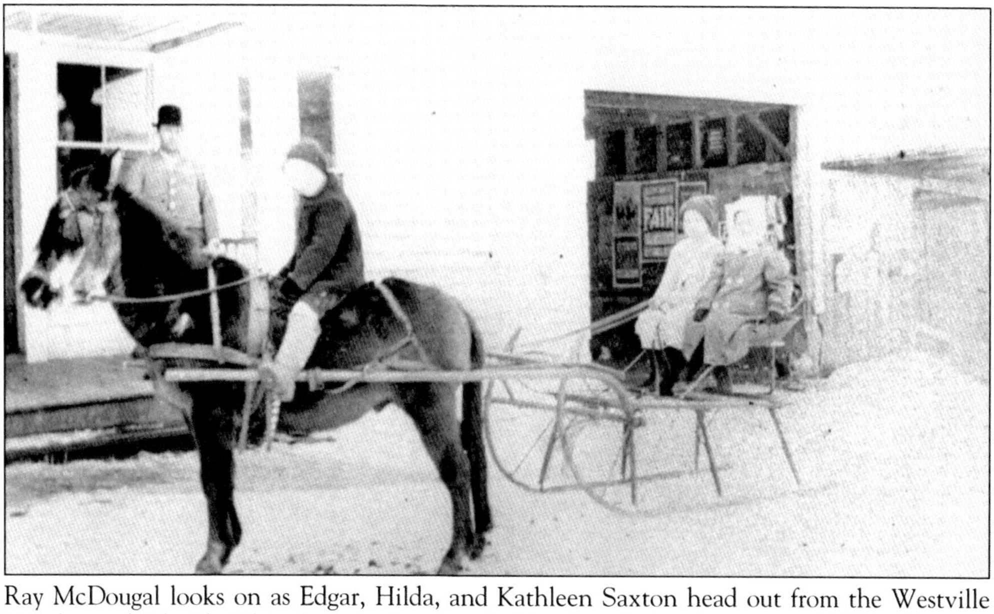

Ray McDougal looks on as Edgar, Hilda, and Kathleen Saxton head out from the Westville Hotel on a sleigh ride. This photograph was probably taken during the winter of 1908. (Courtesy TMHA.)

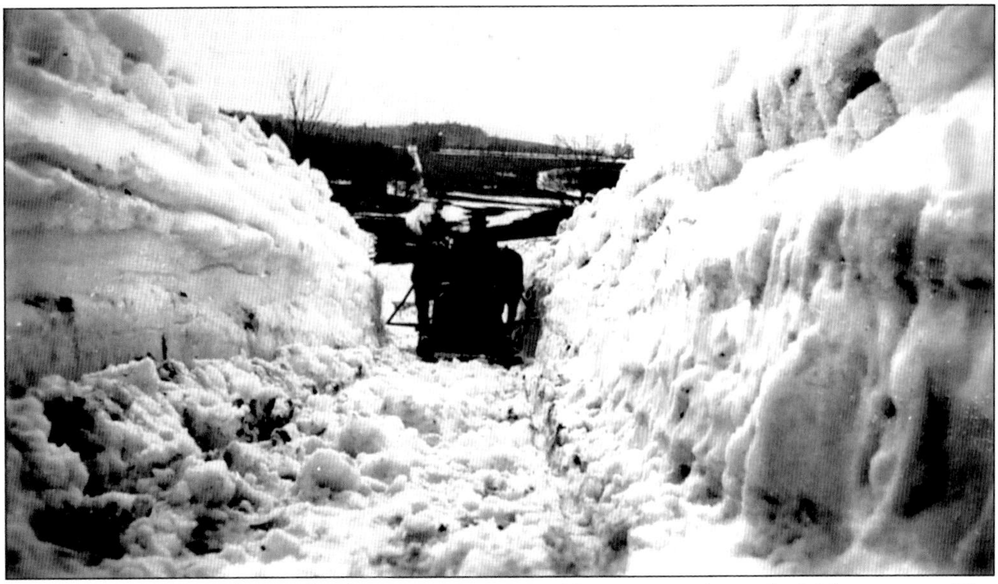

Clearing snow from the roads after a storm was problematic in the early 20th century. The blizzard of March 26, 1920, closed Murphy Hill for some time.

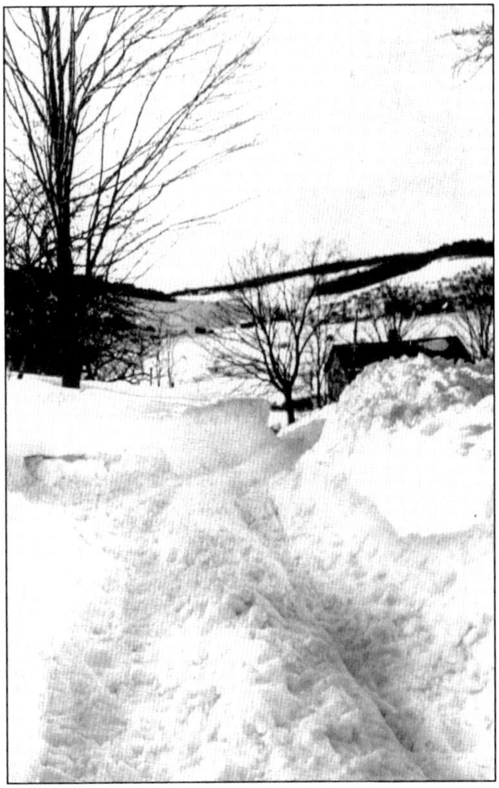

Farms and communities could be isolated for days after a storm. In this 1914 view of Murphy Hill, the house on the right belonged to Adriel Murphy, whose family lends its name to the neighborhood. (Courtesy TMHA.)

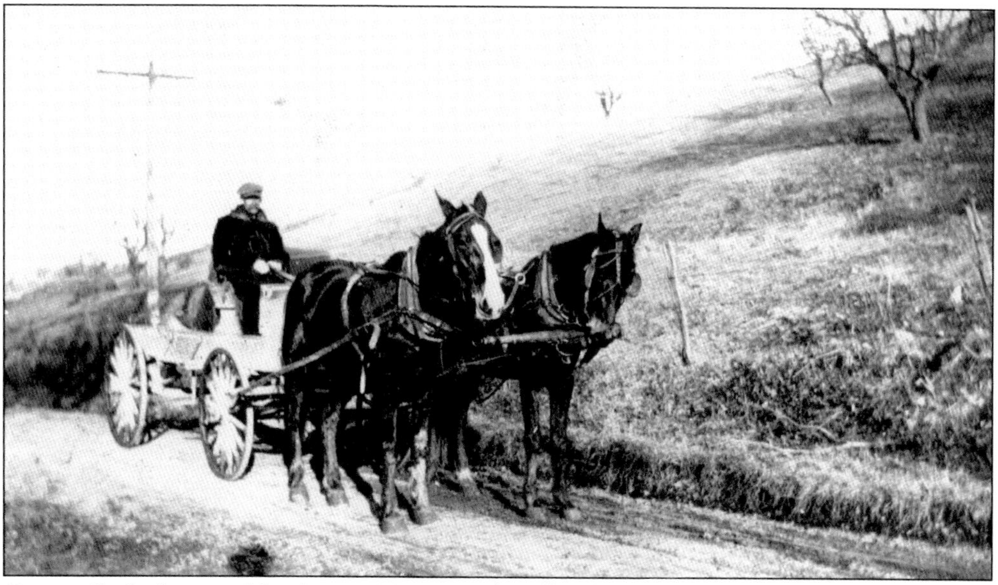

George Garlock named his horses Maggie and Nell. The horses are shown driving the stage from the neighboring village of Cherry Valley.

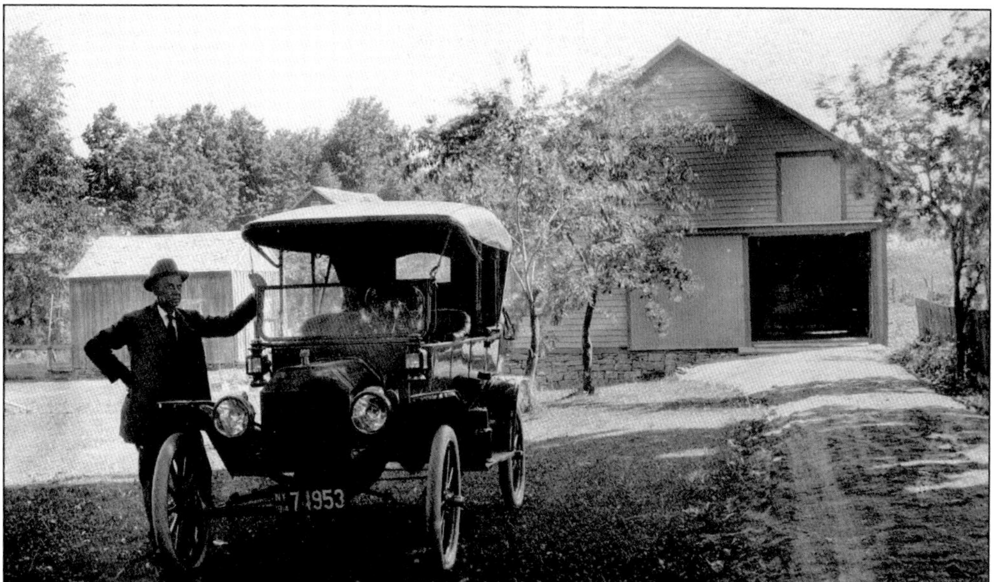

This c. 1914 photograph shows Edward Buel proudly standing with his car. His was the first car owned in the town of Middlefield.

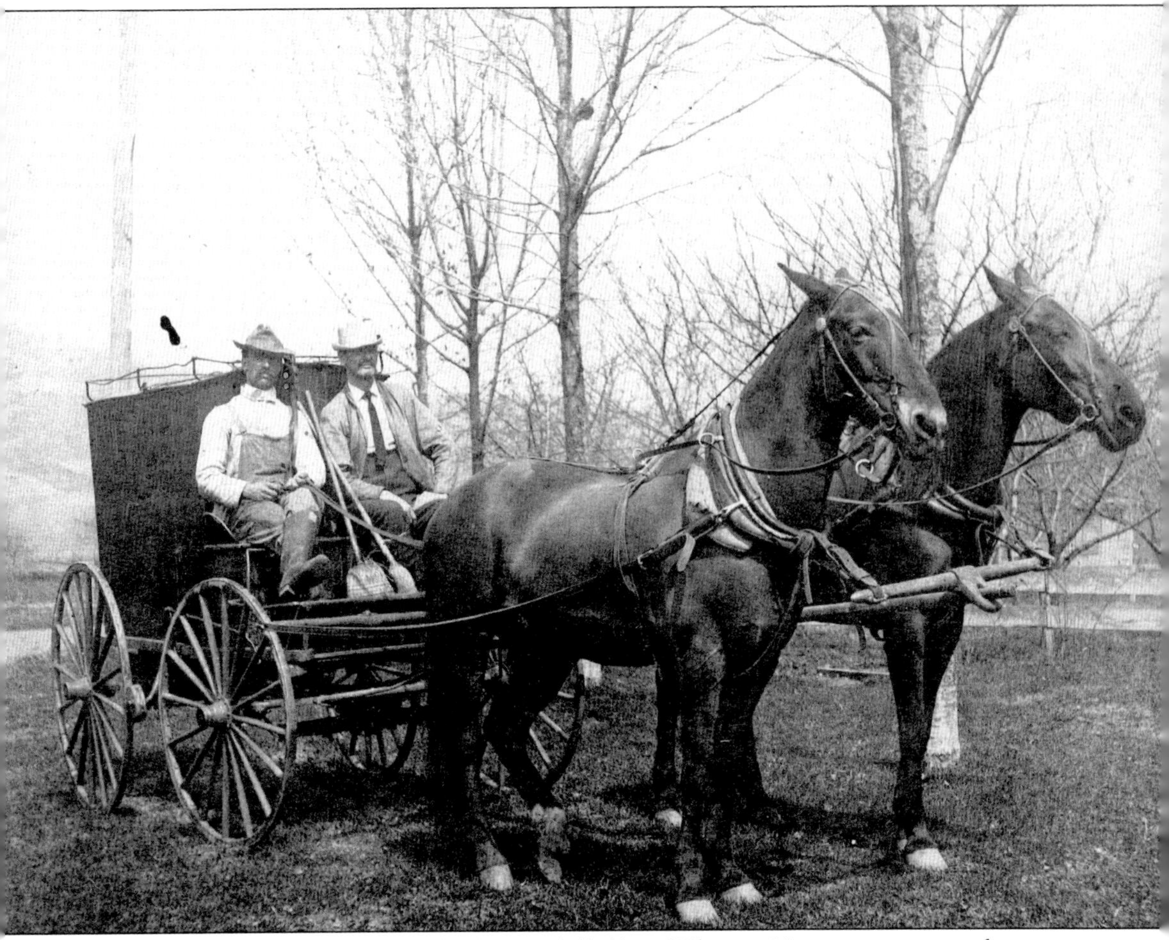

Pictured in their peddler's cart, Charles North (left) and Thomas Hearn, proprietors of a store in the hamlet of Middlefield, often took their wares on the road. To increase sales, merchants often peddled their products at the homes of people who had limited means of getting to a store.

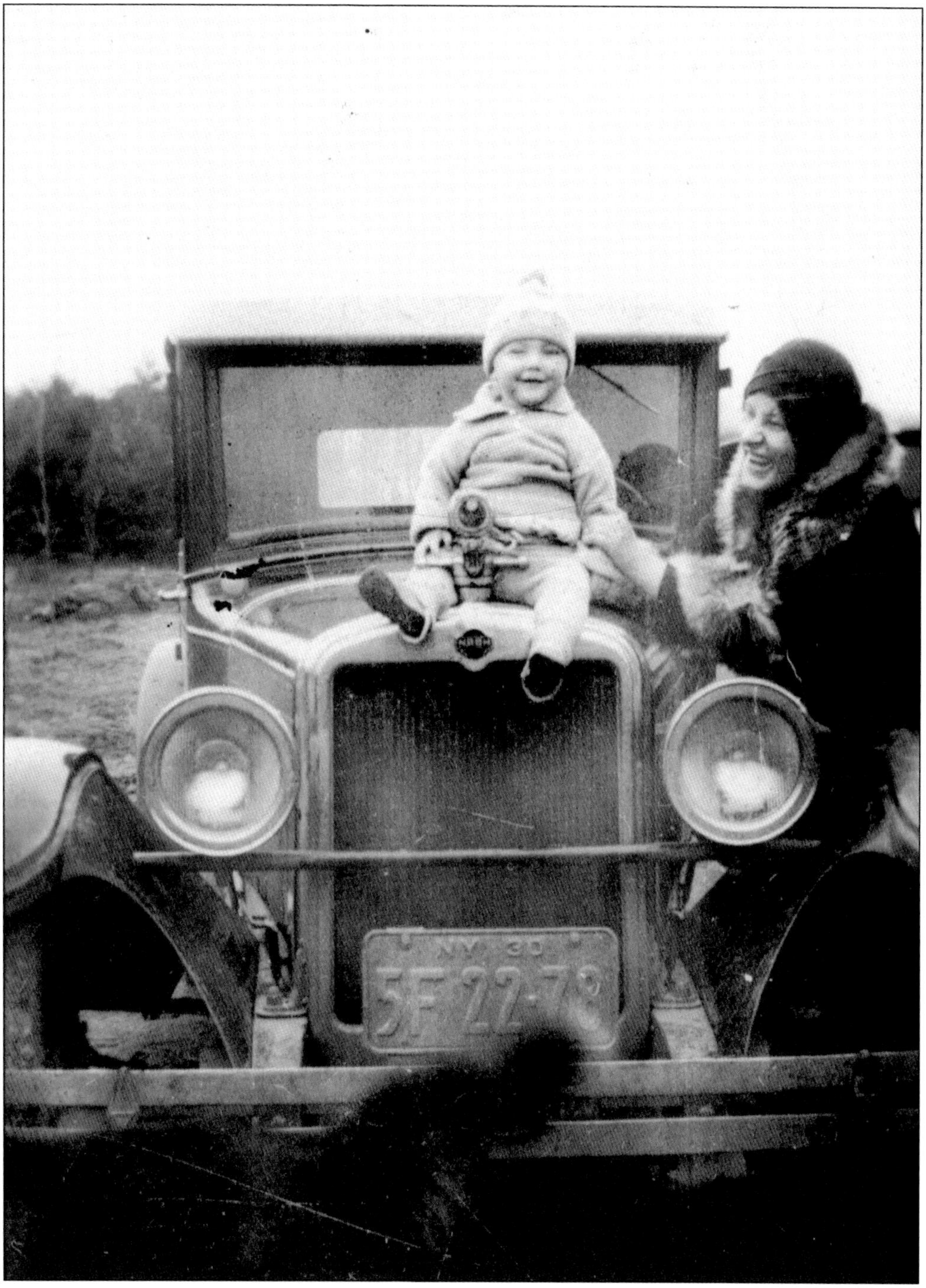

Charles Havens proudly sits atop the family car as his mother, Linda Havens, looks on. This photograph dates from *c.* 1935.

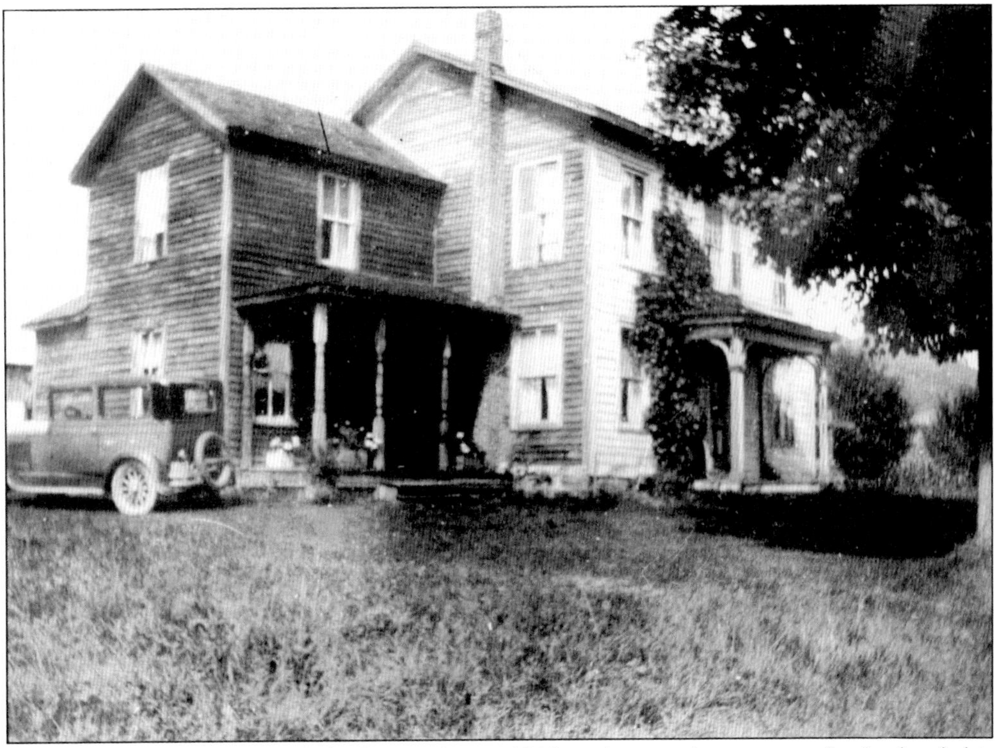

"Our old car by the side of the house Aug. 1928" is the simple note on the back of this photograph. The neighborhood around this house is referred to as Dubbendale, after the Dubben family, whose descendants still farm the area. (Courtesy TMHA.)

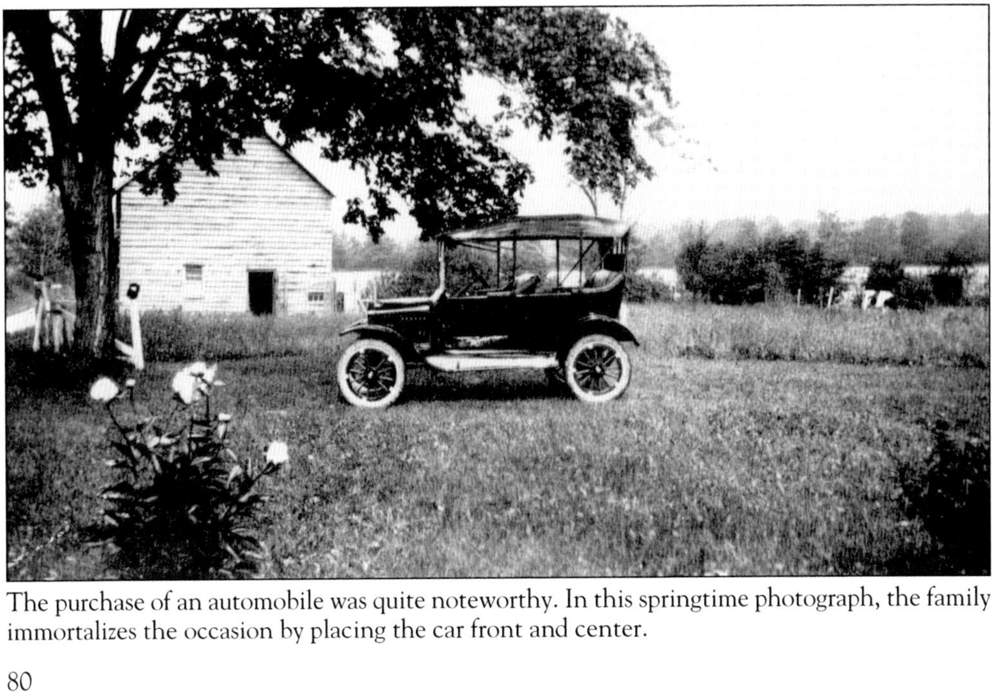

The purchase of an automobile was quite noteworthy. In this springtime photograph, the family immortalizes the occasion by placing the car front and center.

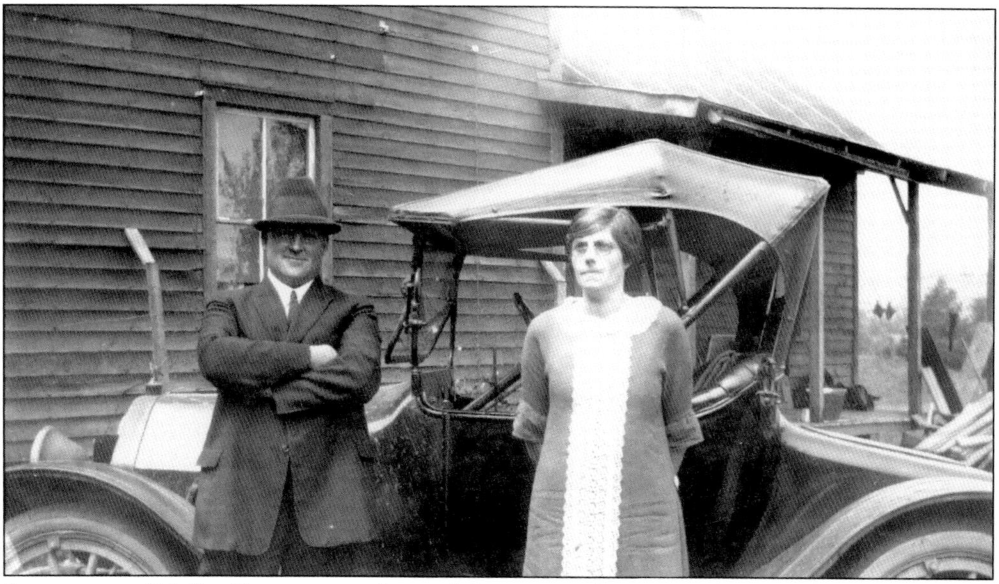

Benjamin and Nellie Slater pose in front of their car at the Mowers house. (Courtesy TMHA.)

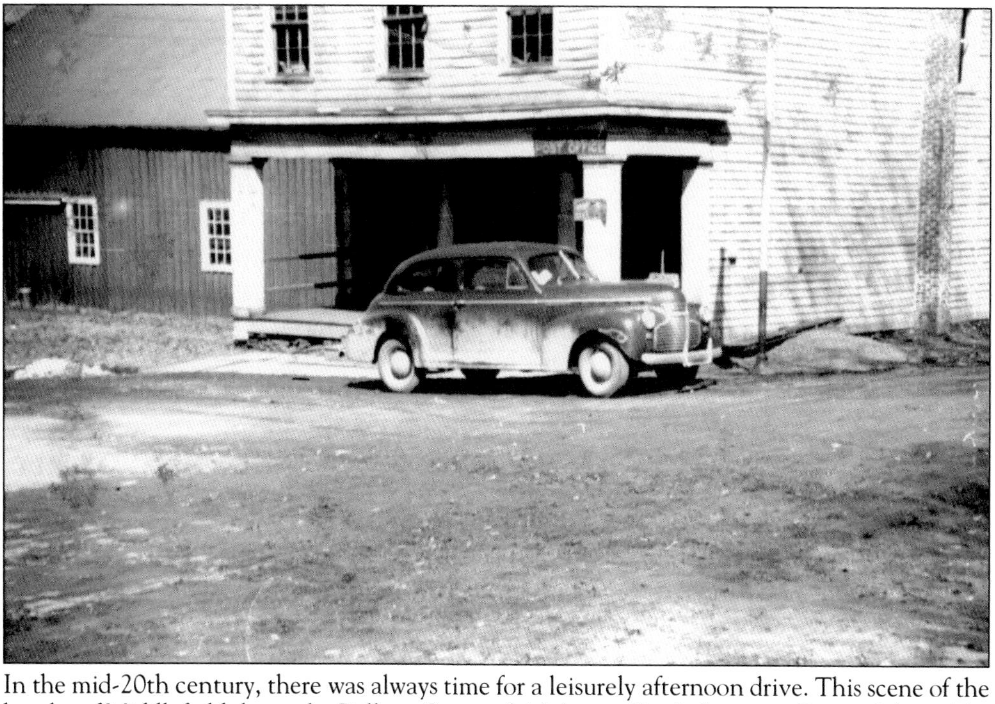

In the mid-20th century, there was always time for a leisurely afternoon drive. This scene of the hamlet of Middlefield shows the Pollette Store, which housed both the post office and the public telephone. On the left is the barn that was later torn down to make way for the firehouse.

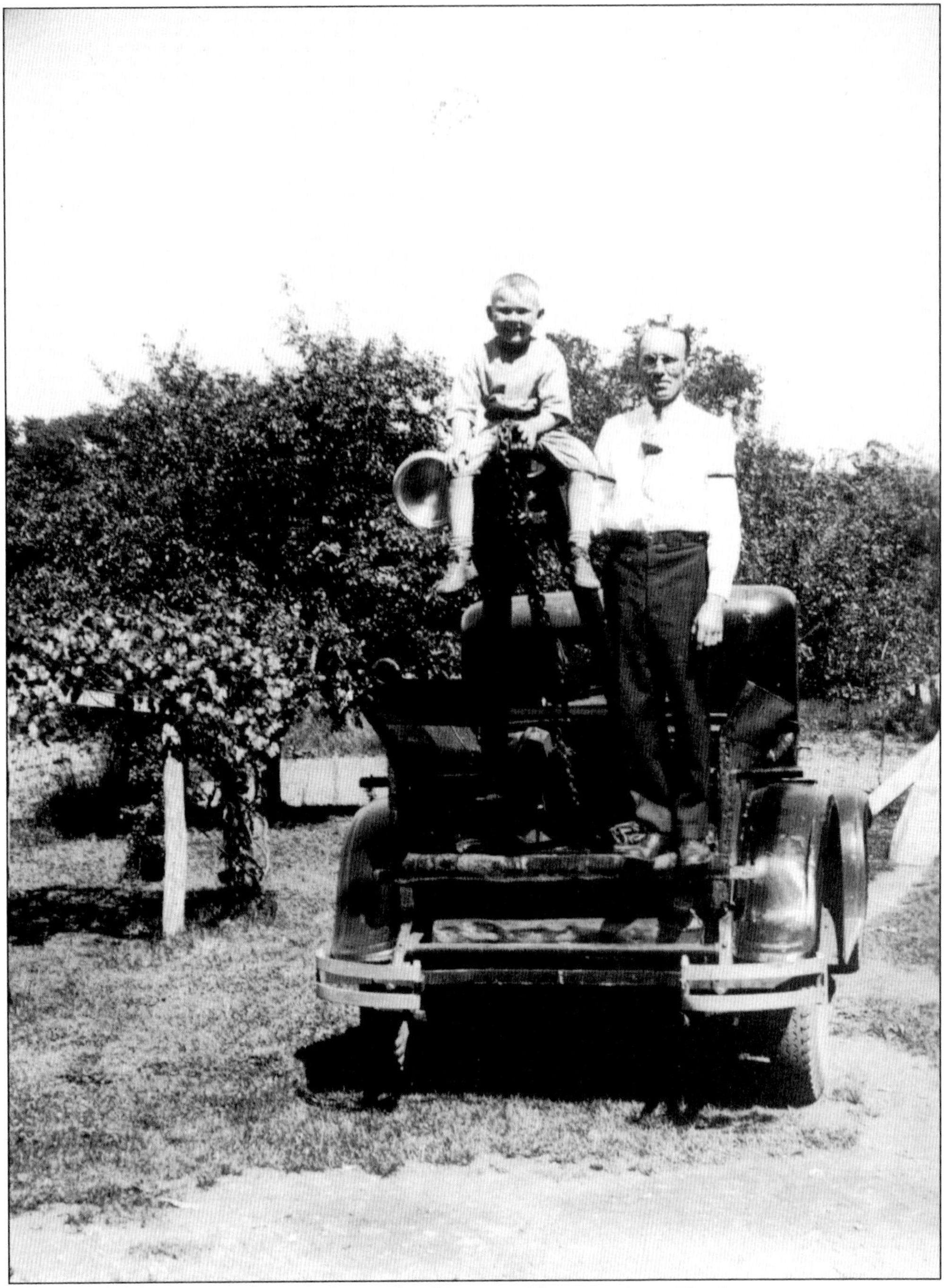
Poised on the boom of a tow truck are Floyd Pitts and his grandson Charles.

Seven

Inns and Taverns

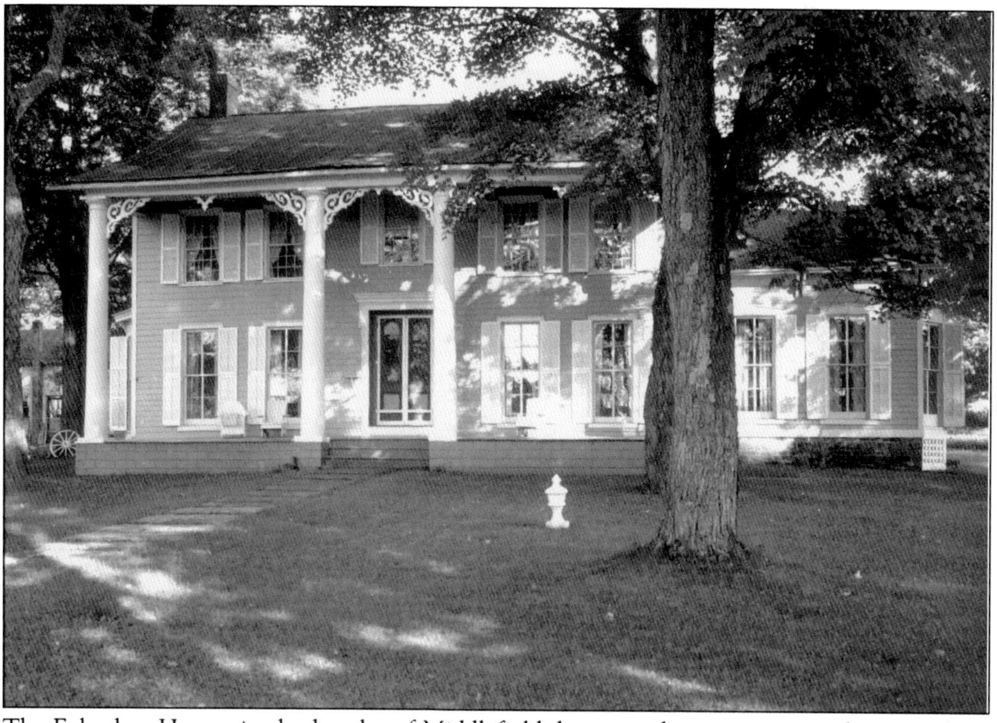

The Folmsbee House, in the hamlet of Middlefield, has served many purposes during its long history. Joshua Pinney, who rented and then purchased the house from George Clarke of Springfield, used it as a tavern from 1803 to 1833, and as the post office while he was postmaster. Benjamin North Jr., the next owner, also ran it as a tavern. In 1824, the house served as the meeting place of the Freemasons after they formed their lodge. Over the years owners have embellished the façade with Victorian ornaments, and one parlor even had its walls painted with a fine mural, possibly by itinerant painter William Price. This photograph was taken c. 1962, shortly before Rodney and Jean Johnson purchased the house.

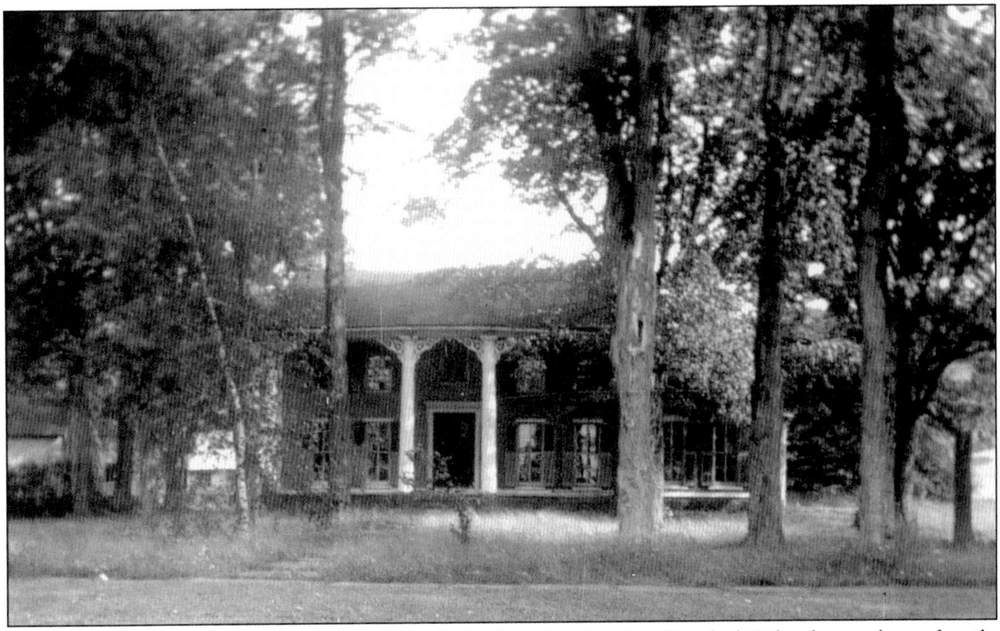

The Folmsbee House is shown in 1956, just before the death of Mabel Folmsbee, whose family had owned the house since 1863. This photograph was taken by Middlefield's first town historian, E. Pomeroy Staats. (Courtesy TMHA.)

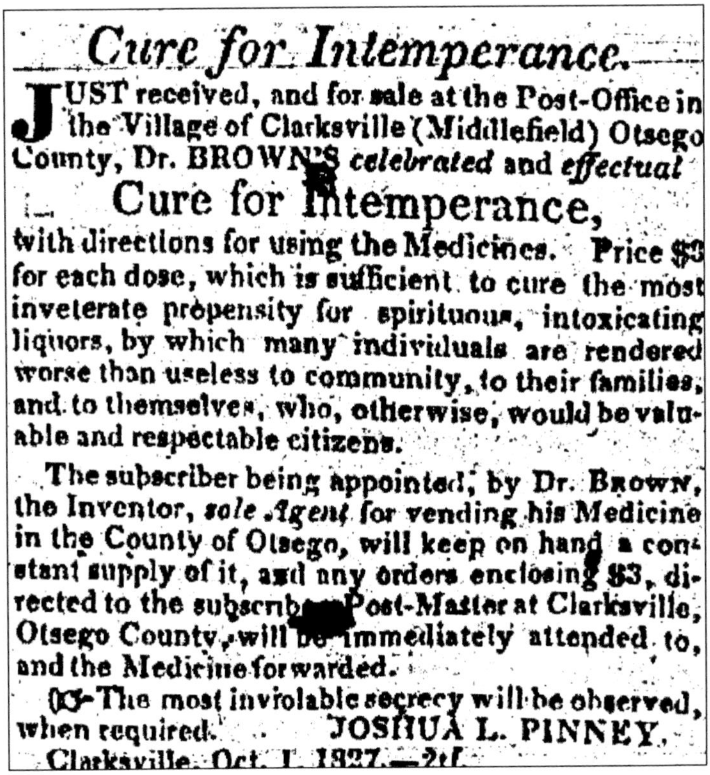

Cure for Intemperance.

JUST received, and for sale at the Post-Office in the Village of Clarksville (Middlefield) Otsego County, Dr. BROWN'S *celebrated* and *effectual*

Cure for Intemperance,

with directions for using the Medicines. Price $3 for each dose, which is sufficient to cure the most inveterate propensity for spirituous, intoxicating liquors, by which many individuals are rendered worse than useless to community, to their families, and to themselves, who, otherwise, would be valuable and respectable citizens.

The subscriber being appointed, by Dr. BROWN, the Inventor, *sole Agent* for vending his Medicine in the County of Otsego, will keep on hand a constant supply of it, and any orders enclosing $3, directed to the subscriber Post-Master at Clarksville, Otsego County, will be immediately attended to, and the Medicine forwarded.

☞The most inviolable secrecy will be observed, when required. JOSHUA L. PINNEY.

Clarksville, Oct. 1, 1827.—2tf.

It is ironic that while he was operating a tavern, Joshua Pinney saw fit to advertise a cure for intemperance. This advertisement promised to cure even "the most inveterate propensity for spirituous, intoxicating liquors." It appeared in the January 28, 1828 edition of the *Freeman's Journal*. To further the irony, Pinney was also operating a still in the 1820s. (Reproduced with permission from the *Freeman's Journal*.)

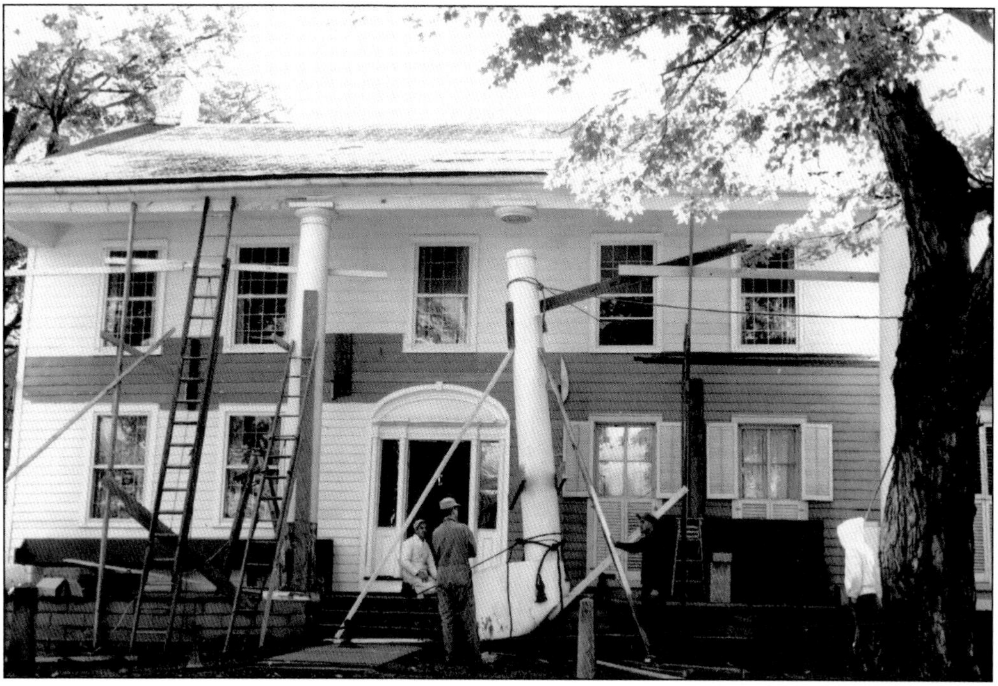

During the restoration of the Pinney Tavern, one of the columns collapsed and nearly crashed into the house due to the extreme state of decay of the base. The scaffolding already in place and attached to the column prevented it from falling.

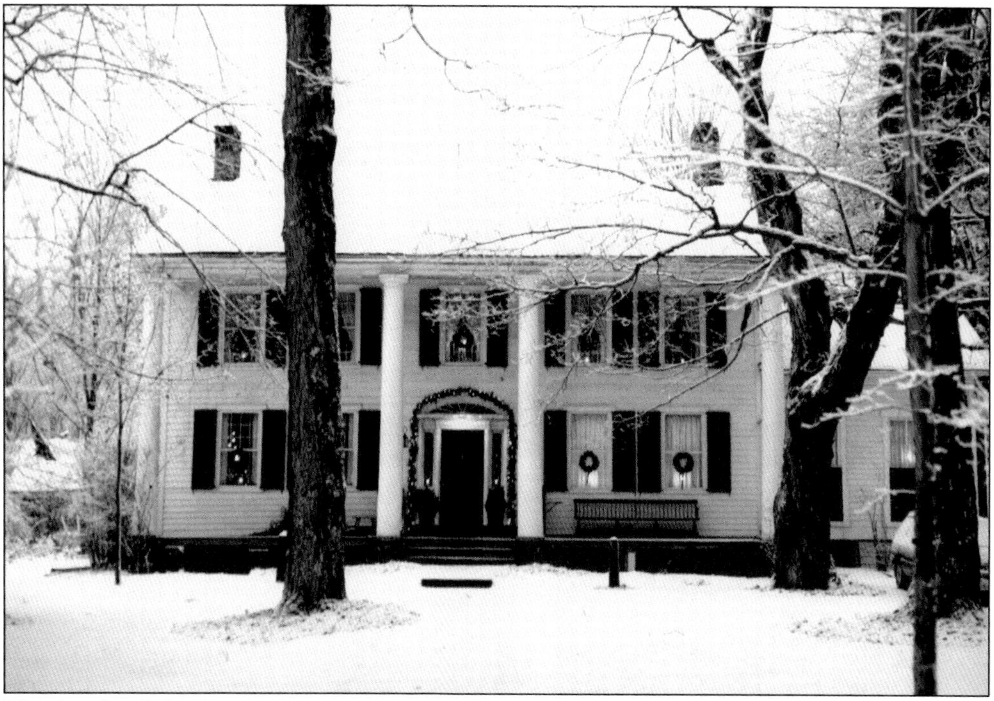

The façade of the Pinney Tavern was completely restored under the care of Rodney and Jean Johnson. Decorated for Christmas, the house truly makes a magical place for a homecoming.

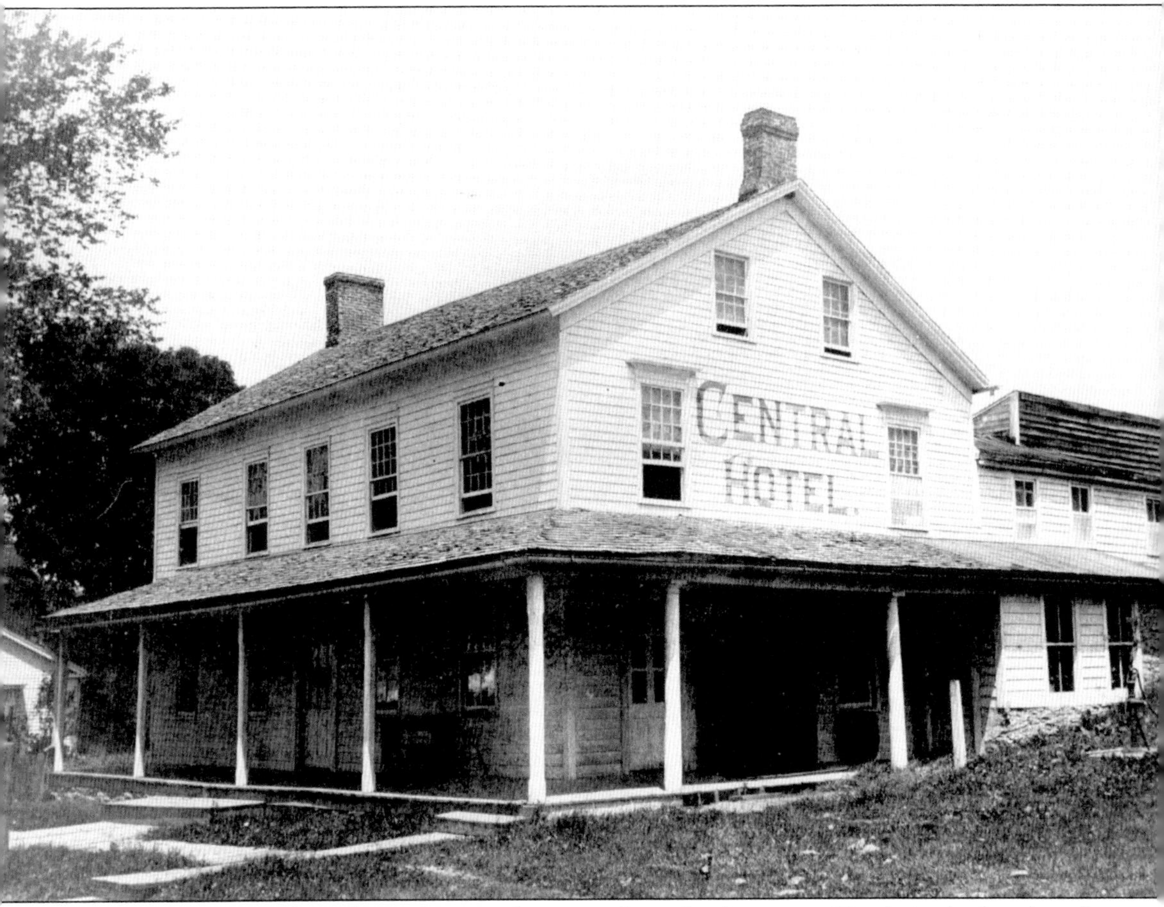

The Central Hotel was located across the street from the American Hotel, in the hamlet of Middlefield. The first deed referencing this house states that Hosea Cummings bought it from George Clarke on April 8, 1822, for $27. On the same day, Cummings sold it to Hannah Howard for $400. The porch obscures some of the fine Federal-style features of the house, which would indicate a construction date as early as 1810. It is the only house in the hamlet to have entablatures above the windows. It served as a tavern for most of the 19th and early 20th centuries. (Courtesy NYSHA.)

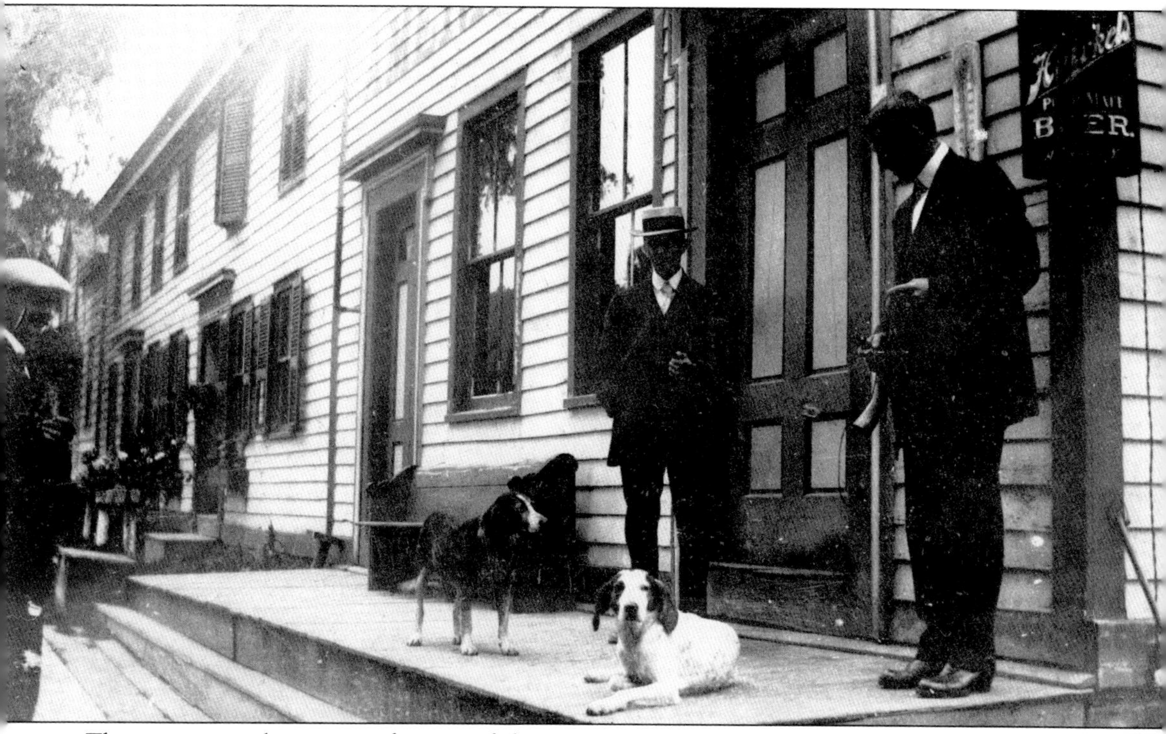

These men may be arriving for one of the many elegant dances that Charles Flint hosted at his hotel. This early-20th-century photograph shows the expanse of the front of the American Hotel. This building is directly across the street from the Central Hotel. It was not uncommon to use church pews in the front of these hotels.

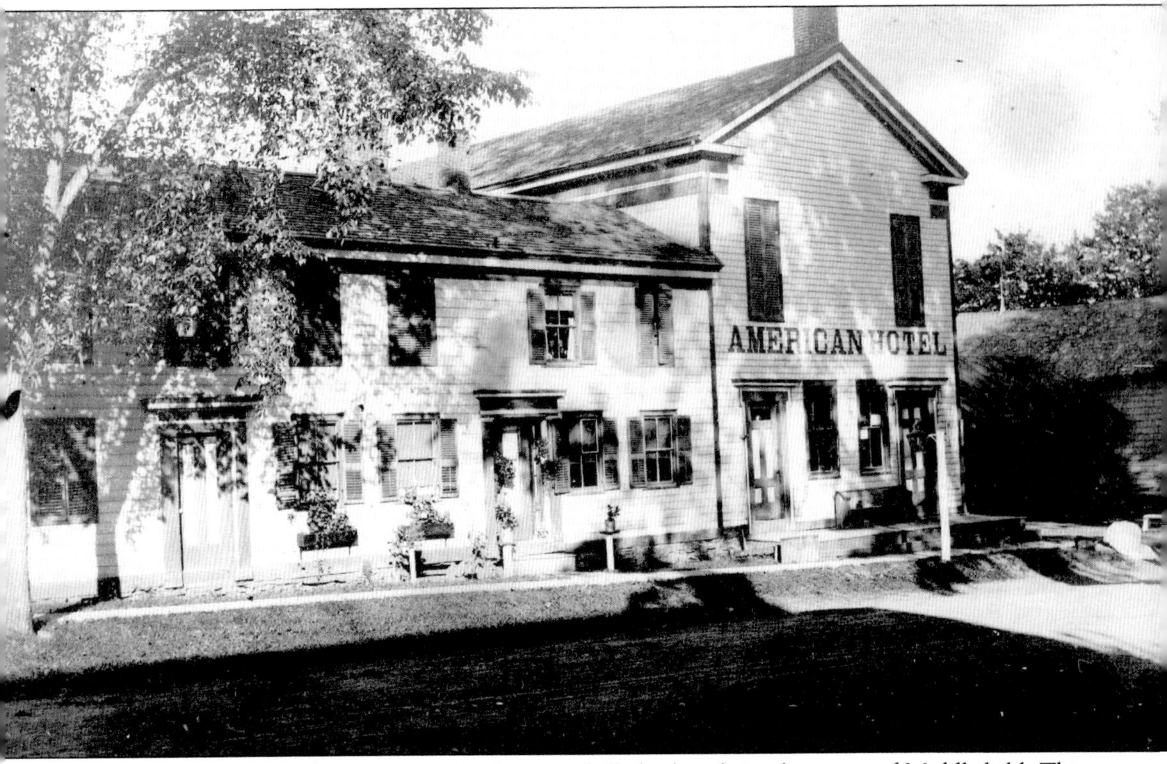

The American Hotel was among the largest of all the hotels in the town of Middlefield. This view shows the hotel during its heyday in the early 1900s.

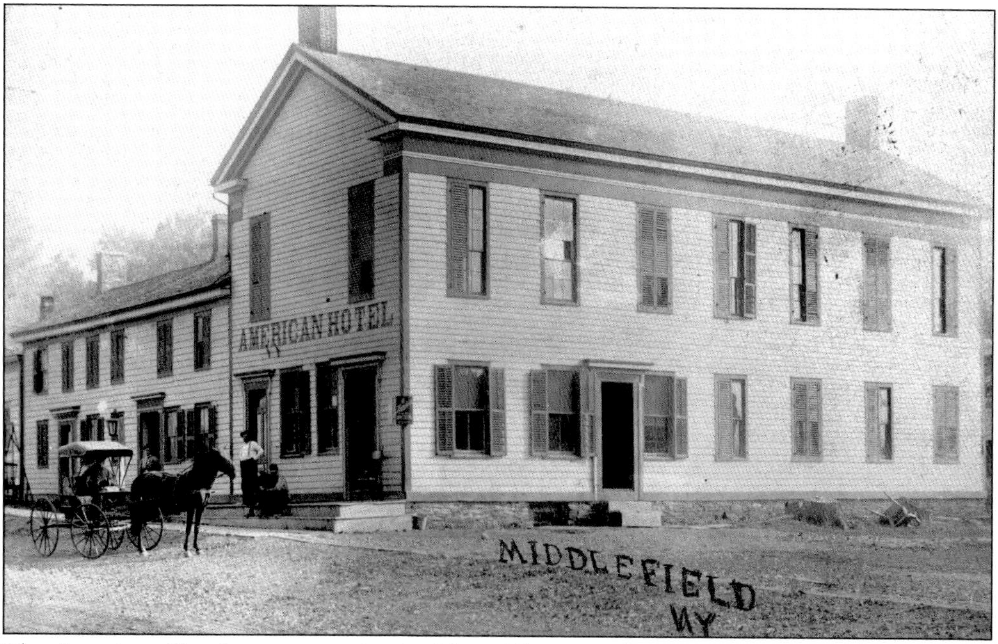

The American Hotel was a towering building. This view shows it *c.* 1900. The hotel burned in 1934.

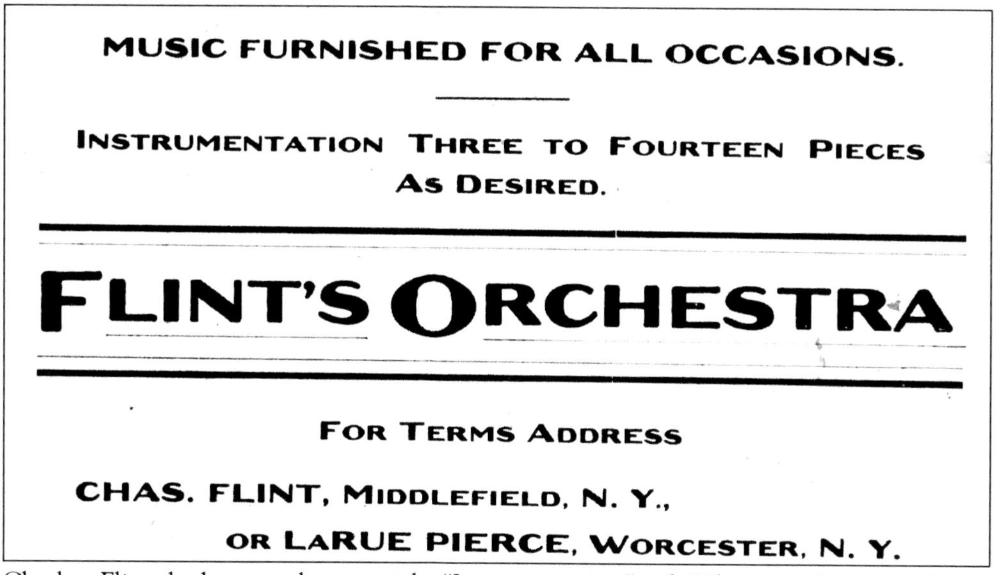

Charles Flint had an orchestra with "Instrumentation" of "Three to Fourteen Pieces As Desired." Among the members of this orchestra were Lee Roberts, who played violin, and Rose Flint, Charles Flint's daughter, who played both piano and percussion.

Social Hop

YOURSELF AND LADY ARE CORDIALLY INVITED TO ATTEND A PRIVATE DANCING PARTY TO BE GIVEN AT THE

AMERICAN * HOTEL,

MIDDLEFIELD, N. Y.,

Wednesday Evening, January 3d, 1894.

MUSIC BY PORTLANDVILLE ORCHESTRA.

COMMITTEE:

C. FOLAND, B. S. PITTS, S. COLE, F. GILLETT, L. A. COSSART, D. PITTS, B. W. DEWER, S. J. PRESTON, E. D. NILES, F. COLMAN, C. MIX, L. COLMAN, H. COSSAART, FRED HOPKINS.

During his ownership of the American Hotel, Charles Flint saw to it that the hotel was the center of society. It was his habit to host elegant balls, community-wide events that required the efforts of many local people working together. Elegant invitation cards were sent out to ensure a large attendance.

Alfred Carey,
Flaar Managcr.

Charles Flint,
Praprietar.

Yourself and ladies are cordially invited to attend the first Annual Ball to be given by

Charles Flint,

in the American Hotel,

Middlefield, N. Y.,

Thursday evening, Jan. twenty fifth, nineteen hundred and six

Music by Flints Orchestra.
Salt Springville, N. Y

Bill, - $1.00.

This is an invitation to the annual ball at the American Hotel on January 25, 1906.

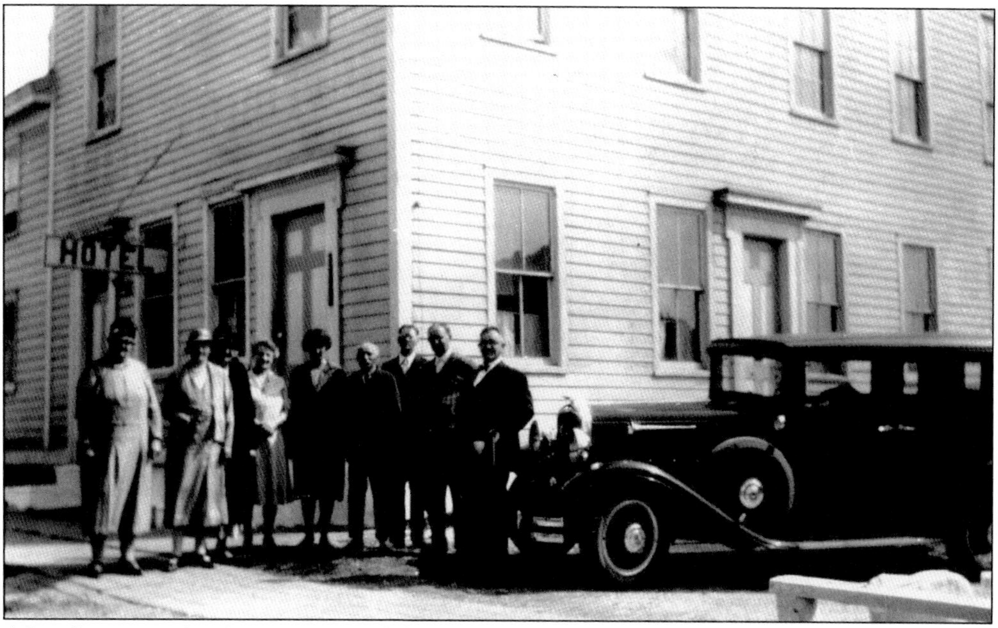

After driving to the American Hotel these ladies and gentlemen pause for a photograph before heading inside. Elegant attire was required when attending one of Charles Flint's balls. In fact, it was only after stealing $75 and two suits from the North and Hearn Store next door on August 15, 1882, that burglars found themselves fit to break into the American Hotel for whiskey and cigars.

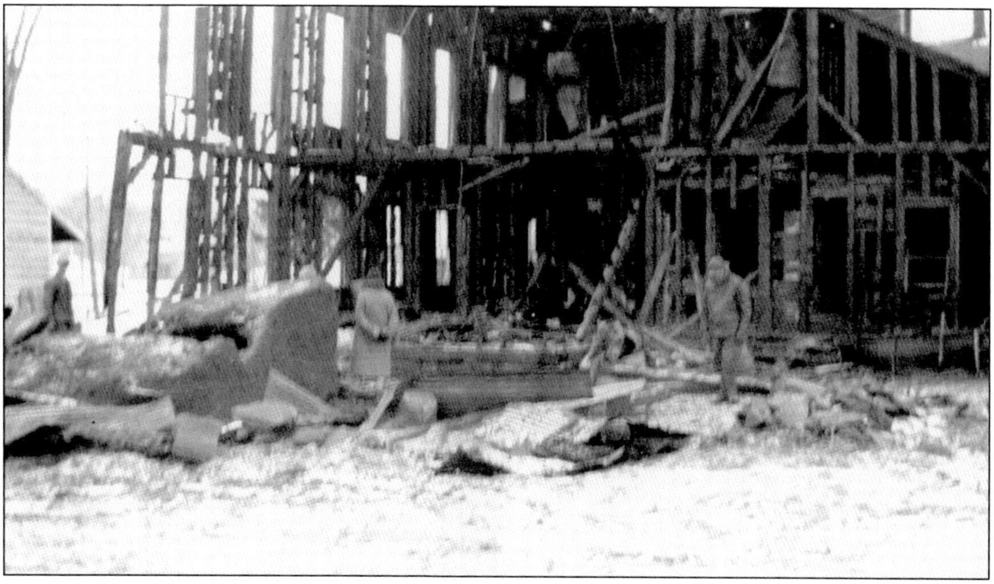

In 1934, fire ravaged the American Hotel—a devastating event for the community. All that was left was a fraction of the once towering building. Charles Flint had recently sold the building to Ford Wedderspoon of Pierstown before Flint died in December 1933. Wedderspoon and Fred Talman had finished storing ice in the icehouse at 6:00 p.m. One half hour later, Frances Roberts reported that the icehouse and woodhouse were in flames. The fire quickly spread to the hotel, which burned for five hours.

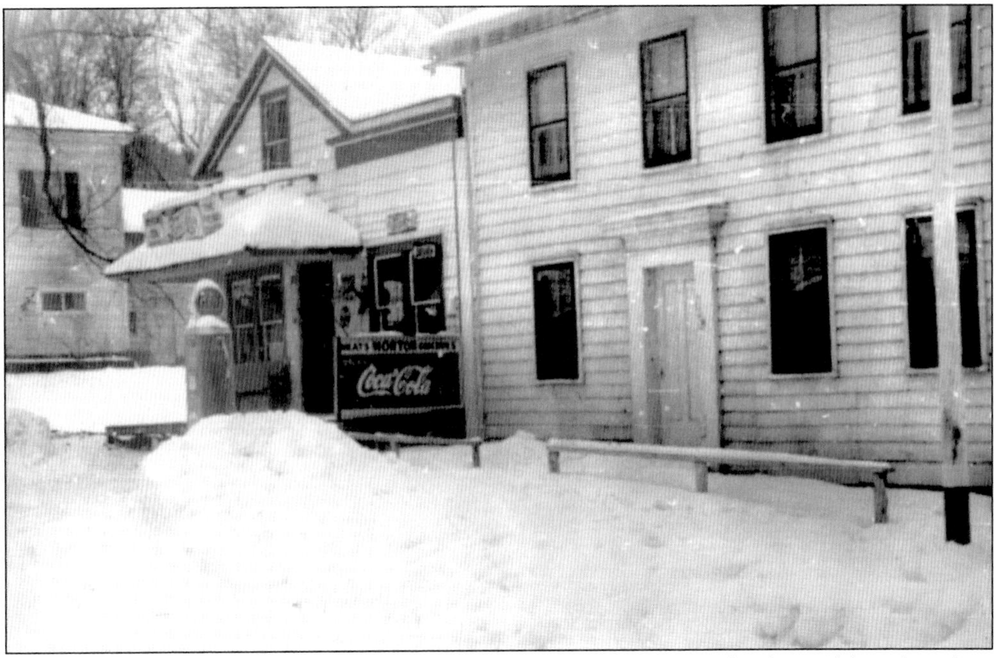

This view of the American Hotel shows it a couple decades after the fire. Although only a fraction of the once grand hotel was left, it still served the community well as Lamb's Store. (Courtesy TMHA.)

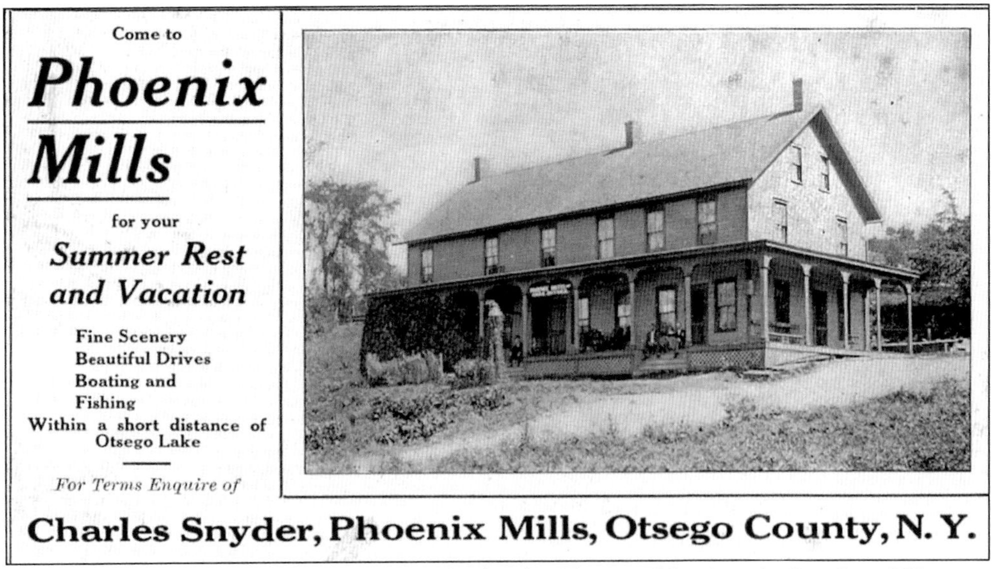

The advertising campaign of Charles Snyder for the Phoenix Hotel in the hamlet of Phoenix Mills still endures with owners of bed-and-breakfast establishments in Middlefield: fine scenery, beautiful drives, boating, and fishing. The natural beauty of Middlefield and Otsego Lake has always been a source of pride. (Courtesy TMHA.)

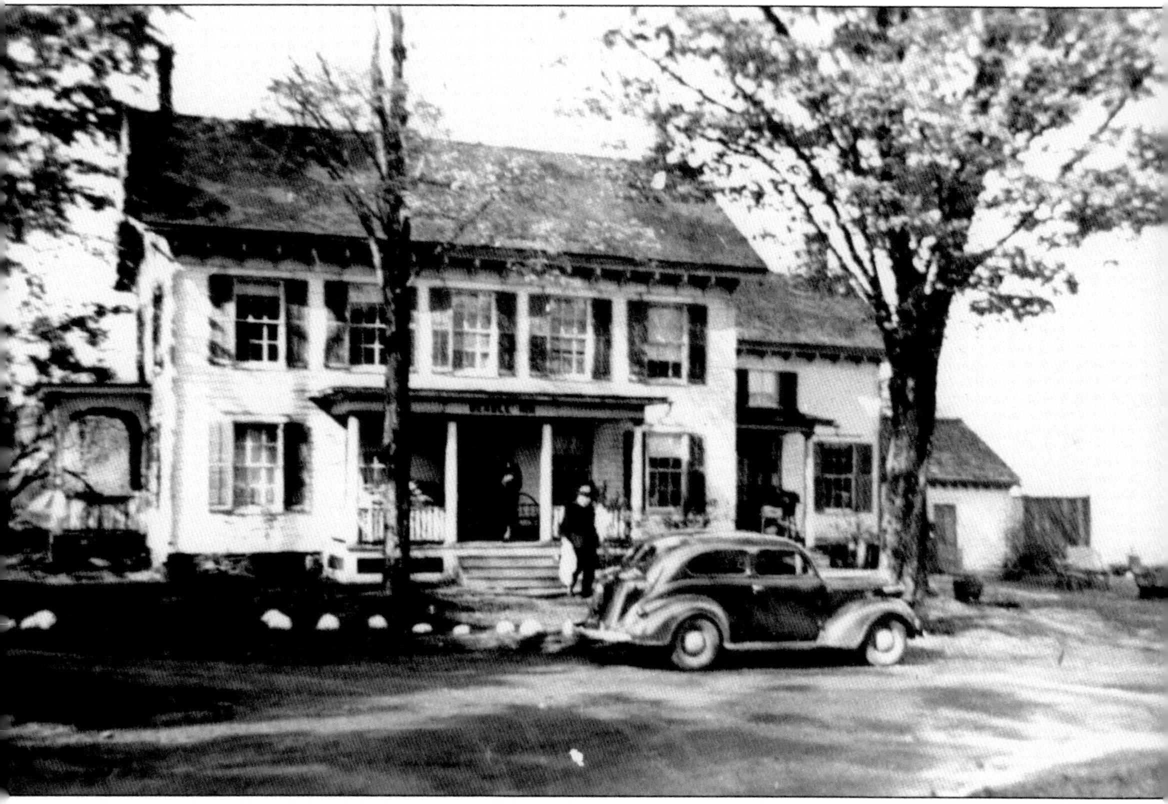

Thomas Rice lived in this house in Whig Corners prior to the Civil War. In 1853, it was purchased by John Coonrad, who eventually sold it to Henry Beadle. For years thereafter it was known as the Beadle Inn. (Courtesy TMHA.)

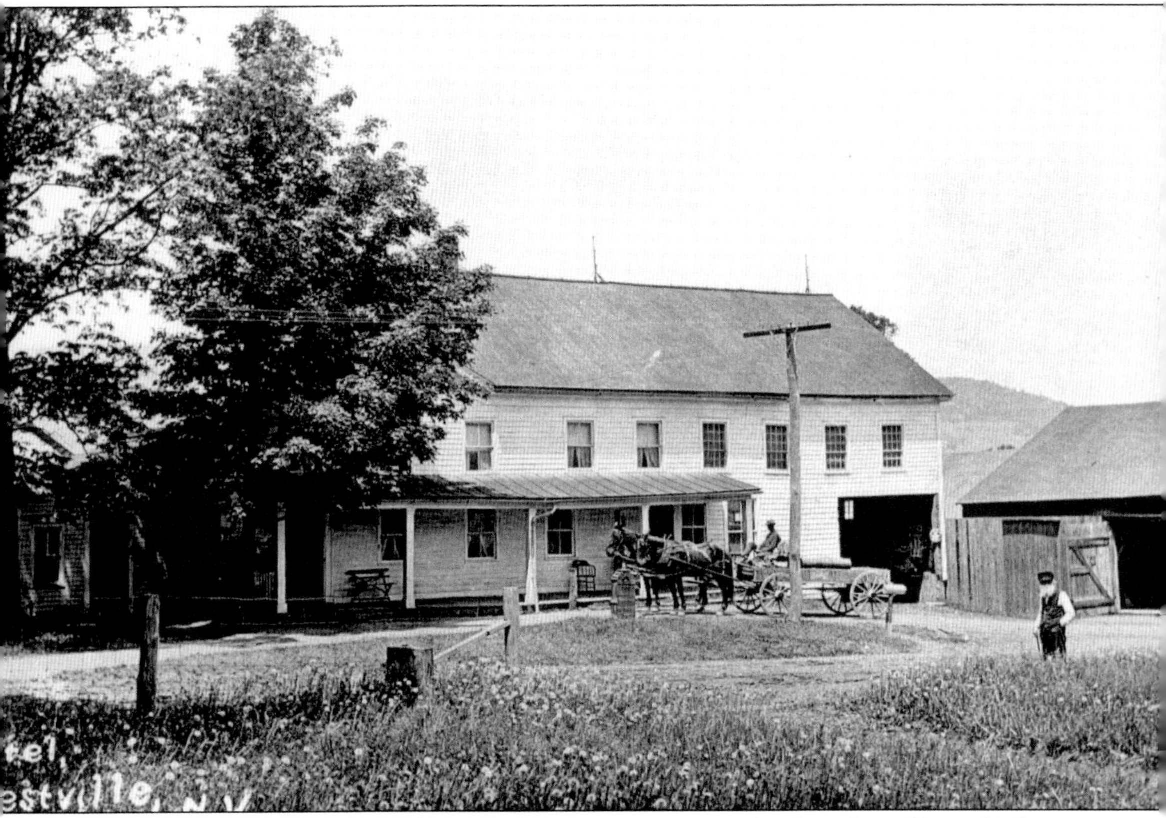

The Westville Hotel proved to be a popular stopping point on the drive from Cherry Valley to Milford. This *c.* 1915 photograph, taken when Warren Brown was proprietor, gives a good idea of the ample size of rural hotels and taverns. (Courtesy TMHA.)

Eight

Community and Customs

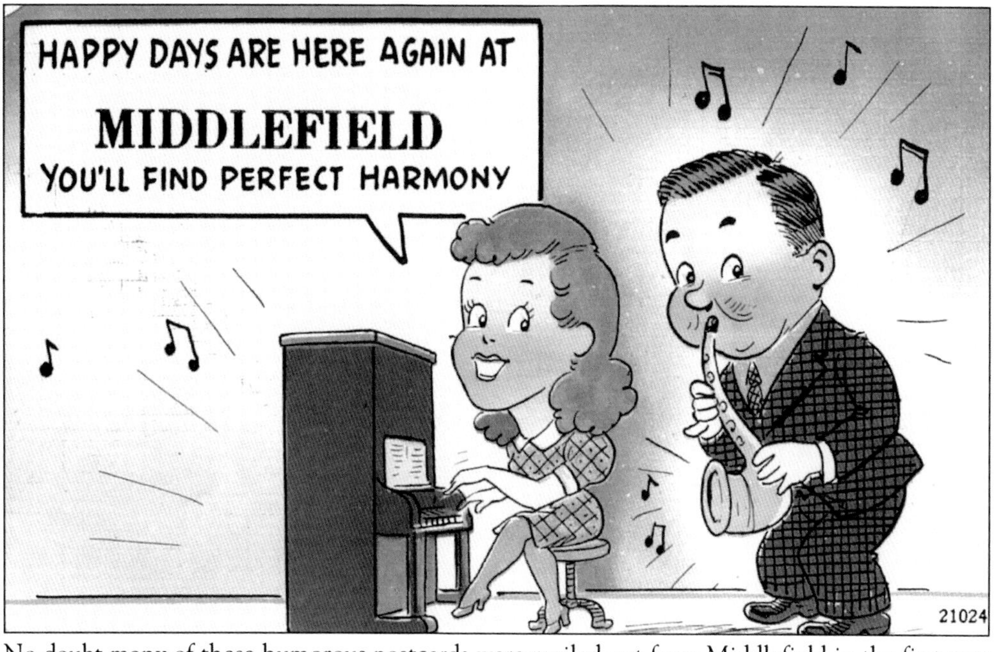

No doubt many of these humorous postcards were mailed out from Middlefield in the first part of the 20th century.

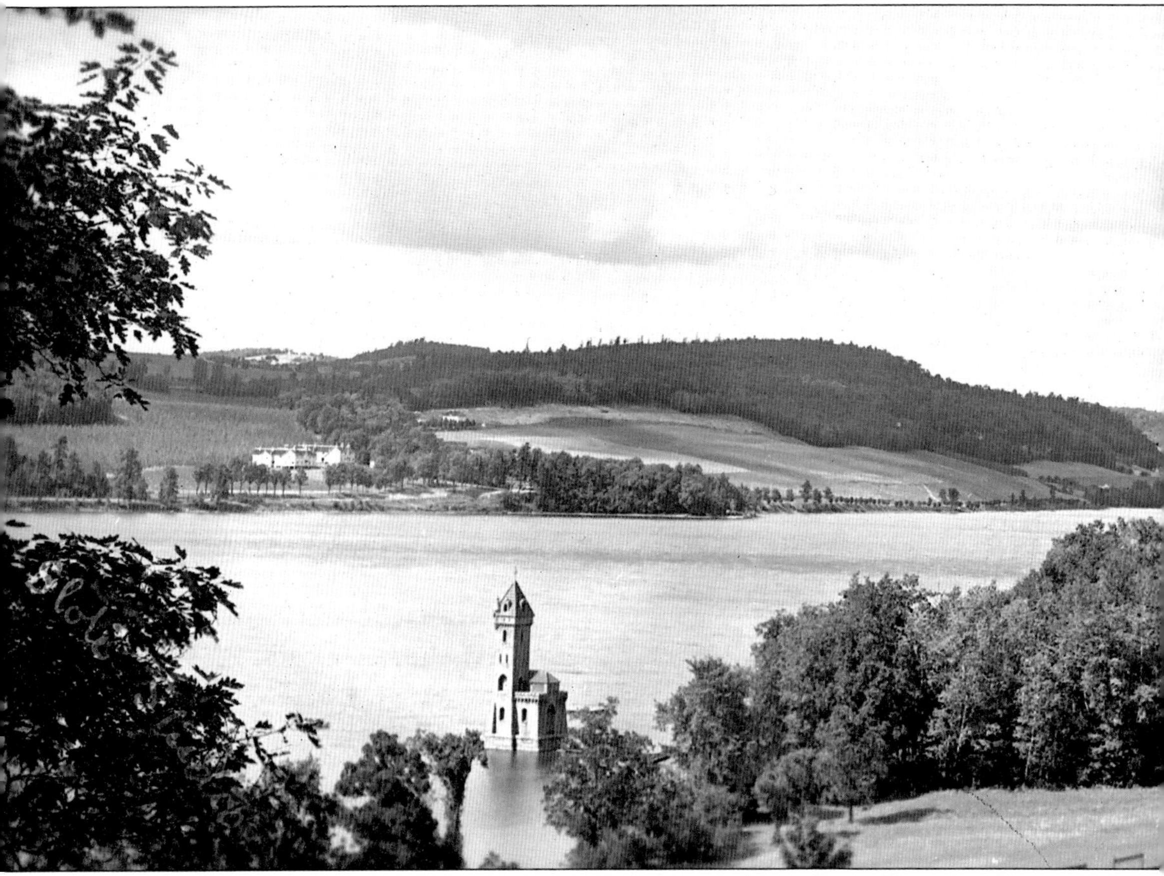

One of the jewels of Middlefield is Otsego Lake, the "Glimmerglass" of James Fenimore Cooper's Leatherstocking Tales. Edward Clark had this medieval folly built in 1876 on Point Judith

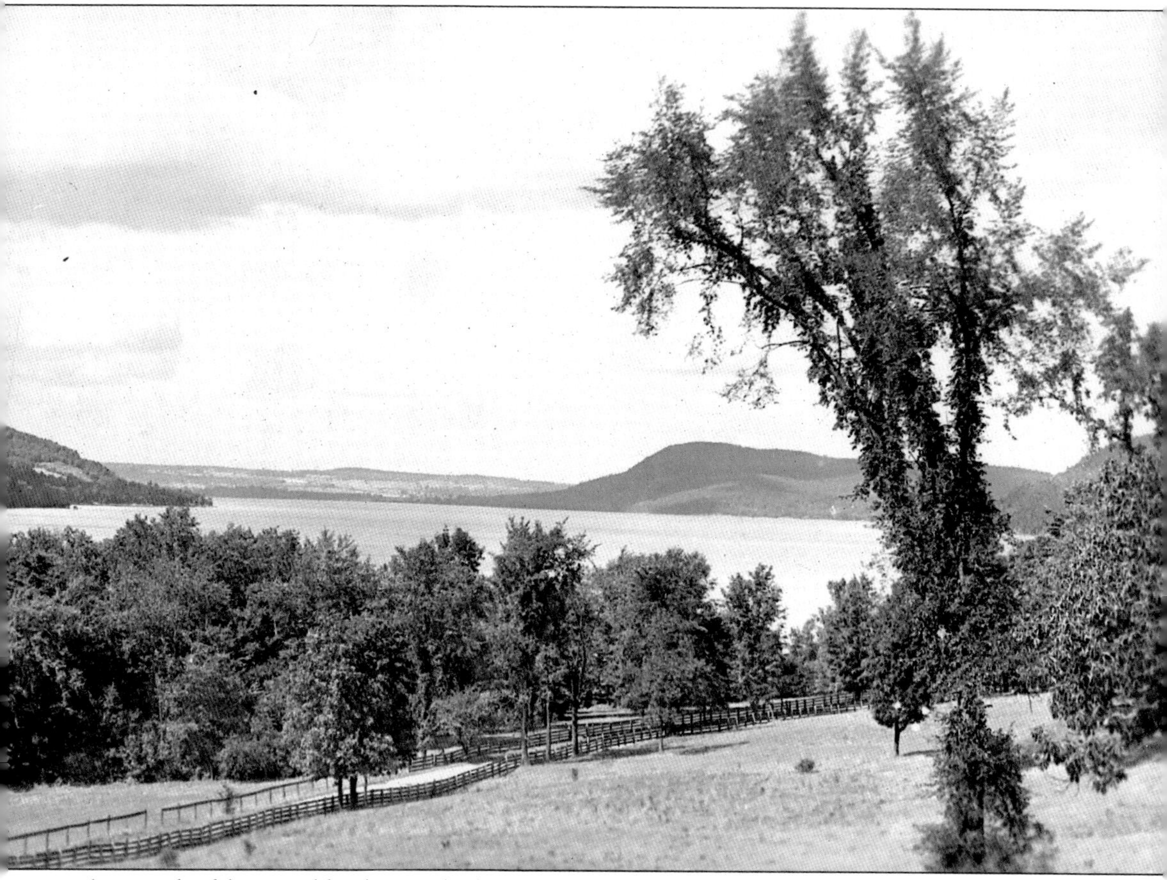

because he felt it would enhance the beauty of the lake. On the opposite side of the lake are the hop fields of Augustus Busch of Anheuser-Busch fame. (Courtesy TMHA.)

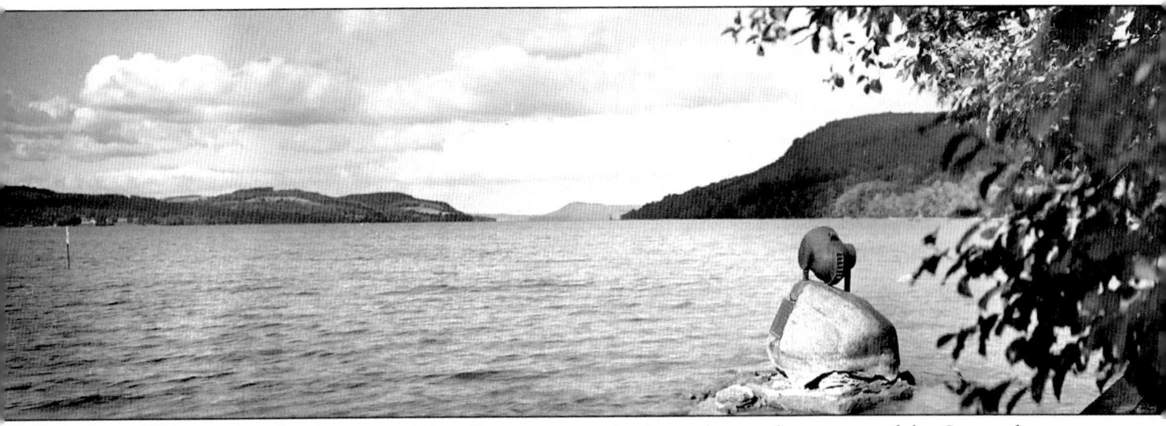

The Daughters of the American Revolution erected this marker at the source of the Susquehanna River. On the right is Middlefield, Otsego Lake's eastern shore. In the distance is Mount Wellington, or the Sleeping Lion. It was here that George Clarke built his great house, Hyde Hall. Clarke was deeply involved in the early development of Middlefield. (Courtesy TMHA.)

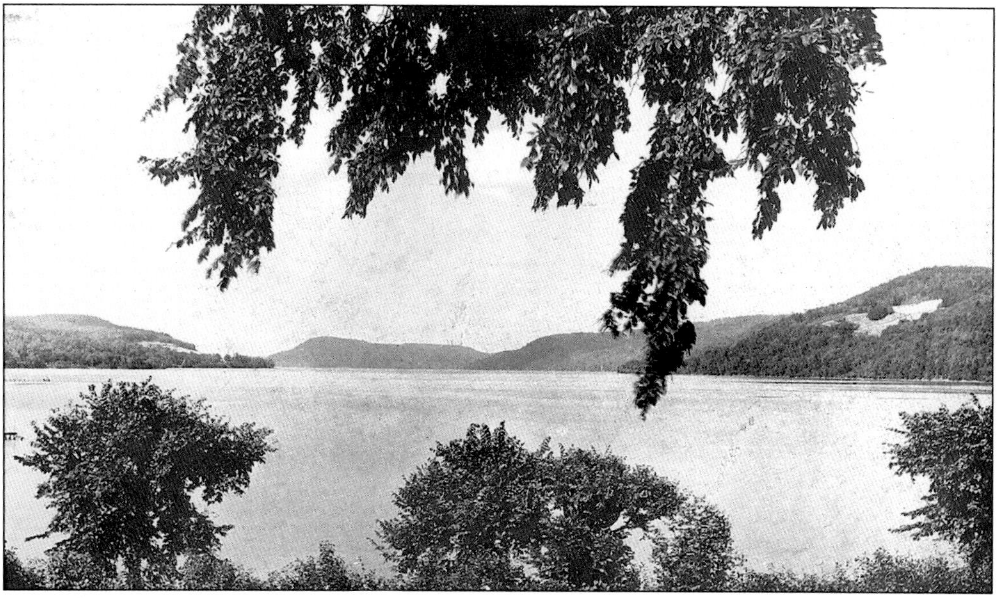

For author James Fenimore Cooper, Otsego Lake was Glimmerglass. The pristine lake forms the western boundary of the town of Middlefield.

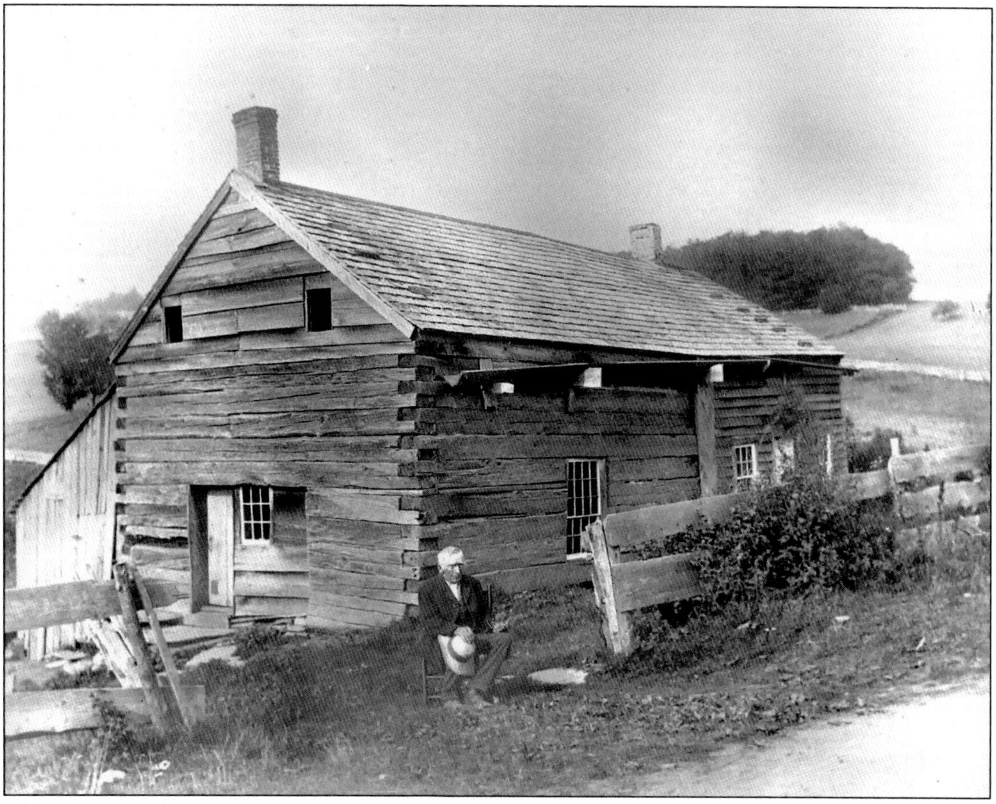

This *c.* 1850 photograph shows the log house built by Peter Davis (1803–1886) early in the 19th century. This house was located on what is now known as the Pete Hendricks Road. Davis was the father of Emily Ann Davis McLean. (Courtesy TMHA.)

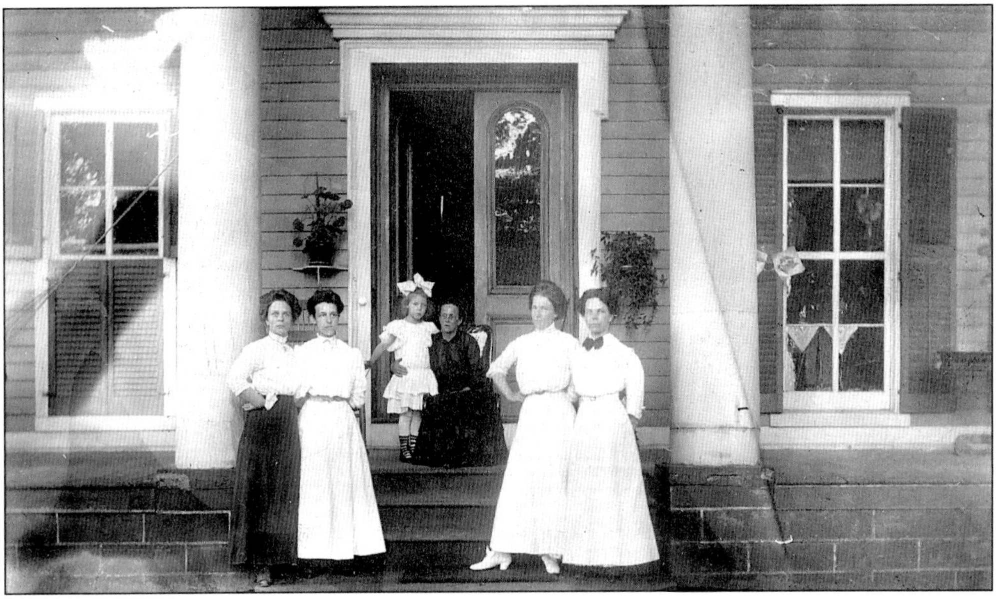

Members of the Briggs family gather outside their stately home *c.* 1910. Over the years this house has been known as the Pinney tavern, Locust Lawn, and the Folmsbee House. It has been used as a tavern, post office, and Masonic Hall. Its grounds have had a blacksmith shop, wagon shop, and doctor's office.

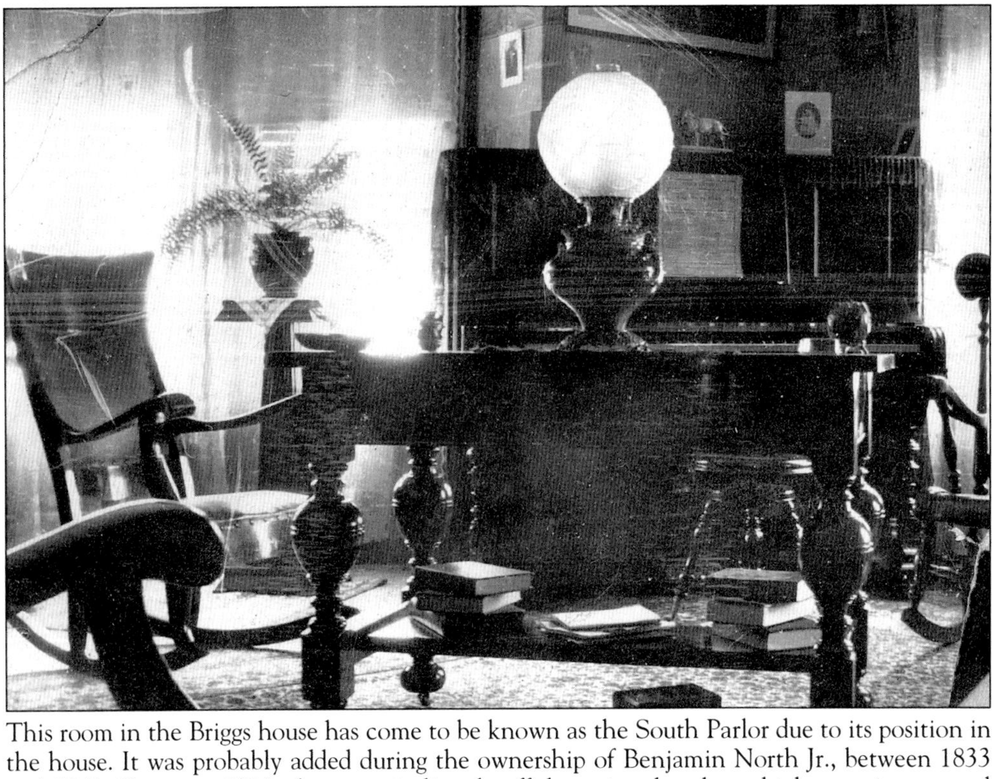

This room in the Briggs house has come to be known as the South Parlor due to its position in the house. It was probably added during the ownership of Benjamin North Jr., between 1833 and 1842. Shown *c.* 1910, the room is directly off the painted parlor, which contains a mural attributed to William Price.

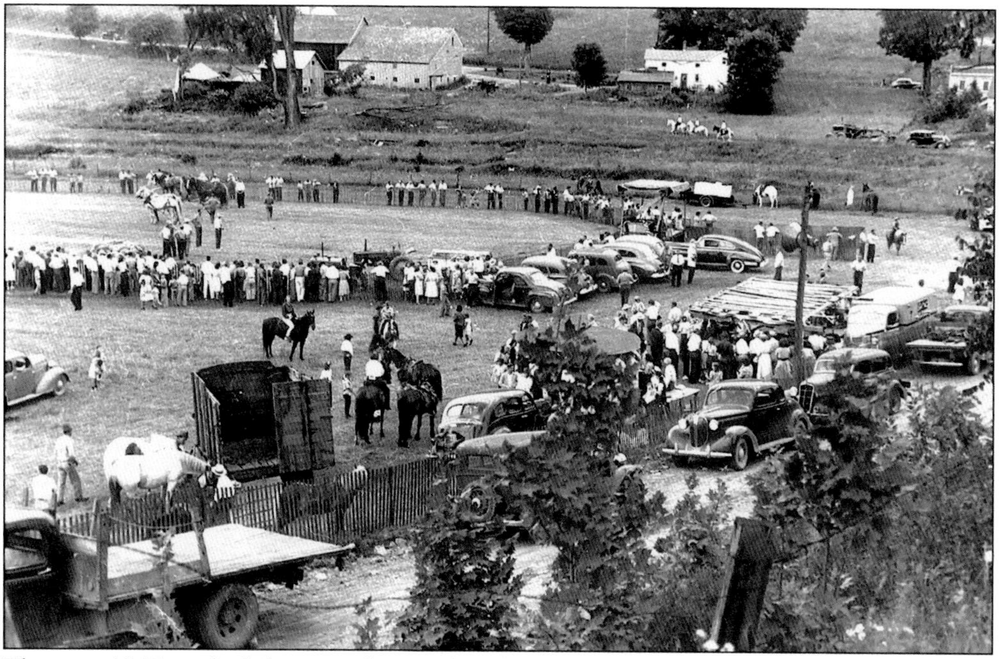

The year 1947 marked the second annual Red Creek Valley Grange Horse Show. This was a very active Grange in the Middlefield community, centered along Red Creek, near Whig Corners. (Courtesy TMHA.)

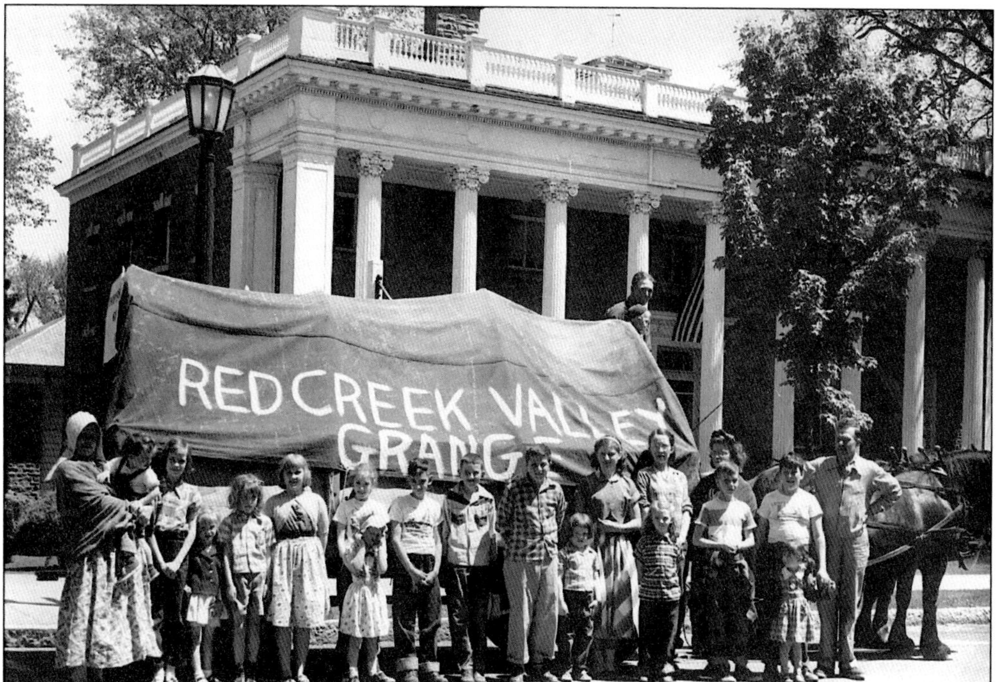

The covered wagon float represents the Red Creek Valley Grange in this Fourth of July parade c. 1954. Pictured atop the wagon are Claud Bliss Jr. and his son Tim. The building in the background is the Cooperstown Village Library. (Courtesy TMHA.)

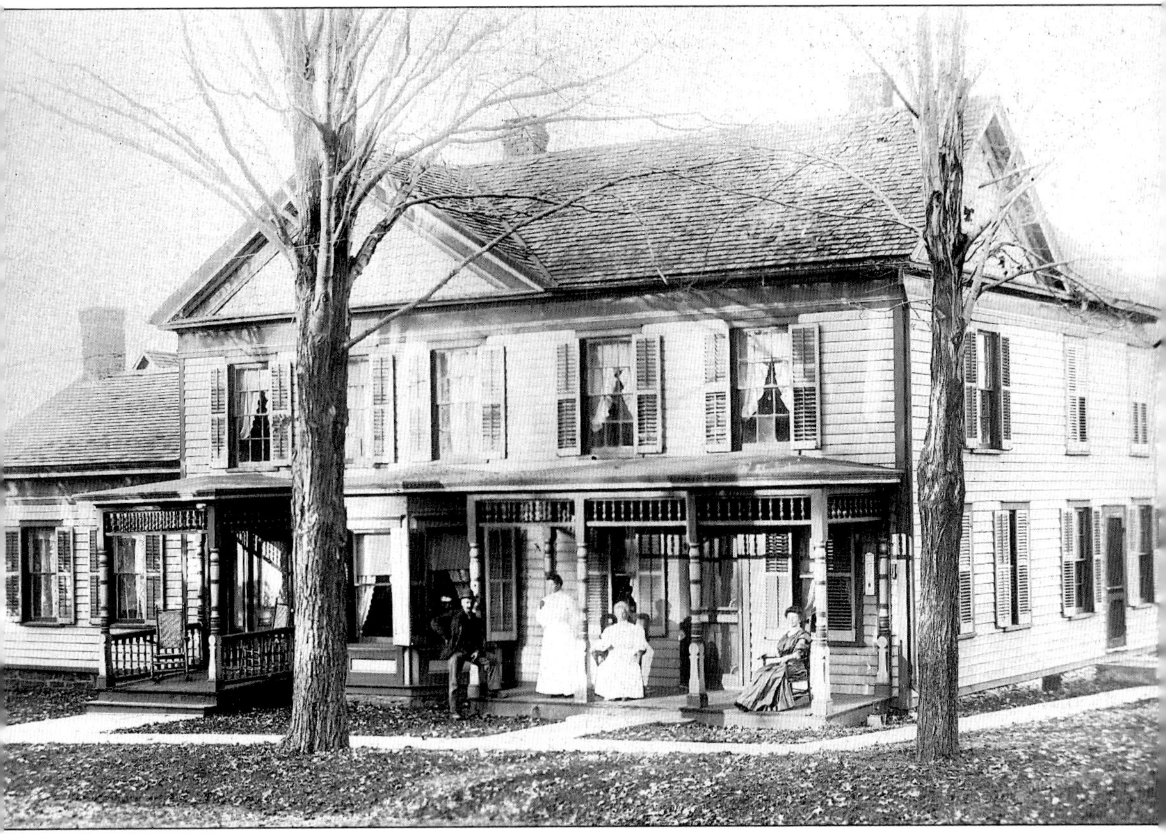

This postcard shows the Buel House, on Whiteman Hill Road in the hamlet of Middlefield. It was sent in October 1908 to Mrs. Harry E. Mitchell, Buel's daughter, in Sharon Springs. During the time the Morton family lived here in 1955, the house was ravaged by fire. The entire right side of the house from the front gable was leveled. The fire was the impetus for forming the Middlefield Volunteer Fire Department.

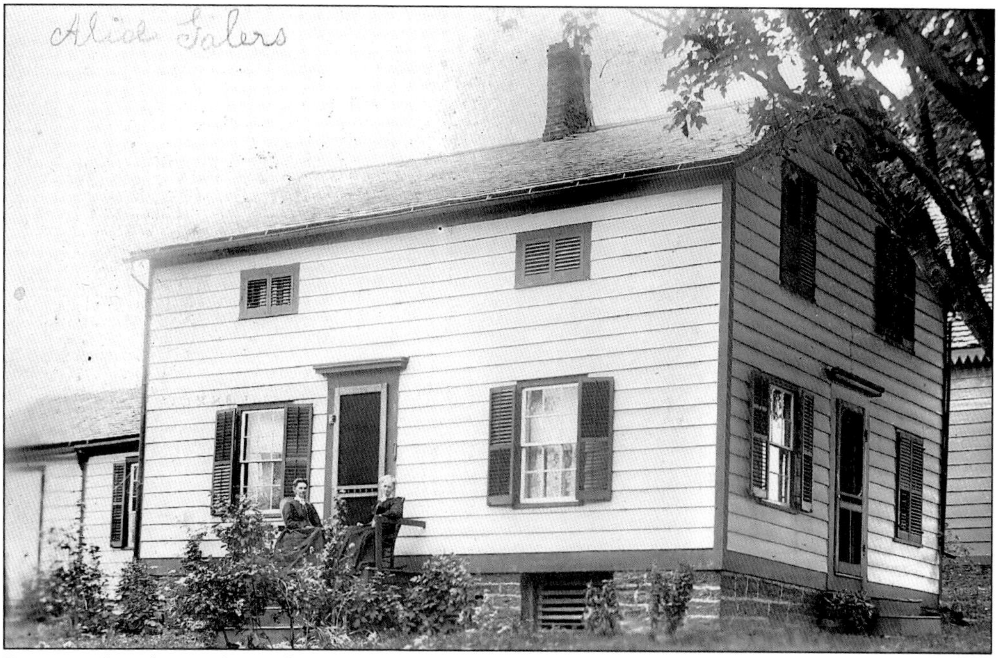

Door gardens have always been popular gathering places. Two Middlefield women sit at their home on Long Patent Road in the hamlet of Middlefield.

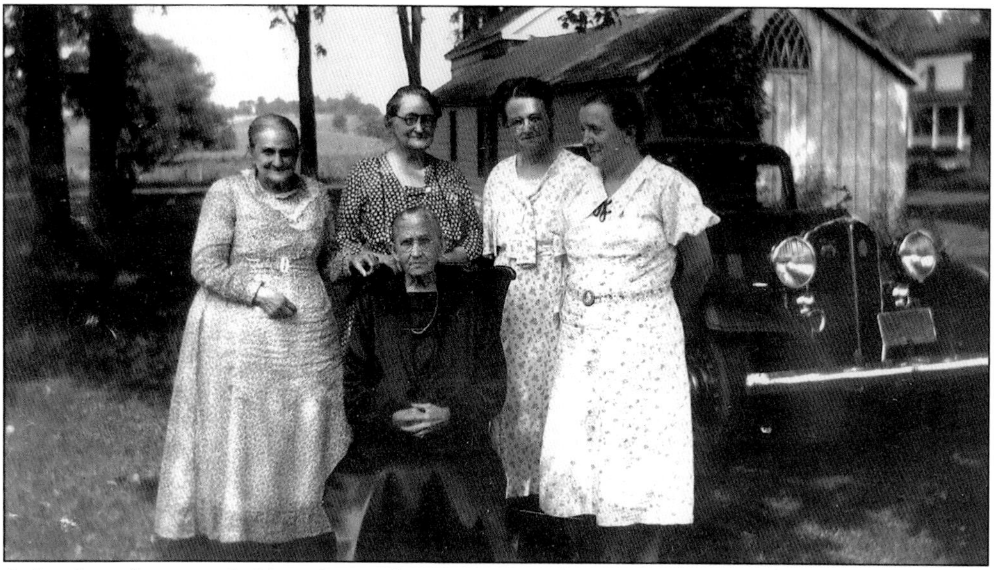

A family gathering is held on September 1, 1937, in the hamlet of Middlefield. It is interesting to note the fine Gothic window in the outbuilding. The window came from the Methodist church at the time of a renovation. The house that can be discerned past the outbuilding was destroyed by fire.

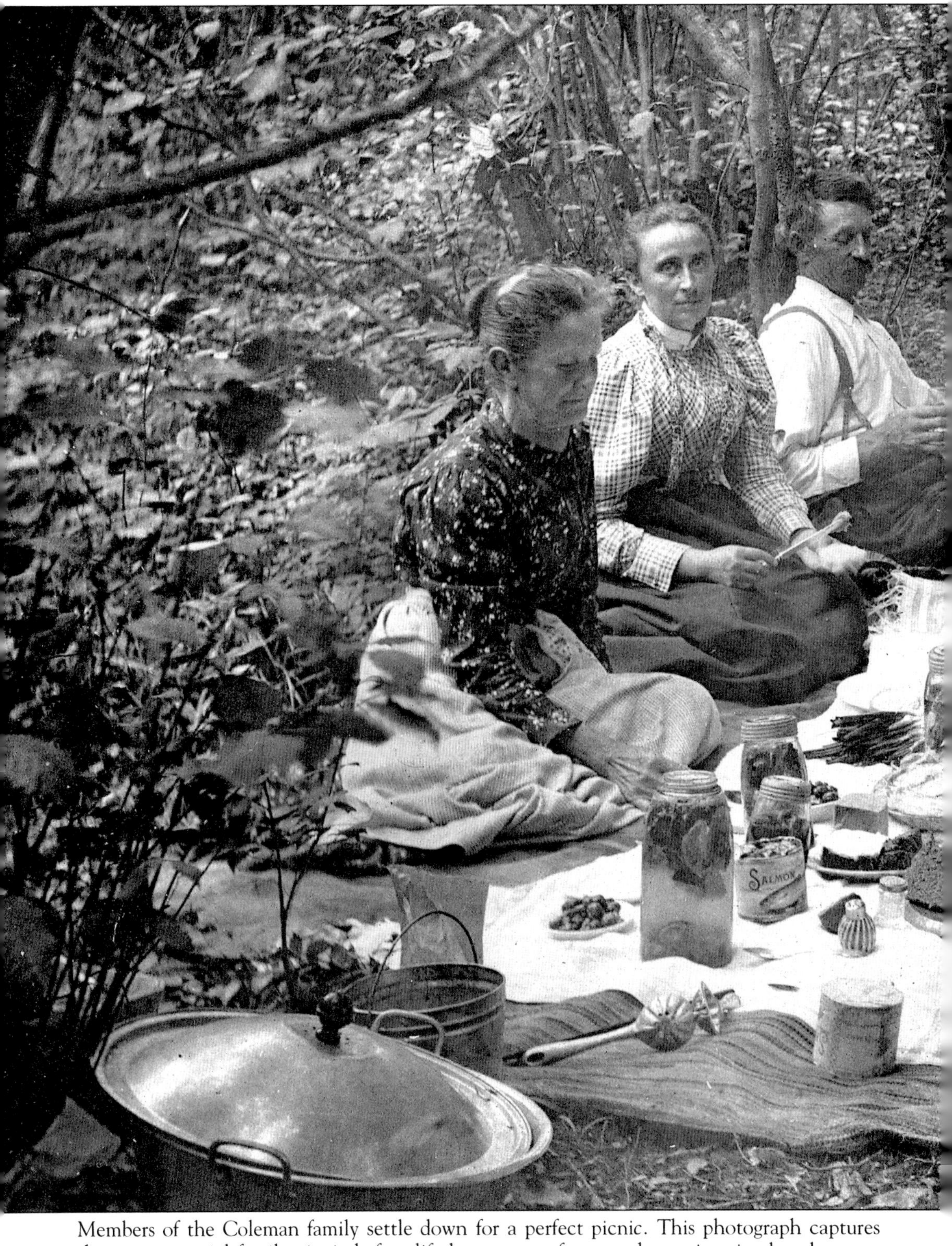

Members of the Coleman family settle down for a perfect picnic. This photograph captures the quintessential family picnic before life became too fast paced to enjoy simpler pleasures.

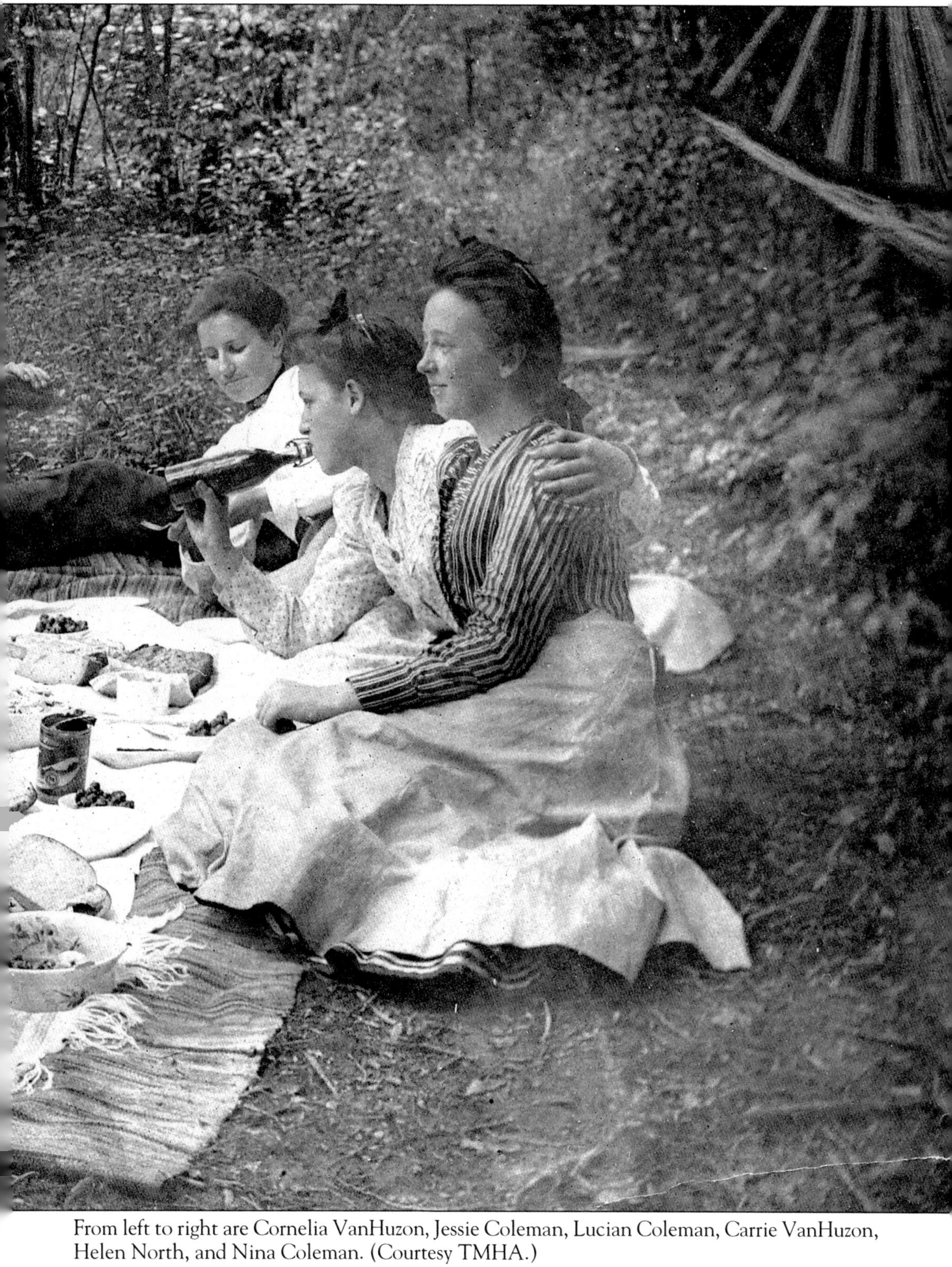

From left to right are Cornelia VanHuzon, Jessie Coleman, Lucian Coleman, Carrie VanHuzon, Helen North, and Nina Coleman. (Courtesy TMHA.)

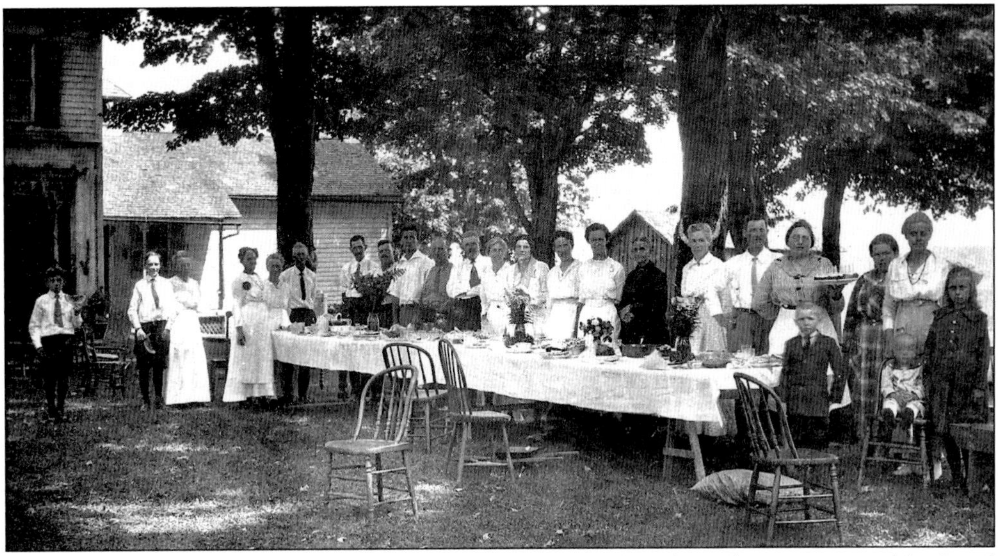

The fourth of July has always been a favorite American holiday. Shown is a neighborhood picnic at the Ottaway home in 1919. (Courtesy TMHA.)

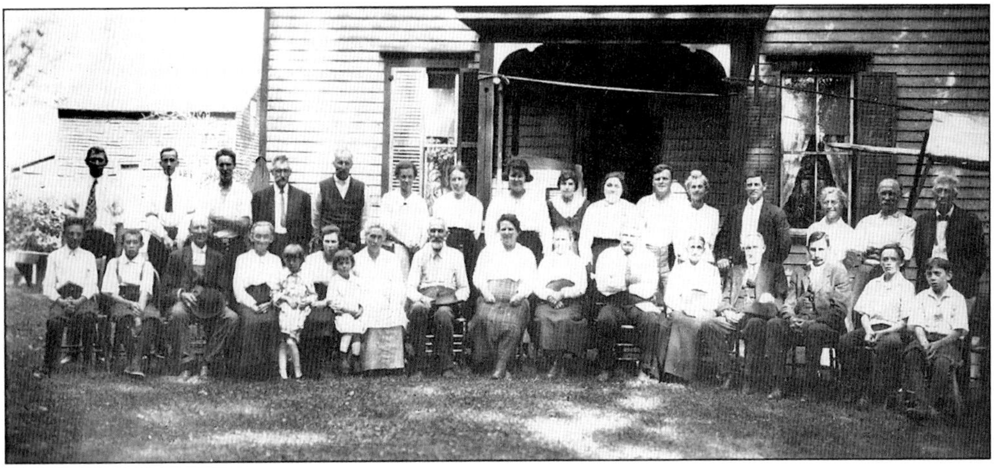

This gathering is being held at Lyman Hinman's house on July 3, 1920, just before the Fourth of July celebration. (Courtesy TMHA.)

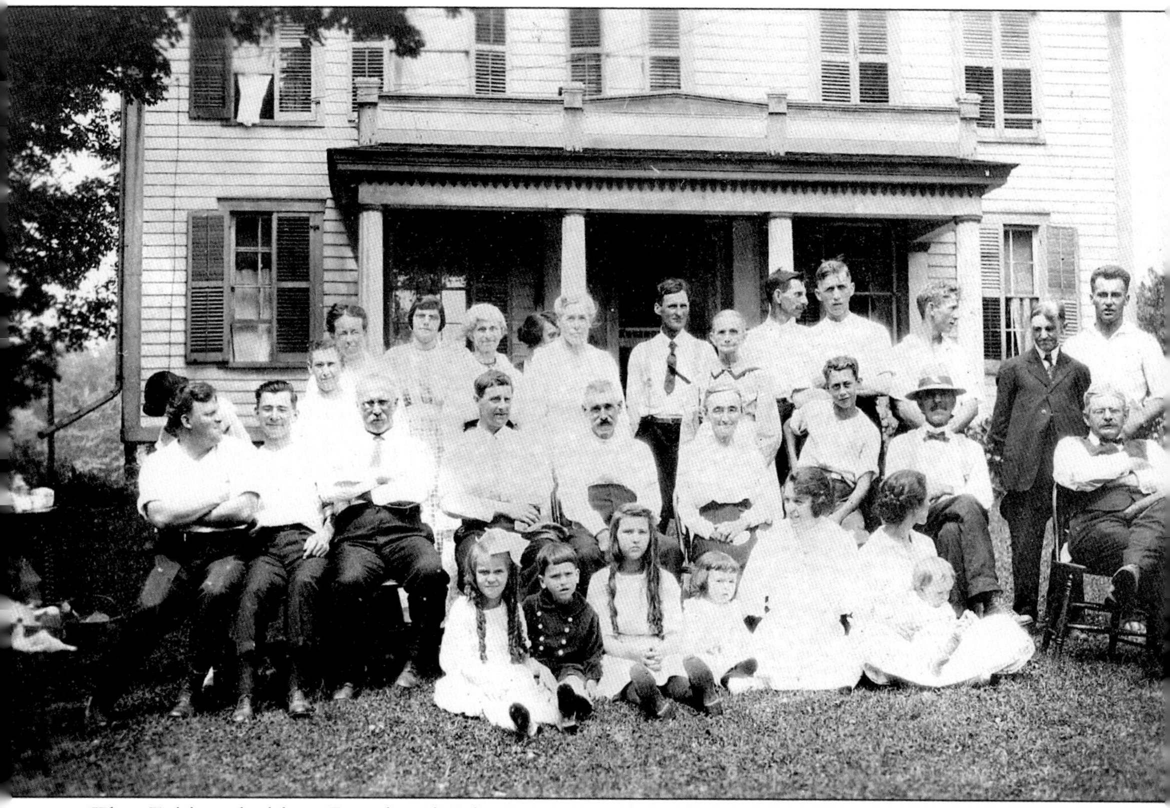

The Ecklers hold a Fourth of July picnic at their home on Ricetown Road in 1921. (Courtesy TMHA.)

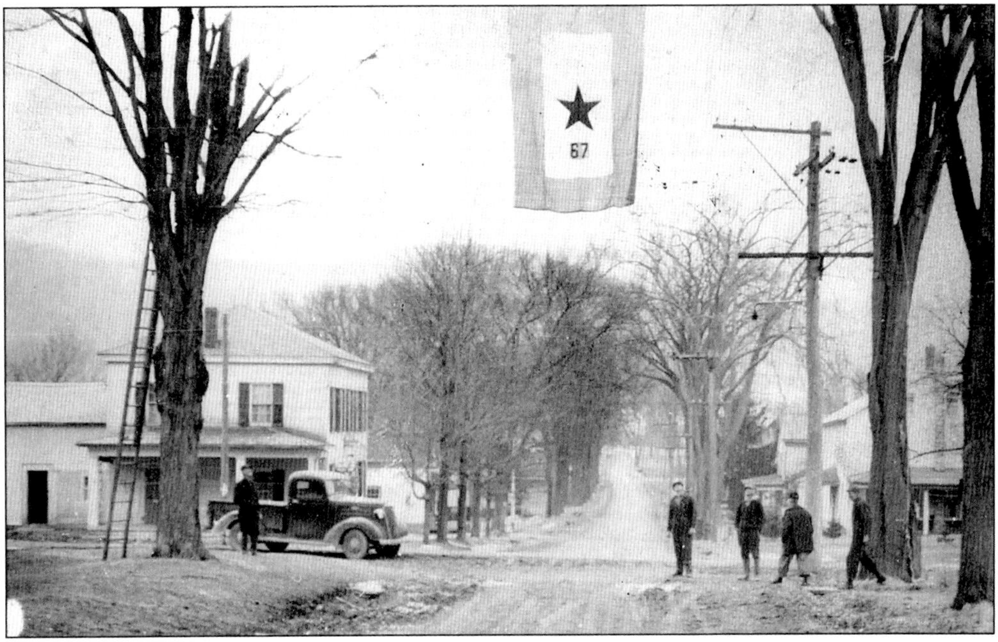

A group of men hang a flag proudly proclaiming that the town of Middlefield had sent 67 men to fight in World War II. This postcard was sent to Mrs. E.J. Buel in Pittsfield. Of these 67 men, 9 came from the hamlet of Middlefield. Looking north through the crossroads one can not help but note the void left by the 1942 fire, which took down the Hearn Store, and the absence of the Cloxton Store, which until it was moved stood about where the ladder is.

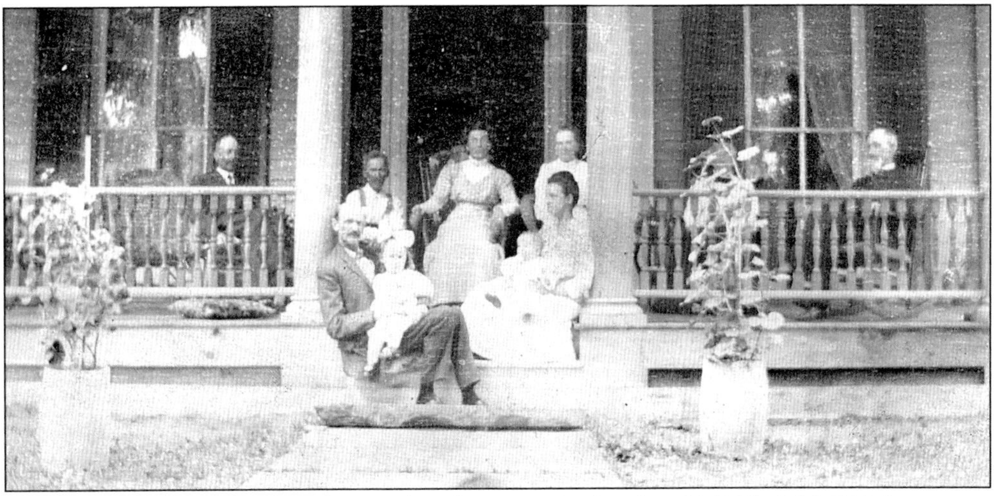

Members of the Pitts family gather at their house in the hamlet of Middlefield. This house was built by Harrison North in 1859.

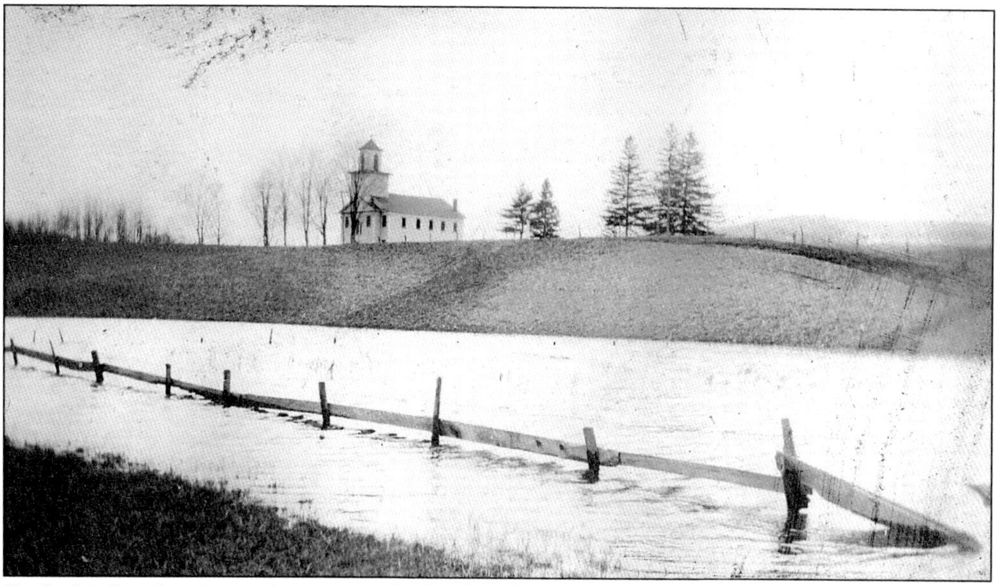

Garlock's Pond is located just outside the hamlet of Middlefield. Perched on the hill is the Baptist church, and just past it in the valley is the hamlet of Middlefield. The rising water level in the spring has flooded the fence.

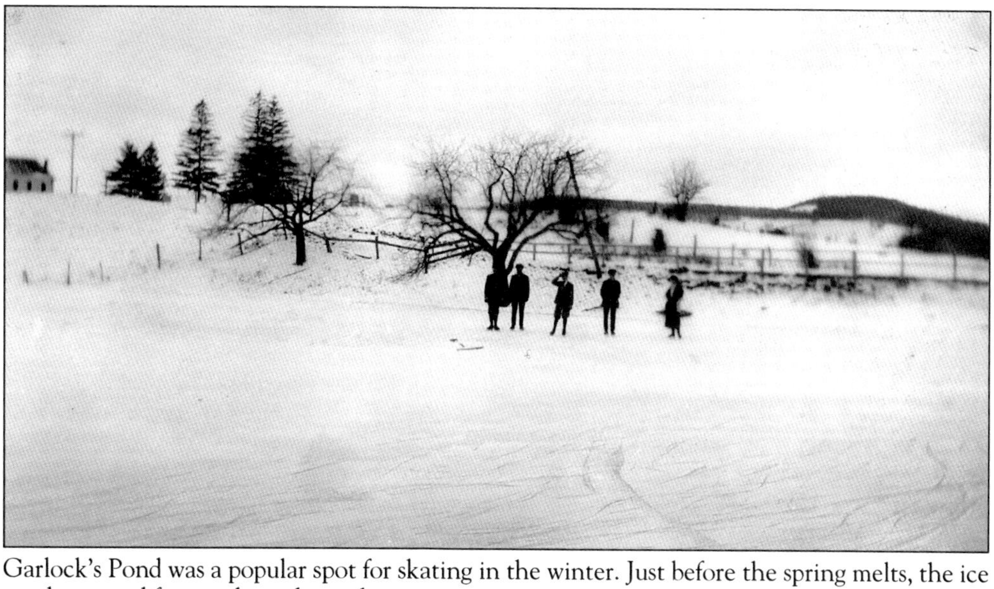

Garlock's Pond was a popular spot for skating in the winter. Just before the spring melts, the ice was harvested for use throughout the summer.

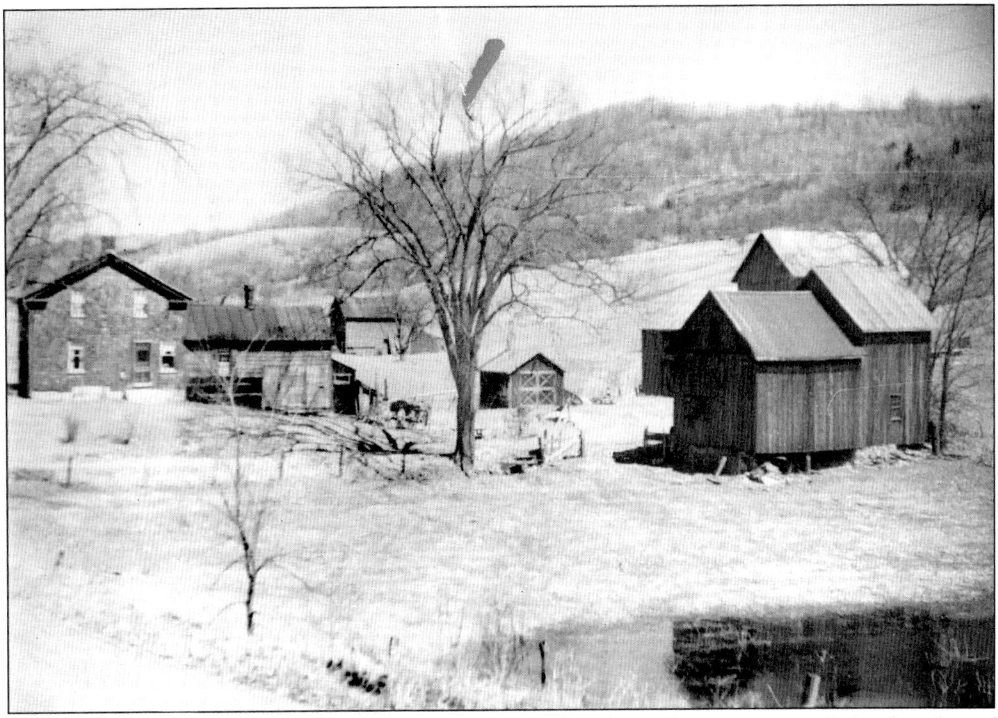

This photograph shows Garlock's farm on Rezen Road on the way out of the hamlet of Middlefield. In the lower right corner is Garlock's Pond. (Courtesy TMHA.)

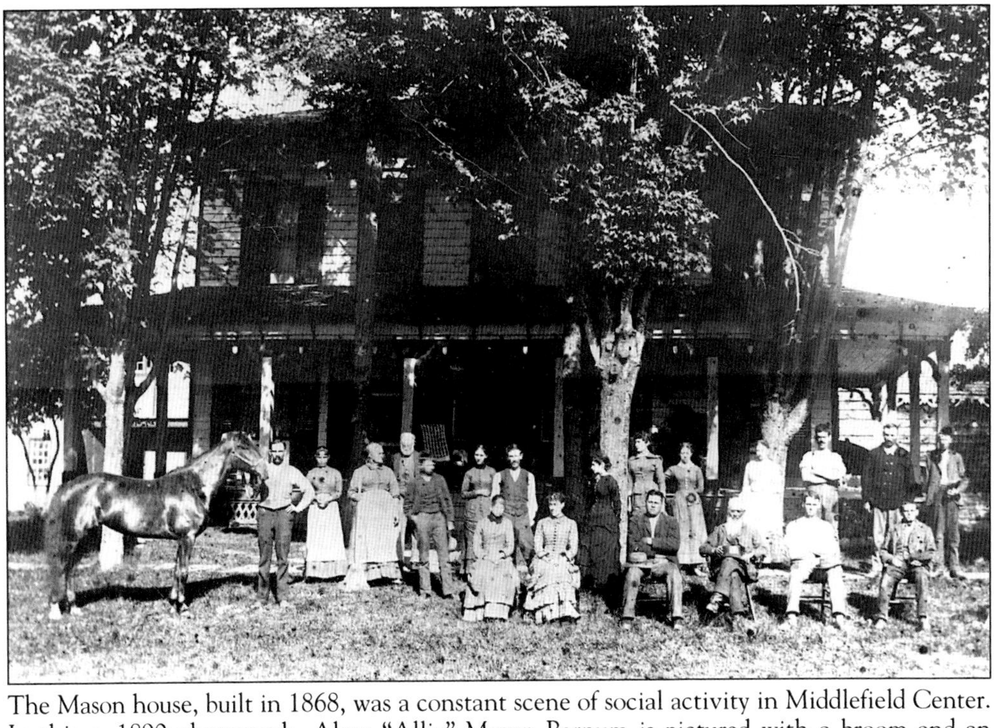

The Mason house, built in 1868, was a constant scene of social activity in Middlefield Center. In this c. 1890 photograph, Alma "Allie" Mason Barnum is pictured with a broom and an apron, surrounded by her guests. (Courtesy TMHA.)

Shown in 1959, shortly before it collapsed, is the once grand Mason House. (Courtesy TMHA.)

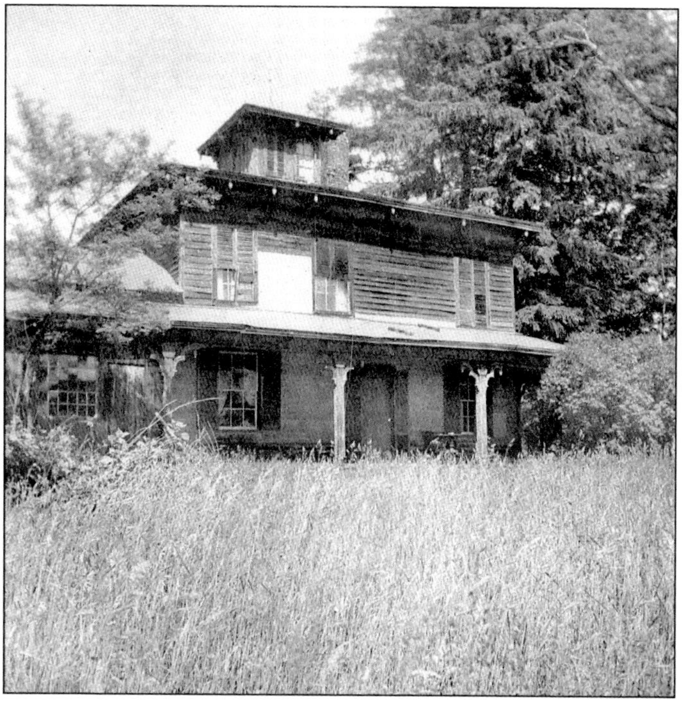

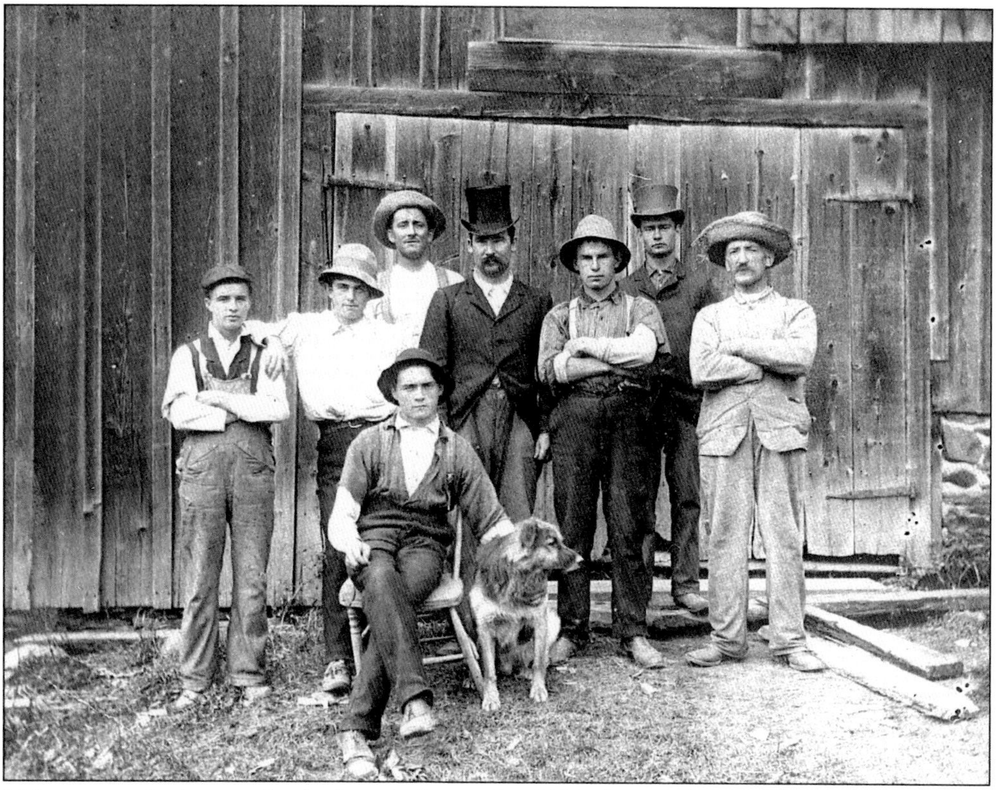

Eight men and a dog pose by the barn in September 1901. Among them is Thomas F. O'Connell, with the mustache and top hat. (Courtesy TMHA.)

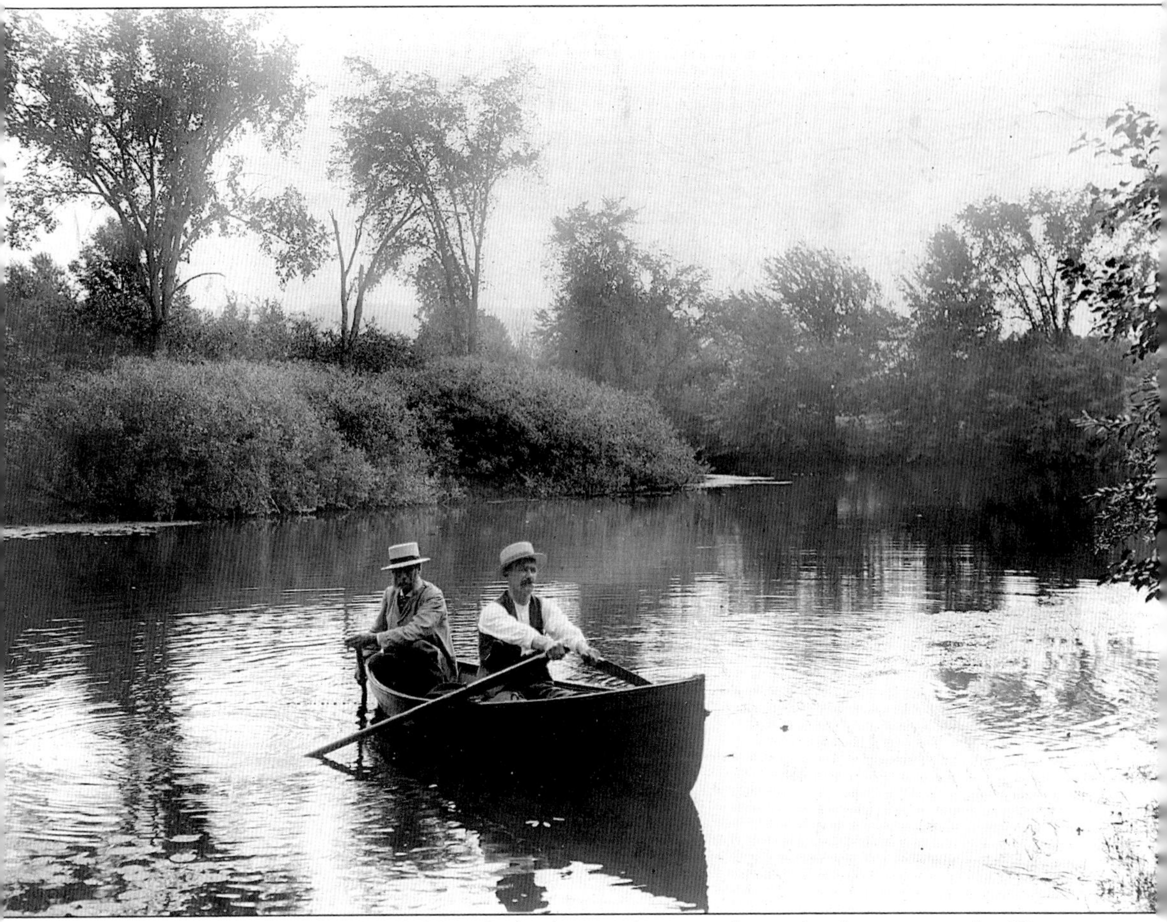

Good friends Adriel Murphy (left) and Charles North enjoy a leisurely afternoon on the Cherry Valley Creek. The creek winds through the town of Middlefield and meets the Susquehanna River as it rushes from Otsego Lake. (Courtesy TMHA.)

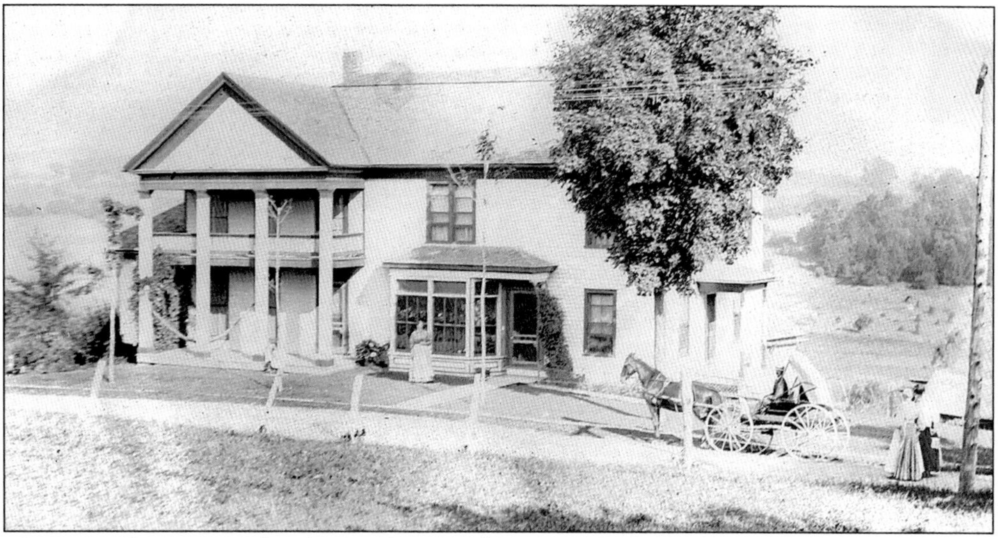

This magnificent example of a Greek Revival house is the Cunningham home in Middlefield Center. (Courtesy TMHA.)

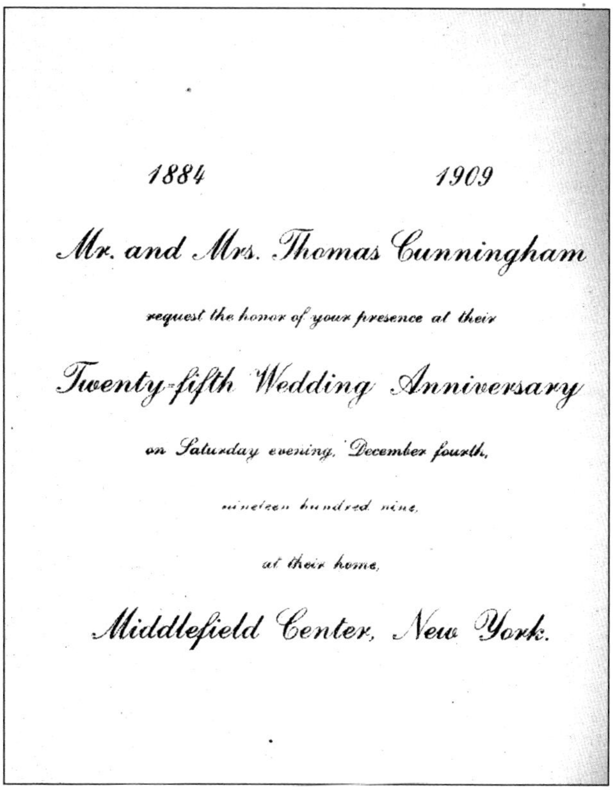

1884 1909

Mr. and Mrs. Thomas Cunningham

request the honor of your presence at their

Twenty-fifth Wedding Anniversary

on Saturday evening, December fourth,

nineteen hundred nine,

at their home,

Middlefield Center, New York.

It is always pleasant to see lovers fall in love to stay. This invitation is for friends of the Cunninghams to come to their house to celebrate their 25th wedding anniversary in 1909.

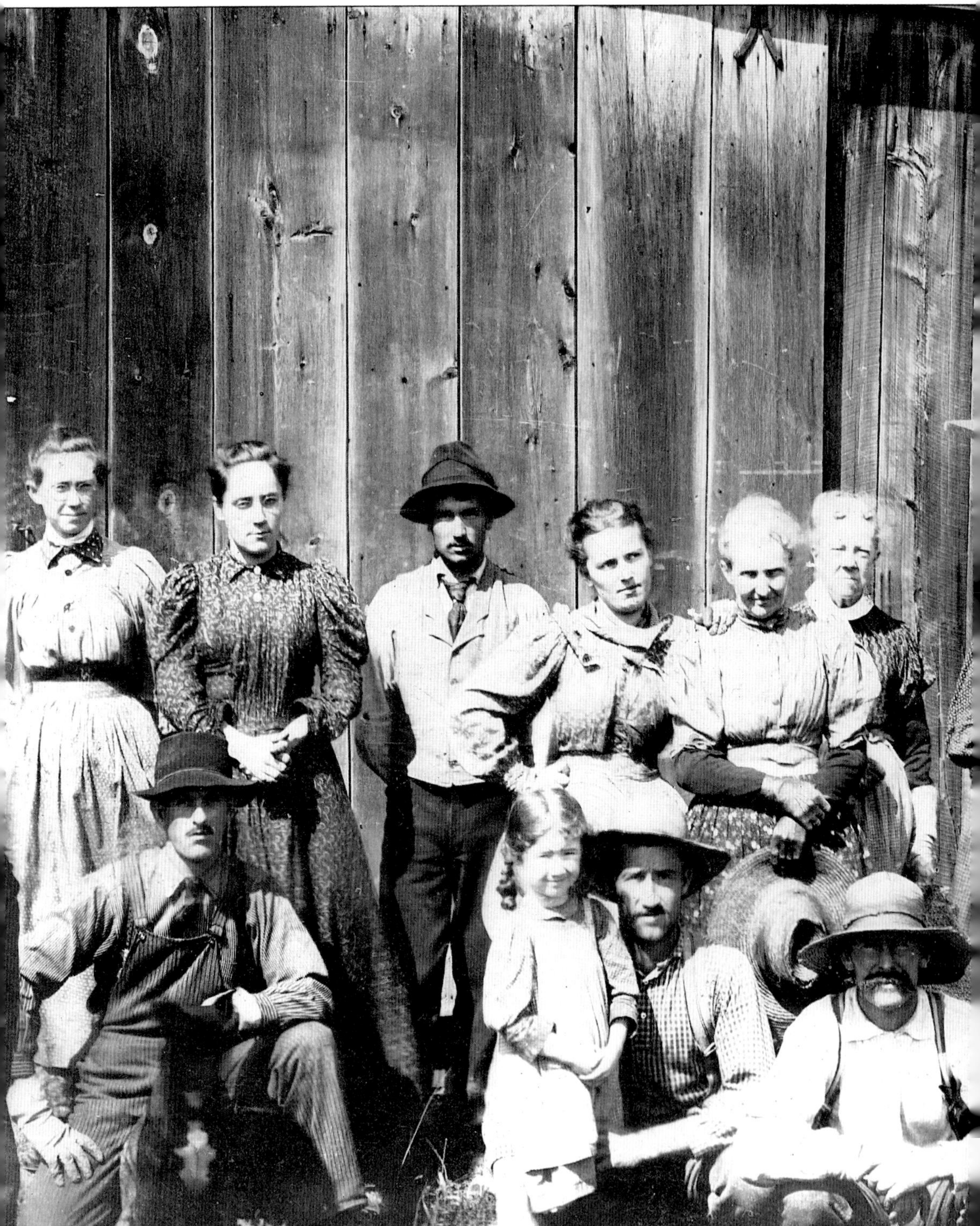

At Middlefield Center, members of the Cunningham family gather outside the barn by the wood pile. Many of them wear hats for shade in the bright midday sun. The family dog, in the

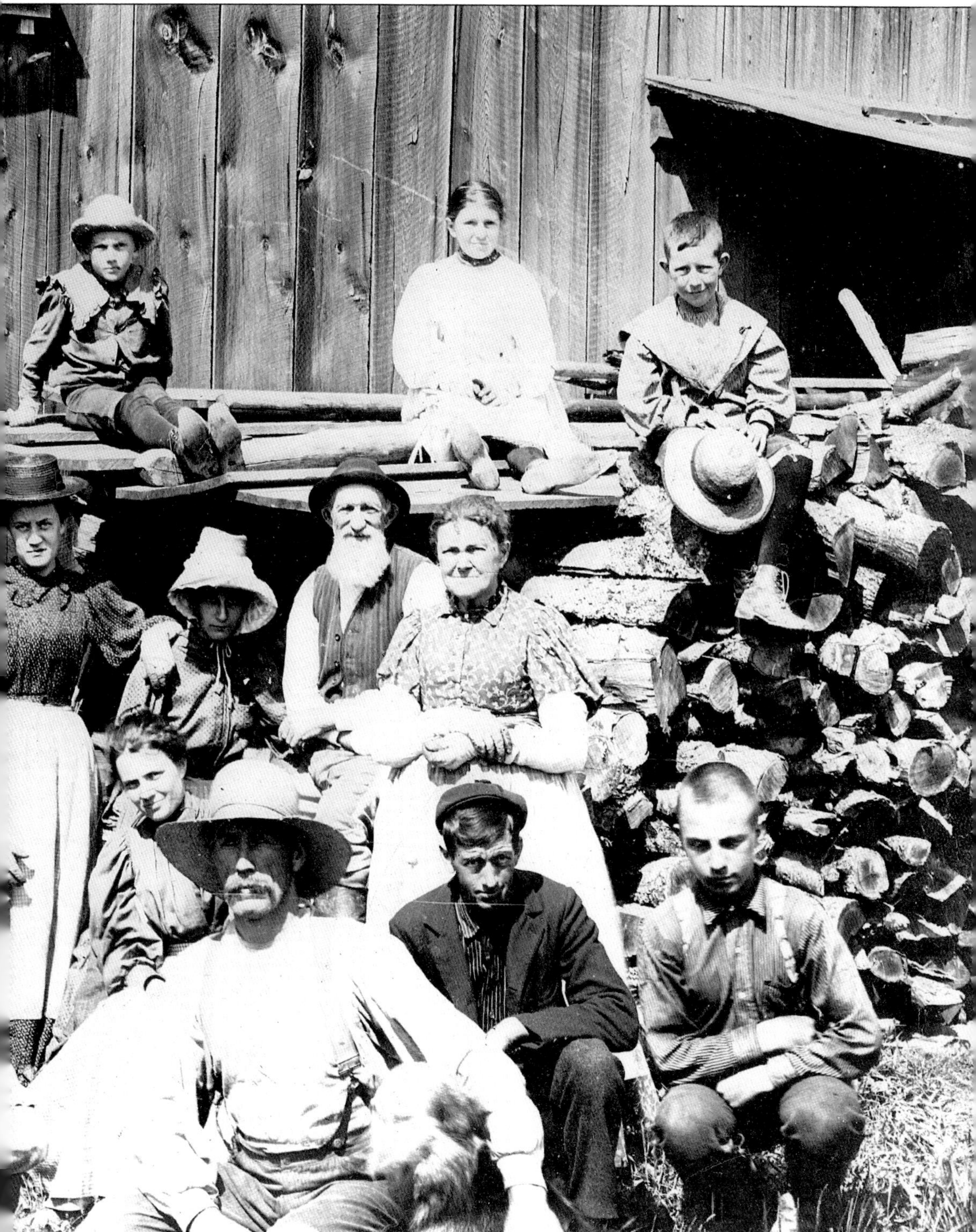

foreground, merely shuts his eyes. (Courtesy TMHA.)

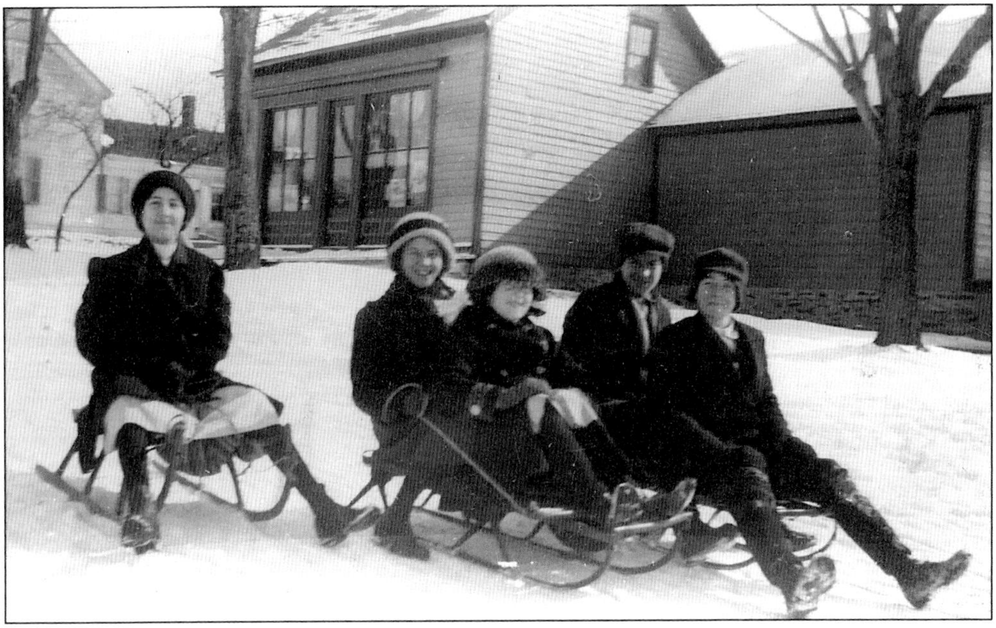

Some of the Cunninghams spend the winter afternoon sledding. The building in the background is the Kellar Boot Shop, in Middlefield Center. (Courtesy TMHA.)

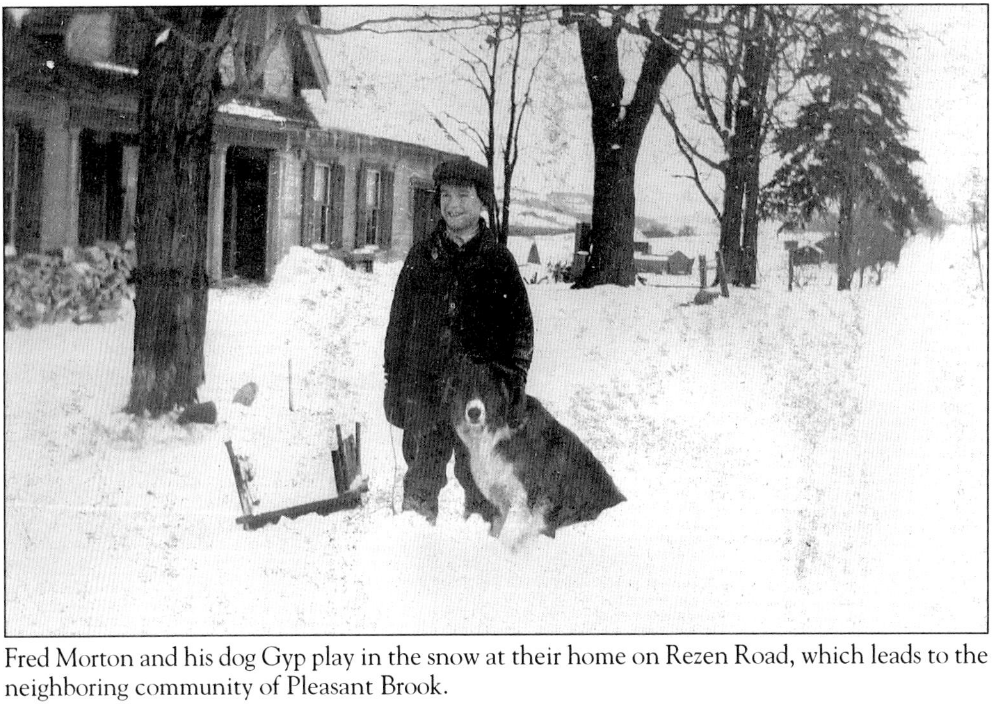

Fred Morton and his dog Gyp play in the snow at their home on Rezen Road, which leads to the neighboring community of Pleasant Brook.

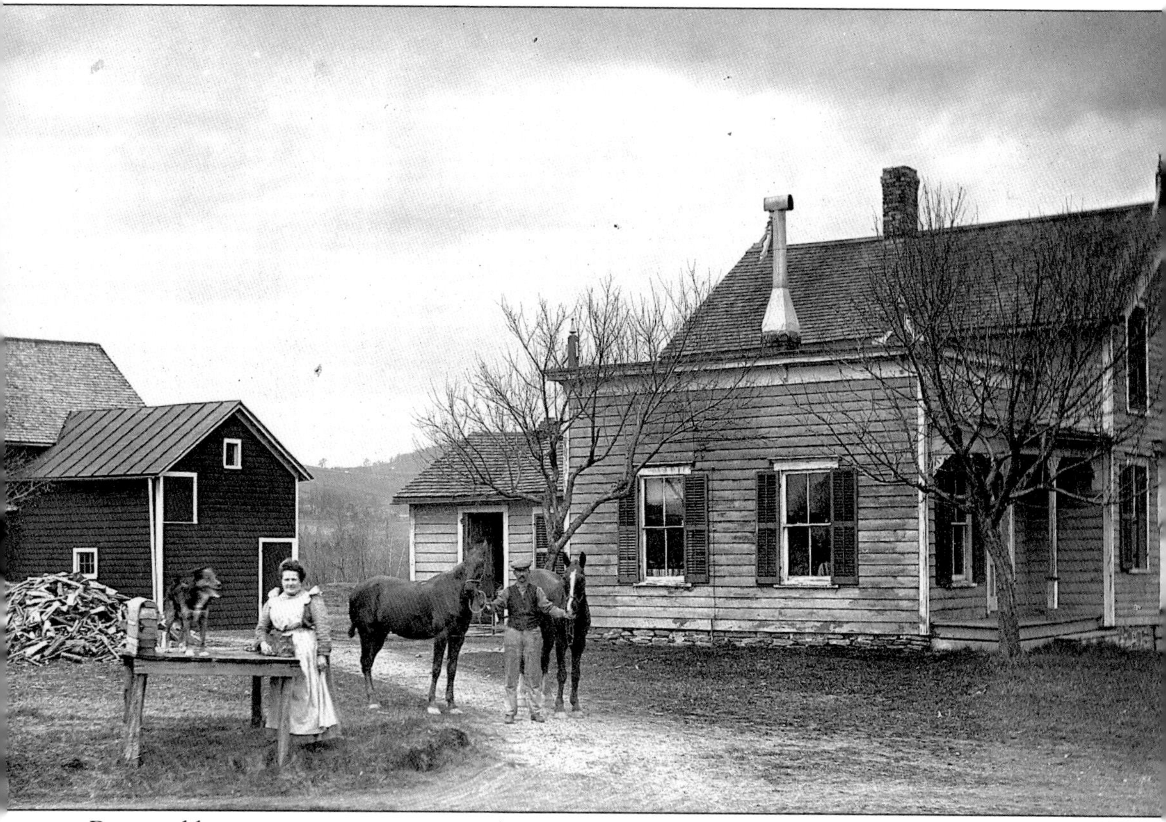

Dogs and horses were common pets. This man and woman had two horses on their farm near Westville, and a dog . . . on the table.

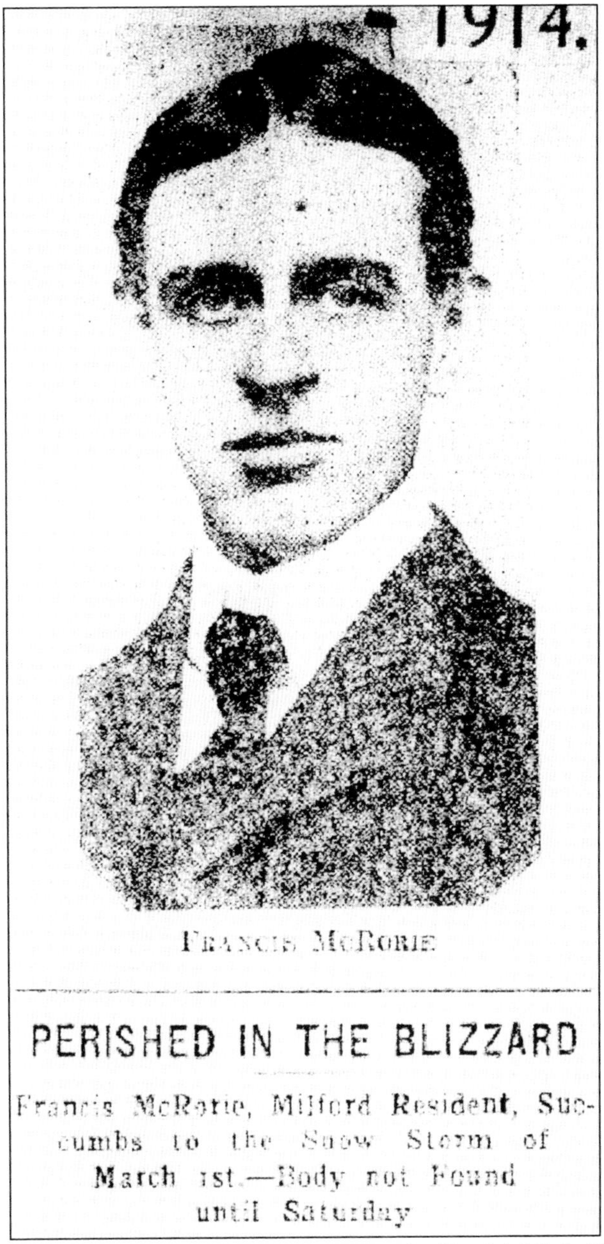

1914.

FRANCIS MCRORIE

PERISHED IN THE BLIZZARD

Francis McRorie, Milford Resident, Succumbs to the Snow Storm of March 1st.—Body not Found until Saturday

No town is without its enduring tale of romantic tragedy. For Middlefield, it is the story of Francis McRorie. He lived in the neighboring village of Milford. On Sunday, March 1, 1914, he traveled to the hamlet of Middlefield to the house of Claire North to visit Lucy Pratt, a lady he was courting. He left that house in his horse and cutter to drive back to Milford so he could open the post office on Monday morning. There was a terrible blizzard blowing, and with no lights to guide him in the darkness, he got off the road. His horse slipped over an embankment and became tangled in a barbed wire fence. In his attempt to cut the horse free, McRorie was kicked in the face. Desperate for help, he left the scene heading to the left. Had he turned right instead he would have soon found shelter in the Dubben hop kiln. The horse was found frozen with its legs in the air. McRorie was buried under a foot of snow, curled on his stomach, frozen.

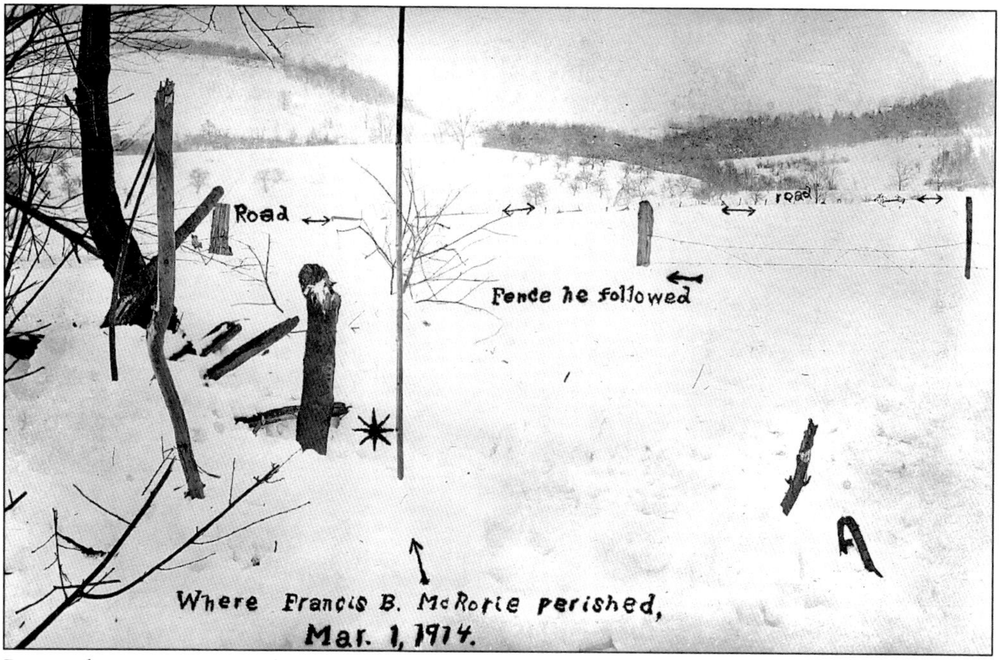

Postcards commemorate the tragedy.

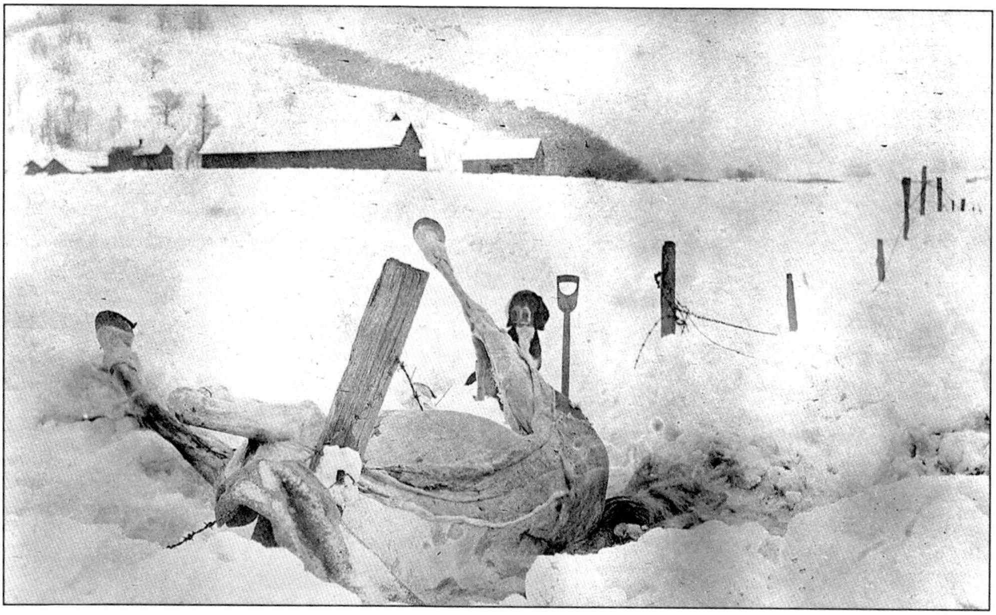

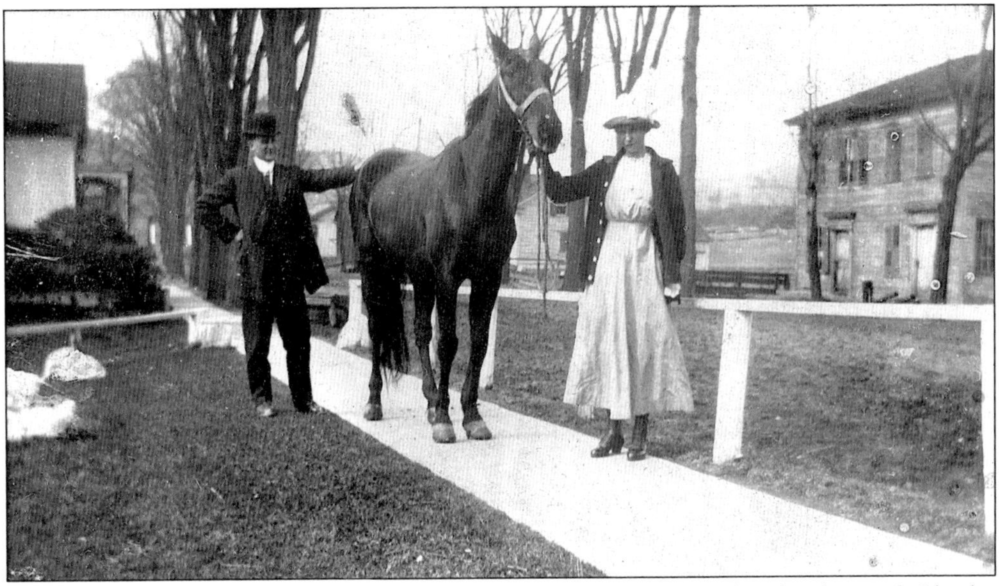

Rose Flint North stands with her horse Old Darby. She was the daughter of Charles Flint, owner of the American Hotel, and the wife of James North. The large house on the right belonged to Lamore Cossart and no longer stands. The horse was laid to rest on August 25, 1915.

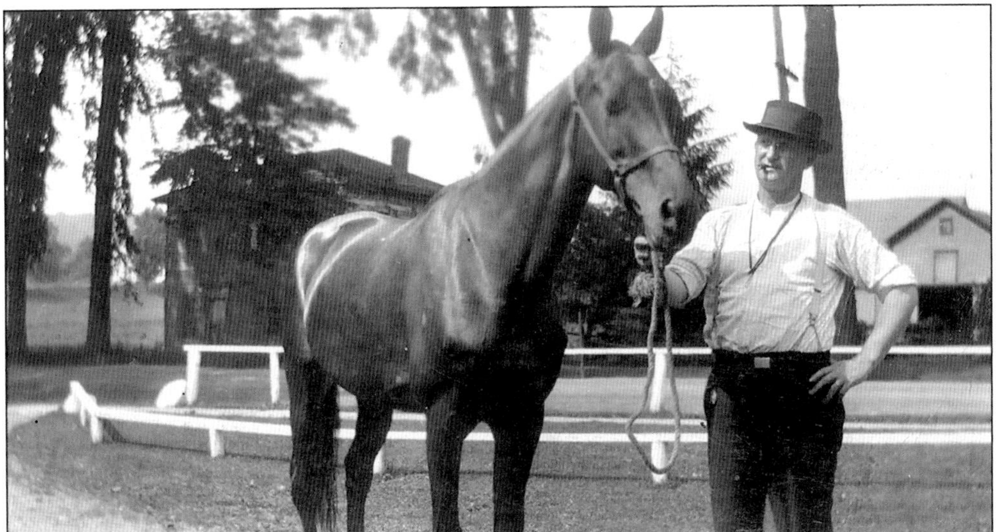

Charles Flint pauses in the driveway of the American Hotel with his horse. The barn in the right background was built c. 1840 by Moses Brown, a business partner of Harrison North. Moses Brown built the barn at the same time that he built his fine Greek Revival house.

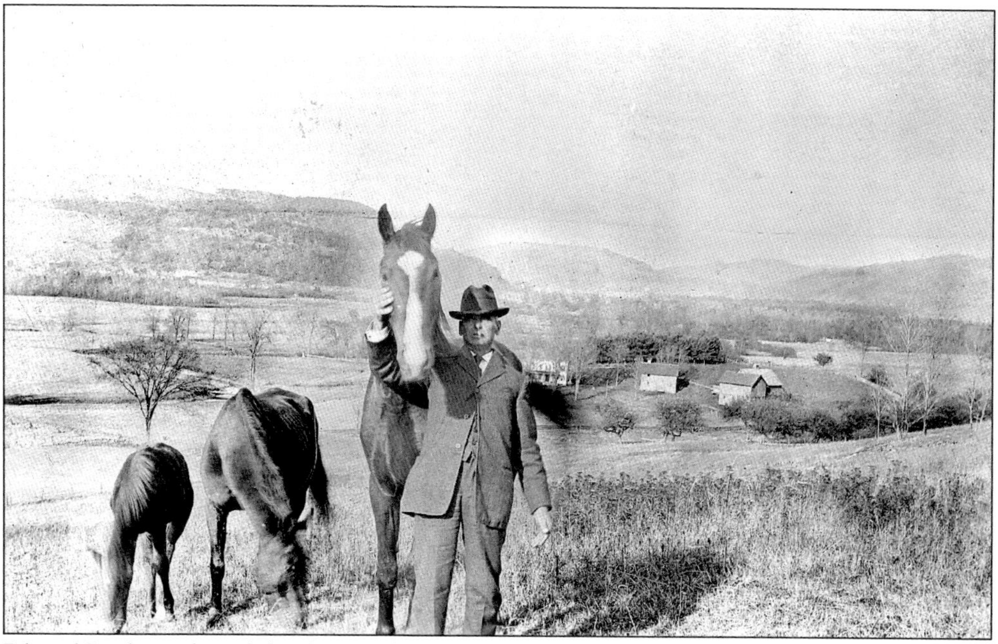

Edward Buel stands with his favorite horses. The house in the right distance may be the North house, also known as the Brick House. The bricks to build it came from a brickyard that once existed along the Cherry Valley Creek near this spot.

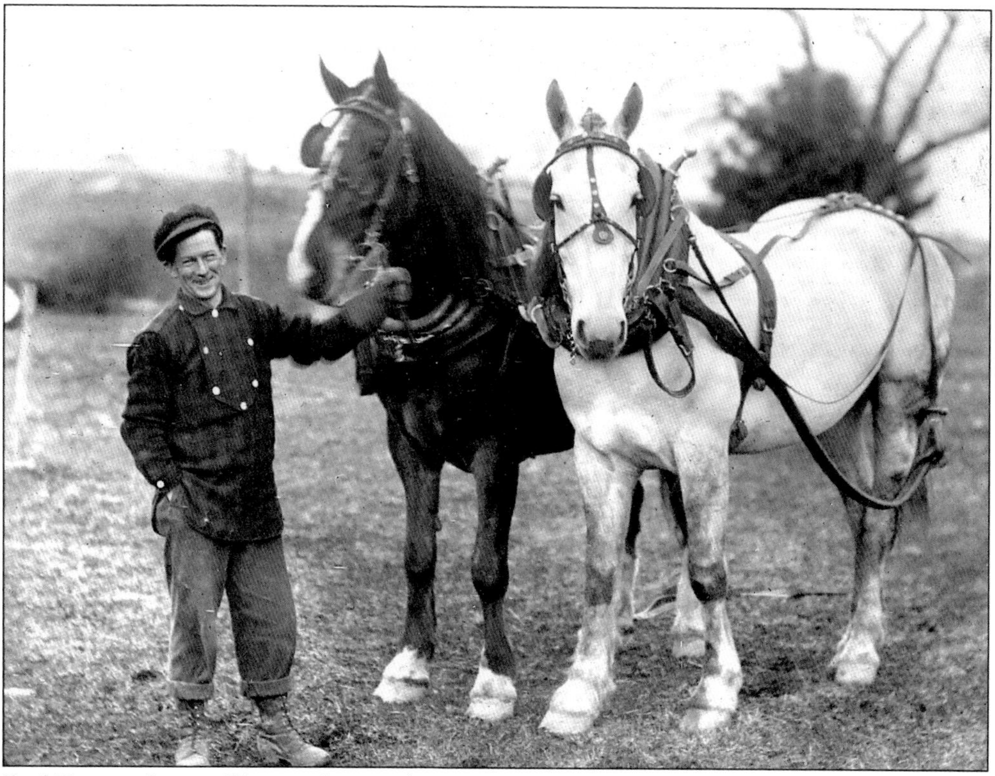

Fred Havens shows off his two horses. (Courtesy TMHA.)

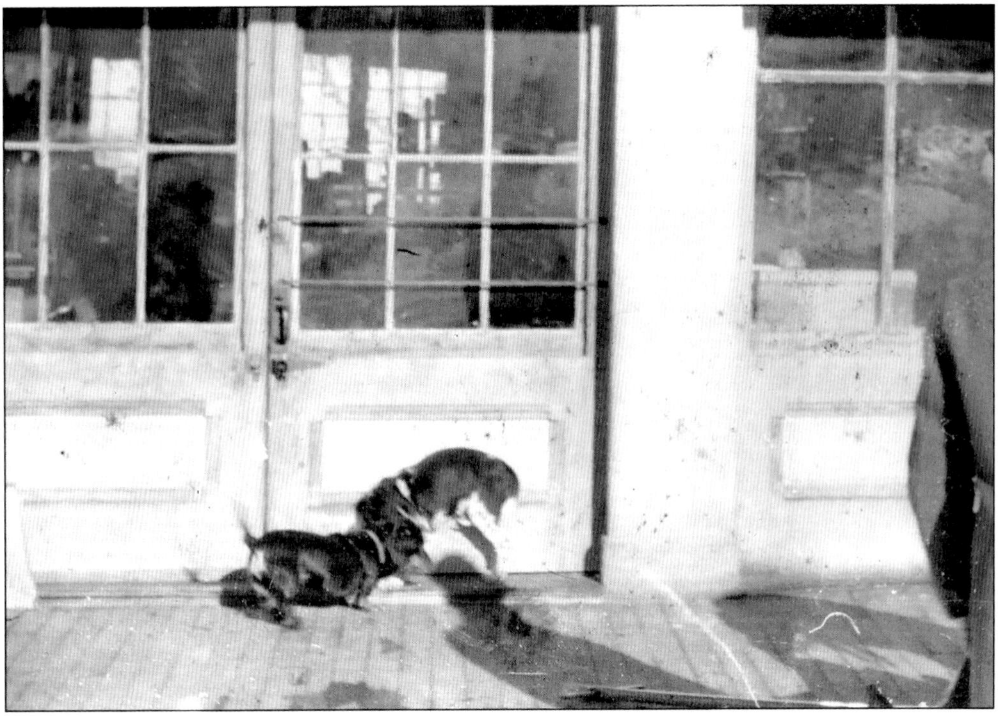

The country store was always a popular gathering place to swap gossip and discuss politics. Even the neighborhood dogs played on the porch of the Pollette Store. This photograph was taken c. 1945, before Thomas Pollette had redone the front windows to improve the display areas.

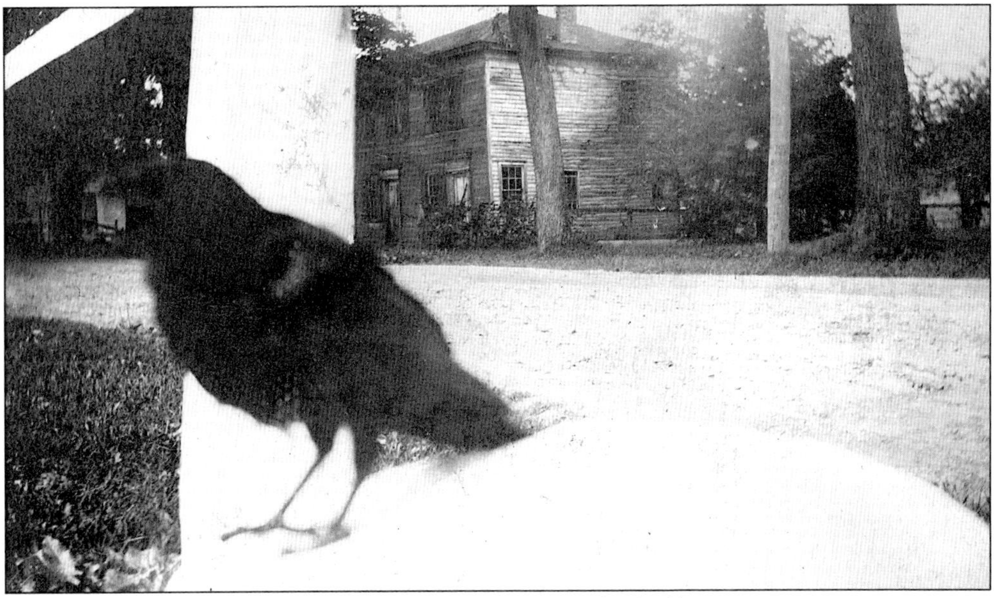

Not all people had the usual pets. Charles Flint was very fond of his pet crow.

Nine

Resting Places

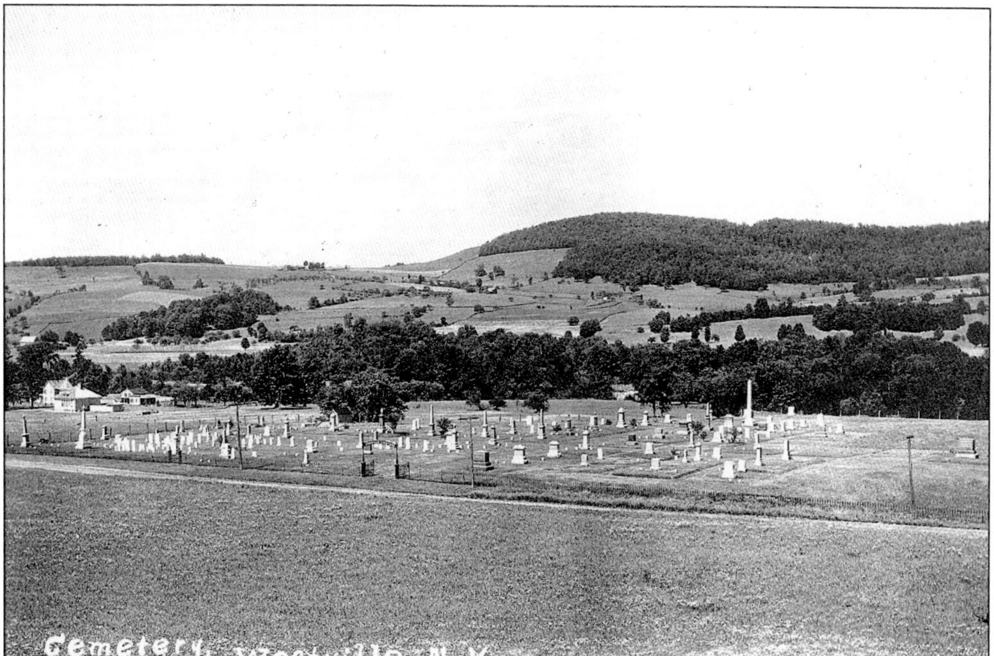

This view taken *c.* 1915 shows the Westville Cemetery with its quiet, contemplative setting. The cemetery was established in 1883, and its first plot was reserved for Albert Coats and his wife, of Westville. In the left distance is the Westville District No. 2 School. (Courtesy TMHA.)

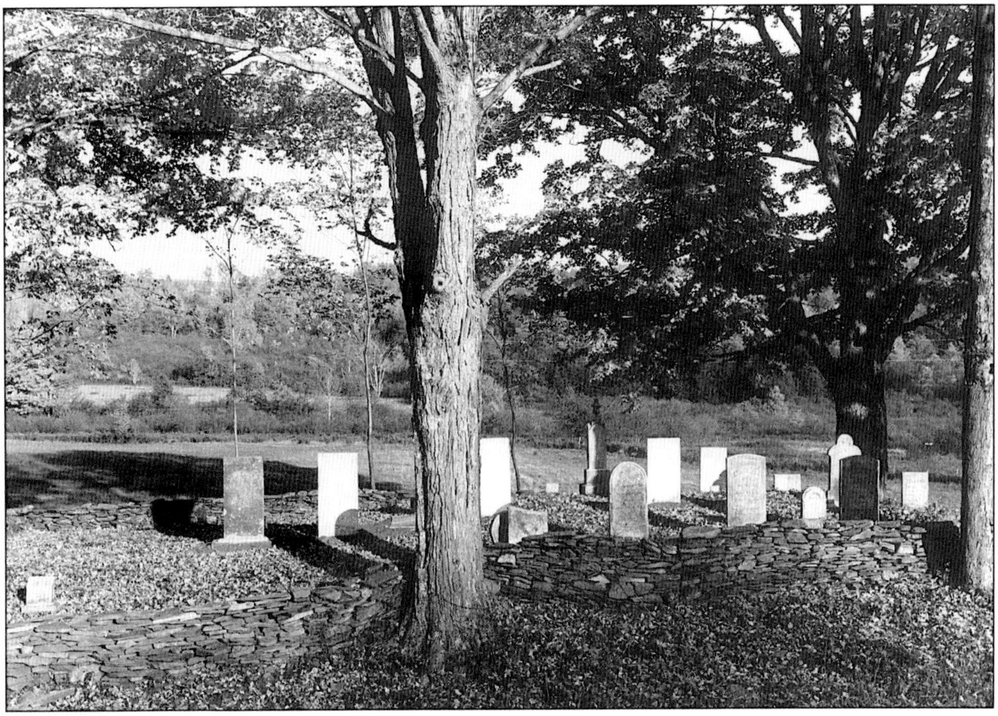

In 1968, a group undertook the restoration of the old Baptist Cemetery in the hamlet of Middlefield. Undergrowth was cleared, and stones were reset. (Courtesy TMHA.)

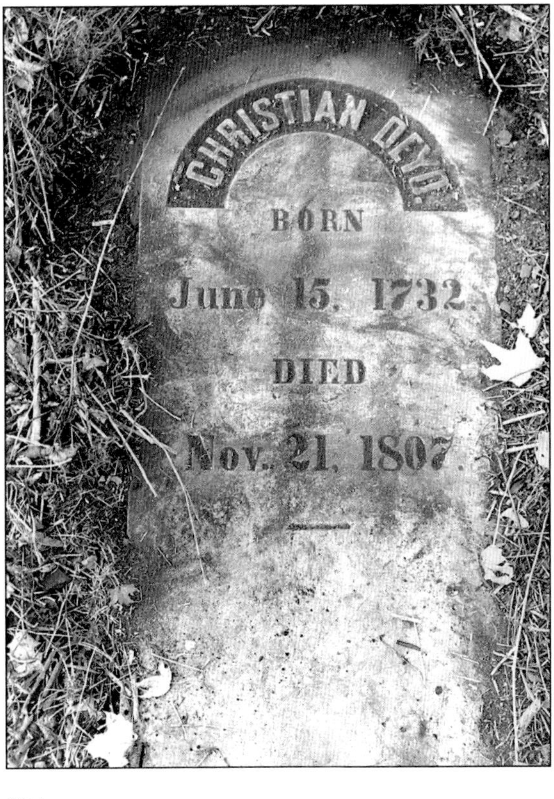

The oldest extant stone in the Baptist Cemetery is for Christian Deyo, who died in 1807. This finely cut stone is a testament to the regard in which Deyo was held. (Courtesy TMHA.)

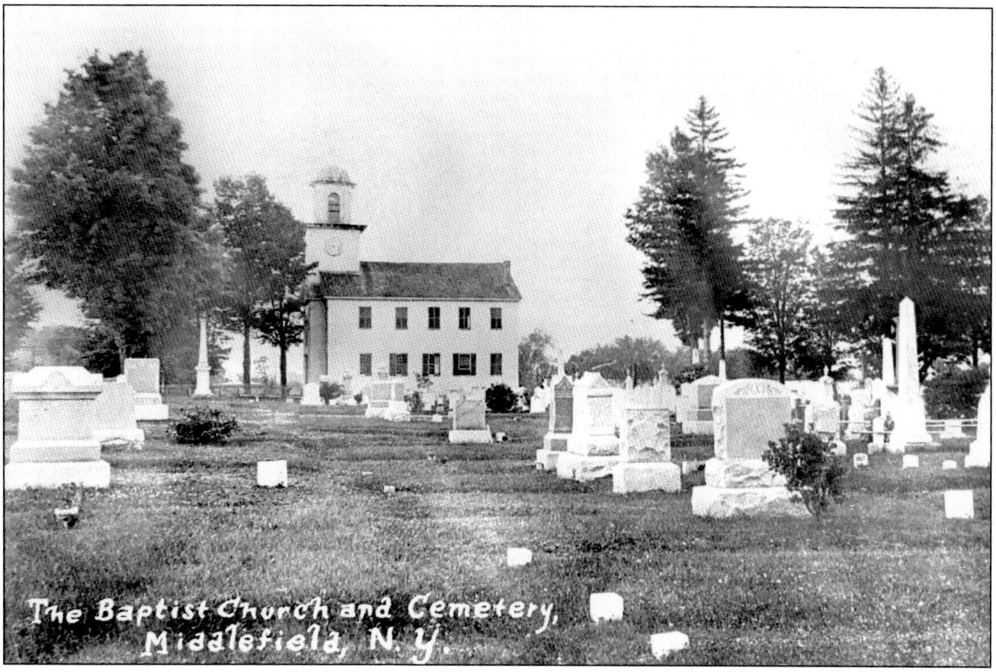

The Baptist church stands beside the Baptist Cemetery in the hamlet of Middlefield. When George Clarke donated this land to the Baptists in 1825 it was with one stipulation: should the Protestant Episcopal Church organize in Middlefield, the Baptists would have to give that congregation half of the land. That would have become very problematic since the Baptists promptly put a cemetery on the remaining land after building their church. (Courtesy TMHA.)

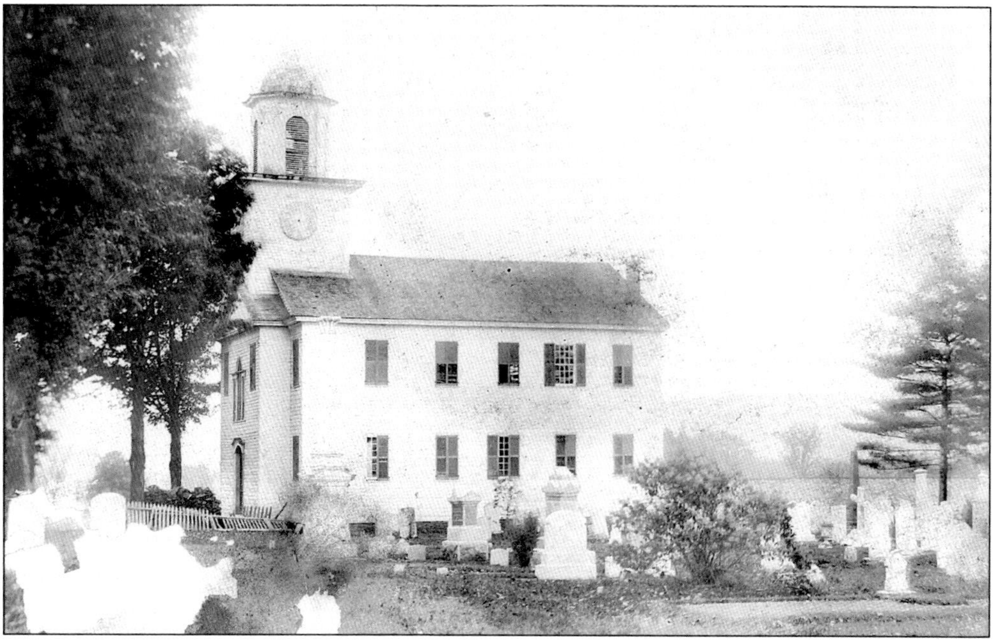

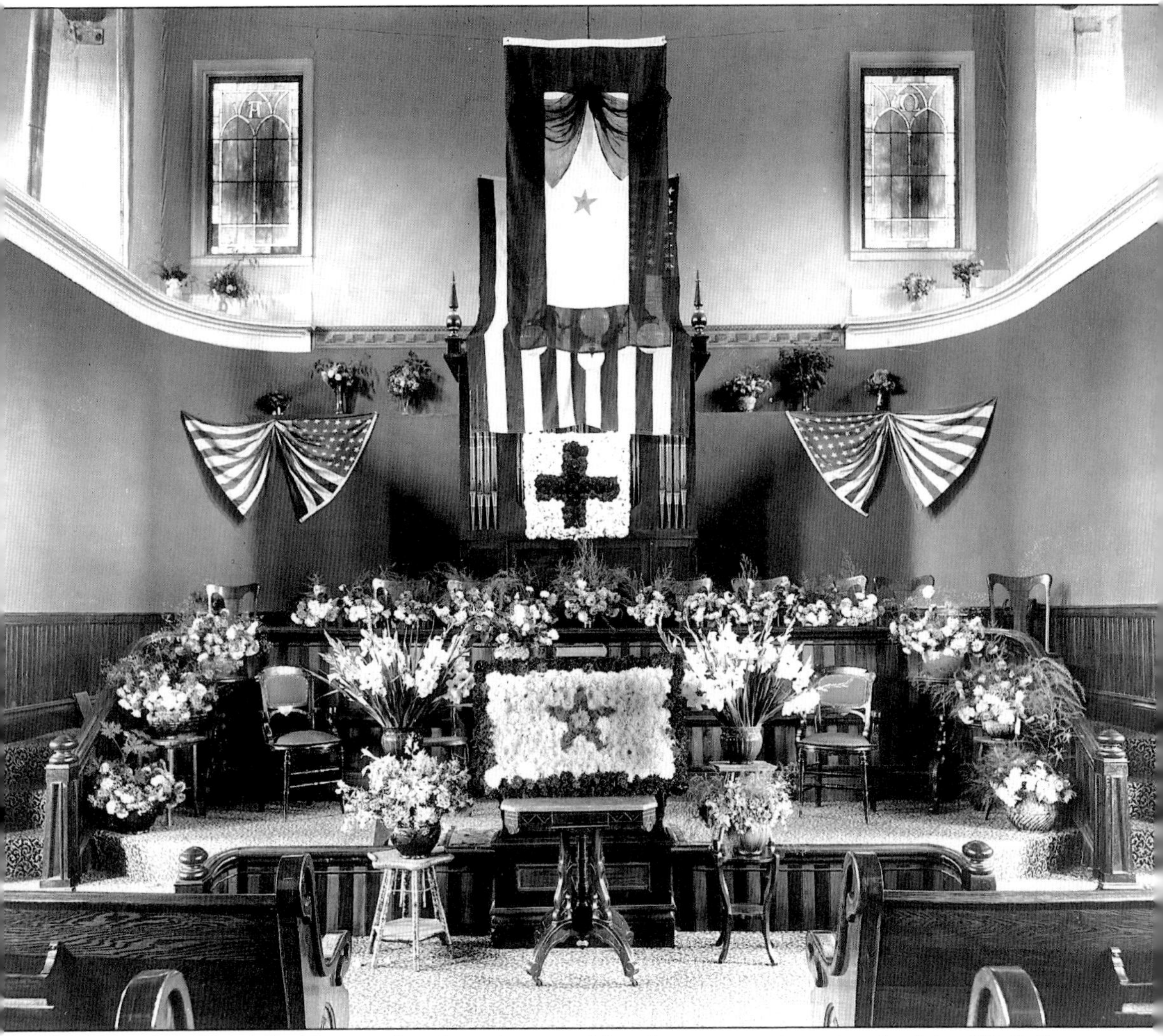

The interior of the Baptist church is decorated for the memorial service for John W. Stiles. Stiles was a member of Company G, 27th Division, 107th Infantry. He was killed in France on August 18, 1918. (Courtesy TMHA.)